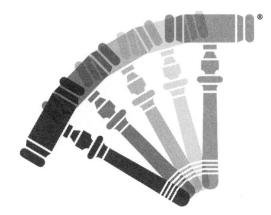

Casenote™ Legal Briefs

HEALTH CARE LAW

Keyed to
Hall, Bobinski, and Orentlicher's
Health Care Law and Ethics, Sixth Edition

PUBLISHERS

1185 Avenue of the Americas, New York, NY 10036
www.aspenpublishers.com

This publication is designed to provide accurate and authoritative information in regard to the subject matter covered. It is sold with the understanding that the publisher is not engaged in rendering legal, accounting, or other professional services. If legal advice or other expert assistance is required, the services of a competent professional person should be sought.

— From a *Declaration of Principles* adopted jointly by
a Committee of the American Bar Association and a
Committee of Publishers and Associates

About Aspen Publishers

Aspen Publishers, headquartered in New York City, is a leading information provider for attorneys, business professionals, and law students. Written by preeminent authorities, our products consist of analytical and practical information covering both U.S. and international topics. We publish in the full range of formats, including updated manuals, books, periodicals, CDs, and online products.

Our proprietary content is complemented by 2,500 legal databases, containing over 11 million documents, available through our Loislaw division. Aspen Publishers also offers a wide range of topical legal and business databases linked to Loislaw's primary material. Our mission is to provide accurate, timely, and authoritative content in easily accessible formats, supported by unmatched customer care.

To order any Aspen Publishers title, go to *www.aspenpublishers.com* or call 1-800-638-8437.

For more information on Loislaw products, go to *www.loislaw.com* or call 1-800-364-2512.

For Customer Care issues, e-mail CustomerCare@aspenpublishers.com; call 1-800-234-1660; or fax 1-800-901-9075.

Aspen Publishers
A Wolters Kluwer Company

FORMAT FOR THE CASENOTE LEGAL BRIEF

PARTY ID: Quick identification of the relationship between the parties.

PALSGRAF v. LONG ISLAND R.R. CO.
Injured bystander (P) v. Railroad company (D)
N.Y. Ct. App., 248 N.Y. 339, 162 N.E. 99 (1928).

NATURE OF CASE: This section identifies the form of action (e.g., breach of contract, negligence, battery), the type of proceeding (e.g., demurrer, appeal from trial court's jury instructions) or the relief sought (e.g., damages, injunction, criminal sanctions).

NATURE OF CASE: Appeal from judgment affirming verdict for plaintiff seeking damages for personal injury.

FACT SUMMARY: This is included to refresh the student's memory and can be used as a quick reminder of the facts.

FACT SUMMARY: Helen Palsgraf (P) was injured on R.R.'s (D) train platform when R.R.'s (D) guard helped a passenger aboard a moving train, causing his package to fall on the tracks. The package contained fireworks which exploded, creating a shock that tipped a scale onto Palsgraf (P).

CONCISE RULE OF LAW: Summarizes the general principle of law that the case illustrates. It may be used for instant recall of the court's holding and for classroom discussion or home review.

CONCISE RULE OF LAW: The risk reasonably to be perceived defines the duty to be obeyed.

FACTS: This section contains all relevant facts of the case, including the contentions of the parties and the lower court holdings. It is written in a logical order to give the student a clear understanding of the case. The plaintiff and defendant are identified by their proper names throughout and are always labeled with a (P) or (D).

FACTS: Helen Palsgraf (P) purchased a ticket to Rockaway Beach from R.R. (D) and was waiting on the train platform. As she waited, two men ran to catch a train that was pulling out from the platform. The first man jumped aboard, but the second man, who appeared as if he might fall, was helped aboard by the guard on the train who had kept the door open so they could jump aboard. A guard on the platform also helped by pushing him onto the train. The man was carrying a package wrapped in newspaper. In the process, the man dropped his package, which fell on the tracks. The package contained fireworks and exploded. The shock of the explosion was apparently of great enough strength to tip over some scales at the other end of the platform, which fell on Palsgraf (P) and injured her. A jury awarded her damages, and R.R. (D) appealed.

ISSUE: The issue is a concise question that brings out the essence of the opinion as it relates to the section of the casebook in which the case appears. Both substantive and procedural issues are included if relevant to the decision.

ISSUE: Does the risk reasonably to be perceived define the duty to be obeyed?

HOLDING AND DECISION: This section offers a clear and in-depth discussion of the rule of the case and the court's rationale. It is written in easy-to-understand language and answers the issue(s) presented by applying the law to the facts of the case. When relevant, it includes a thorough discussion of the exceptions to the case as listed by the court, any major cites to other cases on point, and the names of the judges who wrote the decisions.

HOLDING AND DECISION: (Cardozo, C.J.) Yes. The risk reasonably to be perceived defines the duty to be obeyed. If there is no foreseeable hazard to the injured party as the result of a seemingly innocent act, the act does not become a tort because it happened to be a wrong as to another. If the wrong was not willful, the plaintiff must show that the act as to her had such great and apparent possibilities of danger as to entitle her to protection. Negligence in the abstract is not enough upon which to base liability. Negligence is a relative concept, evolving out of the common law doctrine of trespass on the case. To establish liability, the defendant must owe a legal duty of reasonable care to the injured party. A cause of action in tort will lie where harm, though unintended, could have been averted or avoided by observance of such a duty. The scope of the duty is limited by the range of danger that a reasonable person could foresee. In this case, there was nothing to suggest from the appearance of the parcel or otherwise that the parcel contained fireworks. The guard could not reasonably have had any warning of a threat to Palsgraf (P), and R.R. (D) therefore cannot be held liable. Judgment is reversed in favor of R.R. (D).

CONCURRENCE / DISSENT: All concurrences and dissents are briefed whenever they are included by the casebook editor.

DISSENT: (Andrews, J.) The concept that there is no negligence unless R.R. (D) owes a legal duty to take care as to Palsgraf (P) herself is too narrow. Everyone owes to the world at large the duty of refraining from those acts that may unreasonably threaten the safety of others. If the guard's action was negligent as to those nearby, it was also negligent as to those outside what might be termed the "danger zone." For Palsgraf (P) to recover, R.R.'s (D) negligence must have been the proximate cause of her injury, a question of fact for the jury.

EDITOR'S ANALYSIS: This last paragraph gives the student a broad understanding of where the case "fits in" with other cases in the section of the book and with the entire course. It is a hornbook-style discussion indicating whether the case is a majority or minority opinion and comparing the principal case with other cases in the casebook. It may also provide analysis from restatements, uniform codes, and law review articles. The editor's analysis will prove to be invaluable to classroom discussion.

EDITOR'S ANALYSIS: The majority defined the limit of the defendant's liability in terms of the danger that a reasonable person in defendant's situation would have perceived. The dissent argued that the limitation should not be placed on liability, but rather on damages. Judge Andrews suggested that only injuries that would not have happened but for R.R.'s (D) negligence should be compensable. Both the majority and dissent recognized the policy-driven need to limit liability for negligent acts, seeking, in the words of Judge Andrews, to define a framework "that will be practical and in keeping with the general understanding of mankind." The Restatement (Second) of Torts has accepted Judge Cardozo's view.

QUICKNOTES: Conveniently defines legal terms found in the case and summarizes the nature of any statutes, codes, or rules referred to in the text.

QUICKNOTES

FORESEEABILITY – The reasonable anticipation that damage is a likely result from certain acts or omissions.
NEGLIGENCE - Failure to exercise that degree of care which a person of ordinary prudence would exercise under similar circumstances.
PROXIMATE CAUSE – Something which in natural and continuous sequence, unbroken by any new intervening cause, produces an event, and without which the injury would not have occurred.

NOTE TO STUDENTS

Aspen Publishers is proud to offer *Casenote Legal Briefs*–continuing thirty years of publishing America's best-selling legal briefs.

Casenote Legal Briefs are designed to help you save time when briefing assigned cases. Organized under convenient headings, they show you how to abstract the basic facts and holdings from the text of the actual opinions handed down by the courts. Used as part of a rigorous study regime, they can help you spend more time analyzing and critiquing points of law than on copying out bits and pieces of judicial opinions into your notebook or outline.

Casenote Legal Briefs should never be used as a substitute for assigned casebook readings. They work best when read as a follow-up to reviewing the underlying opinions themselves. Students who try to avoid reading and digesting the judicial opinions in their casebooks or on-line sources will end up shortchanging themselves in the long run. The ability to absorb, critique, and restate the dynamic and complex elements of case law decisions is crucial to your success in law school and beyond. It cannot be developed vicariously.

Casenote Legal Briefs represent but one of the many offerings in Aspen's Study Aid Timeline, which includes:

- Casenotes *Legal Briefs*
- Emanuel *Outlines*
- *Examples & Explanations* Series
- *Introduction to Law* Series
- Emanuel *Law in a Flash* Flashcards
- Emanuel *CrunchTime* Series

Each of these series is designed to provide you with easy-to-understand explanations of complex points of law. Each volume offers guidance on the principles of legal analysis and, consulted regularly, will hone your ability to spot relevant issues. We have titles that will help you prepare for class, prepare for your exams, and enhance your general comprehension of the law along the way.

To find out more about Aspen Study Aid publications, visit us on-line at www.aspenpublishers.com or e-mail us at legaledu@aspenpubl.com. We'll be happy to assist you.

Free access to Briefs and Updates on-line!

Download the cases you want in your notes or outlines using the full cut-and-paste feature accompanying our on-line briefs. On-line briefs will also contain the latest updates. Please fill out this form for full access to these useful features. No photocopies of this form will be accepted.

① **Name:** _____ **Phone: (___)** _____

Address: _____ **Apt.:** _____

City: _____ **State:** _____ **ZIP Code:** _____

Law School: _____ **Year (circle one): 1st   2nd   3rd**

② **Cut out the UPC found on the lower left-hand corner of the back cover of this book. Staple the UPC inside this box. Only the original UPC from the book cover will be accepted. (No photocopies or store stickers are allowed.)**

> **Attach UPC inside this box.**

③ **E-mail:** _____ **(Print LEGIBLY or you may not get access!)**

④ **Title (course subject) of this book** _____

⑤ **Used with which casebook (provide author's name):** _____

⑥ **Mail the completed form to:**   Aspen Publishers, Inc.
Legal Education Division
Casenote On-line Access
1185 Avenue of the Americas
New York, NY 10036

I understand that on-line access is granted solely to the purchaser of this book for the academic year in which it was purchased. Any other usage is not authorized and will result in immediate termination of access. Sharing of codes is strictly prohibited.

_____
Signature

Upon receipt of this completed form, you will be e-mailed codes so that you may access the Briefs and Updates for this Casenote Legal Brief. On-line Briefs and Updates may not be available for all titles. For a full list of available titles please check www.aspenpublishers.com/casenotes.

HOW TO BRIEF A CASE

A. DECIDE ON A FORMAT AND STICK TO IT

Structure is essential to a good brief. It enables you to arrange systematically the related parts that are scattered throughout most cases, thus making manageable and understandable what might otherwise seem to be an endless and unfathomable sea of information. There are, of course, an unlimited number of formats that can be utilized. However, it is best to find one that suits your needs and stick to it. Consistency breeds both efficiency and the security that when called upon you will know where to look in your brief for the information you are asked to give.

Any format, as long as it presents the essential elements of a case in an organized fashion, can be used. Experience, however, has led *Casenotes* to develop and utilize the following format because of its logical flow and universal applicability.

NATURE OF CASE: This is a brief statement of the legal character and procedural status of the case (e.g., "Appeal of a burglary conviction").

There are many different alternatives open to a litigant dissatisfied with a court ruling. The key to determining which one has been used is to discover *who is asking this court for what.*

This first entry in the brief should be kept as *short as possible.* The student should use the court's terminology if the student understands it. But since jurisdictions vary as to the titles of pleadings, the best entry is the one that apprises the student of who wants what in this proceeding, not the one that sounds most like the court's language.

CONCISE RULE OF LAW: A statement of the general principle of law that the case illustrates (e.g., "An acceptance that varies any term of the offer is considered a rejection and counteroffer").

Determining the rule of law of a case is a procedure similar to determining the issue of the case. Avoid being fooled by red herrings; there may be a few rules of law mentioned in the case excerpt, but usually only one is *the* rule with which the casebook editor is concerned. The techniques used to locate the issue, described below, may also be utilized to find the rule of law. Generally, your best guide is simply the chapter heading. It is a clue to the point the casebook editor seeks to make and should be kept in mind when reading every case in the respective section.

FACTS: A synopsis of only the essential facts of the case, i.e., those bearing upon or leading up to the issue.

The facts entry should be a short statement of the events and transactions that led one party to initiate legal proceedings against another in the first place. While some cases conveniently state the salient facts at the beginning of the decision, in other instances they will have to be culled from hiding places throughout the text, even from concurring and dissenting opinions. Some of the "facts" will often be in dispute and should be so noted. Conflicting evidence may be briefly pointed up. "Hard" facts must be included. Both must be *relevant* in order to be listed in the facts entry. It is impossible to tell what is relevant until the entire case is read, as the ultimate determination of the rights and liabilities of the parties may turn on something buried deep in the opinion.

The facts entry should never be longer than one to three *short* sentences.

It is often helpful to identify the role played by a party in a given context. For example, in a construction contract case the identification of a party as the "contractor" or "builder" alleviates the need to tell that that party was the one who was supposed to have built the house.

It is always helpful, and a good general practice, to identify the "plaintiff" and the "defendant." This may seem elementary and uncomplicated, but, especially in view of the creative editing practiced by some casebook editors, it is sometimes a difficult or even impossible task. Bear in mind that the *party presently* seeking something from this court may not be the plaintiff, and that sometimes only the cross-claim of a defendant is treated in the excerpt. Confusing or misaligning the parties can ruin your analysis and understanding of the case.

ISSUE: A statement of the general legal question answered by or illustrated in the case. For clarity, the issue is best put in the form of a question capable of a "yes" or "no" answer. In reality, the issue is simply the Concise Rule of Law put in the form of a question (e.g., "May an offer be accepted by performance?").

The major problem presented in discerning what is *the* issue in the case is that an opinion usually purports to raise and answer several questions. However, except for rare cases, only one such question is really the issue in the case. Collateral issues not necessary to the resolution of the matter in controversy are handled by the court by language known as *"obiter dictum"* or merely *"dictum."* While dicta may be included later in the brief, it has no place under the issue heading.

To find the issue, the student again asks *who wants what* and then goes on to ask *why did that party succeed or fail in getting it.* Once this is determined, the "why" should be turned into a question.

The complexity of the issues in the cases will vary, but in all cases a single-sentence question should sum up the issue. *In a few cases,* there will be two, or even more rarely, three issues of equal importance to the resolution of the case. Each should be expressed in a single-sentence question.

Since many issues are resolved by a court in coming to a final disposition of a case, the casebook editor will reproduce the portion of the opinion containing the issue or issues most relevant to the area of law under scrutiny. A noted law professor gave this advice: "Close the book; look at the title on the cover." Chances are, if it is Property, the student need not concern himself with whether, for example, the federal government's treatment of the plaintiff's land really raises a federal question sufficient to support jurisdiction on this ground in federal court.

The same rule applies to chapter headings designating sub-areas within the subjects. They tip the student off as to what the text is designed to teach. The cases are arranged in a casebook to show a progression or development of the law, so that the preceding cases may also help.

It is also most important to remember to *read the notes and questions* at the end of a case to determine what the editors wanted the student to have gleaned from it.

HOLDING AND DECISION: This section should succinctly explain the rationale of the court in arriving at its decision. In capsulizing the "reasoning" of the court, it should always include an application of the general rule or rules of law to the specific facts of the case. Hidden justifications come to light in this entry; the reasons for the state of the law, the public policies, the biases and prejudices, those considerations that influence the justices' thinking and, ultimately, the outcome of the case. At the end, there should be a short indication of the disposition or procedural resolution of the case (e.g., "Decision of the trial court for Mr. Smith (P) reversed").

The foregoing format is designed to help you "digest" the reams of case material with which you will be faced in your law school career. Once mastered by practice, it will place at your fingertips the information the authors of your casebooks have sought to impart to you in case-by-case illustration and analysis.

B.   BE AS ECONOMICAL AS POSSIBLE IN BRIEFING CASES

Once armed with a format that encourages succinctness, it is as important to be economical with regard to the time spent on the actual reading of the case as it is to be economical in the writing of the brief itself. This does not mean "skimming" a case. Rather, it means reading the case with an "eye" trained to recognize into which "section" of your brief a particular passage or line fits and having a system for quickly and precisely marking the case so that the passages fitting any one particular part of the brief can be easily identified and brought together in a concise and accurate manner when the brief is actually written.

It is of no use to simply repeat everything in the opinion of the court; the student should only record enough information to trigger his or her recollection of what the court said. Nevertheless, an accurate statement of the "law of the case," i.e., the legal principle applied to the facts, is absolutely essential to class preparation and to learning the law under the case method.

To that end, it is important to develop a "shorthand" that you can use to make margin notations. These notations will tell you at a glance in which section of the brief you will be placing that particular passage or portion of the opinion.

Some students prefer to underline all the salient portions of the opinion (with a pencil or colored underliner marker), making marginal notations as they go along. Others prefer the color-coded method of underlining, utilizing different colors of markers to underline the salient portions of the case, each separate color being used to represent a different section of the brief. For example, blue underlining could be used for passages relating to the concise rule of law, yellow for those relating to the issue, and green for those relating to the holding and decision, etc. While it has its advocates, the color-coded method can be confusing and time-consuming (all that time spent on changing colored markers). Furthermore, it can interfere with the continuity and concentration many students deem essential to the reading of a case for maximum comprehension. In the end, however, it is a matter of personal preference and style. Just remember, whatever method you use, underlining must be used sparingly or its value is lost.

For those who take the marginal notation route, an efficient and easy method is to go along underlining the key portions of the case and placing in the margin alongside them the following "markers" to indicate where a particular passage or line "belongs" in the brief you will write:

N   (NATURE OF CASE)
CR   (CONCISE RULE OF LAW)
I   (ISSUE)
HC   (HOLDING AND DECISION, relates to the CONCISE RULE OF LAW behind the decision)
HR   (HOLDING AND DECISION, gives the RATIONALE or reasoning behind the decision)
HA   (HOLDING AND DECISION, APPLIES the general principle(s) of law to the facts of the case to arrive at the decision)

Remember that a particular passage may well contain information necessary to more than one part of your brief, in which case you simply note that in the margin. If you are using the color-coded underlining method instead of margin notation, simply make asterisks or checks in the margin next to the passage in question in the colors that indicate the additional sections of the brief where it might be utilized.

The economy of utilizing "shorthand" in marking cases for briefing can be maintained in the actual brief writing process itself by utilizing "law student shorthand" within the brief. There are many commonly used words and phrases for which abbreviations can be substituted in your briefs (and in your class notes also). You can develop abbreviations that are personal to you and which will save you a lot of time. A reference list of briefing abbreviations will be found elsewhere in this book.

C. USE BOTH THE BRIEFING PROCESS AND THE BRIEF AS A LEARNING TOOL

Now that you have a format and the tools for briefing cases efficiently, the most important thing is to make the time spent in briefing profitable to you and to make the most advantageous use of the briefs you create. Of course, the briefs are invaluable for classroom reference when you are called upon to explain or analyze a particular case. However, they are also useful in reviewing for exams. A quick glance at the fact summary should bring the case to mind, and a rereading of the concise rule of law should enable you to go over the underlying legal concept in your mind, how it was applied in that particular case, and how it might apply in other factual settings.

As to the value to be derived from engaging in the briefing process itself, there is an immediate benefit that arises from being forced to sift through the essential facts and reasoning from the court's opinion and to succinctly express them in your own words in your brief. The process ensures that you understand the case and the point that it illustrates, and that means you will be ready to absorb further analysis and information brought forth in class. It also ensures you will have something to say when called upon in class. The briefing process helps develop a mental agility for getting to the *gist* of a case and for identifying, expounding on, and applying the legal concepts and issues found there. Of most immediate concern, that is the mental process on which you must rely in taking law school examinations. Of more lasting concern, it is also the mental process upon which a lawyer relies in serving his clients and in making his living.

ABBREVIATIONS FOR BRIEFING

acceptance .... acp
affirmed .... aff
answer .... ans
assumption of risk .... a/r
attorney .... atty
beyond a reasonable doubt .... b/r/d
bona fide purchaser .... BFP
breach of contract .... br/k
cause of action .... c/a
common law .... c/l
Constitution .... Con
constitutional .... con
contract .... K
contributory negligence .... c/n
cross x
cross-complaint .... x/c
cross-examination .... x/ex
cruel and unusual punishment .... c/u/p
defendant .... D
dismissed .... dis
double jeopardy .... d/j
due process .... d/p
equal protection .... e/p
equity .... eq
evidence .... ev
exclude .... exc
exclusionary rule .... exc/r
felony .... f/n
freedom of speech .... f/s
good faith .... g/f
habeas corpus .... h/c
hearsay .... hr
husband .... H
in loco parentis .... ILP
injunction .... inj
inter vivos .... I/v
joint tenancy .... j/t
judgment .... judgt
jurisdiction .... jur
last clear chance LCC
long-arm statute .... LAS
majority view .... maj
meeting of minds .... MOM
minority view .... min
Miranda warnings .... Mir/w
Miranda rule .... Mir/r
negligence .... neg
notice .... ntc
nuisance .... nus
obligation .... ob
obscene .... obs

offer .... O
offeree .... OE
offeror .... OR
ordinance .... ord
pain and suffering .... p/s
parol evidence .... p/e
plaintiff .... P
prima facie .... p/f
probable cause .... p/c
proximate cause .... px/c
real property .... r/p
reasonable doubt .... r/d
reasonable man .... r/m
rebuttable presumption .... rb/p
remanded .... rem
res ipsa loquitur .... RIL
respondeat superior .... r/s
Restatement .... RS
reversed .... rev
Rule Against Perpetuities .... RAP
search and seizure .... s/s
search warrant .... s/w
self-defense .... s/d
specific performance .... s/p
statute of limitations .... S/L
statute of frauds .... S/F
statute .... S
summary judgment .... s/j
tenancy in common .... t/c
tenancy at will .... t/w
tenant .... t
third party .... TP
third party beneficiary .... TPB
transferred intent .... TI
unconscionable .... uncon
unconstitutional .... unconst
undue influence .... u/e
Uniform Commercial Code .... UCC
unilateral .... uni
vendee .... VE
vendor .... VR
versus v
void for vagueness .... VFV
weight of the evidence .... w/e
weight of authority .... w/a
wife .... W
with .... w/
within .... w/i
without prejudice .... w/o/p
without .... w/o
wrongful death .... wr/d

TABLE OF CASES

CHAPTER 1
INTRODUCTION

QUICK REFERENCE RULES OF LAW

1. **Overview Cases.** Once an individual has been diagnosed as presenting an emergency medical condition, the hospital must provide that treatment necessary to prevent the material deterioration of the individual's condition or provide for an appropriate transfer. (In re Baby K)

2. **Overview Cases.** Since a patient's health care payor is not responsible for discharge determinations, liability will not attach to the payor for a negligent discharge. (Wickline v. State)

3. **Overview Cases.** A court may not order an individual to undergo a Caesarian section to save the baby's life. (In re A.C.)

4. **Overview Cases.** Courts should refrain from intervening in a competitive situation which may upset the balance of the market in cases where there exists no evidence of barriers constraining normal operation of the market. (Federal Trade Commission v. Tenet Health Care Corp.)

IN RE BABY K

Hospital (P) v. Parents of anencephalic infant (D)
16 F.3d 590 (4th Cir. 1994).

NATURE OF CASE: Appeal from declaratory judgment that hospitals must provide stabilizing care to any individual presenting an emergency medical condition.

FACT SUMMARY: When an anencephalic infant was born at a hospital and the mother did not agree with doctors as to the appropriate level of care, the hospital sought a declaratory judgment that it was not required to provide respiratory support or other aggressive treatments for the infant.

CONCISE RULE OF LAW: Once an individual has been diagnosed as presenting an emergency medical condition, the hospital must provide that treatment necessary to prevent the material deterioration of the individual's condition or provide for an appropriate transfer.

FACTS: Baby K was born with anencephaly, a congenital malformation that rendered her permanently unconscious. The physicians recommended that, since most such infants die within a few days of birth due to breathing difficulties, only supportive care in the form of nutrition, hydration, and warmth be provided. Baby K's mother insisted that mechanical breathing assistance also be provided whenever the infant developed difficulty breathing, which the physicians opposed. As a result of this disagreement with the physicians, the hospital unsuccessfully sought to have the infant transferred to another hospital. The infant was later transferred to a nursing home but returned to the hospital's emergency room three times due to breathing difficulties. The hospital filed an action to resolve the issue of whether it was obligated to provide emergency medical treatment that it deemed medically and ethically inappropriate. The district court found that under the Emergency Medical Treatment and Active Labor Act (EMTALA) the hospital, like all hospitals that have entered into Medicare provider agreements, had a duty to screen for emergency medical conditions and to provide such treatment as may be necessary or transfer the patient. The hospital appealed.

ISSUE: Once an individual has been diagnosed as presenting an emergency medical condition, must the hospital provide that treatment necessary to prevent the material deterioration of the individual's condition or provide for an appropriate transfer?

HOLDING AND DECISION: (Wilkins, J.) Yes. Once an individual has been diagnosed as presenting an emergency medical condition, the hospital must provide that treatment necessary to prevent the material deterioration of the individual's condition or provide for an appropriate transfer. Since Baby K's breathing

difficulty qualifies as an emergency medical condition and transfer was not an option since the mother had not requested it, the hospital was required to provide stabilizing care. Although the prevailing standard of medical care for infants with anencephaly is to provide only warmth, nutrition, and hydration, due to their extremely limited life expectancy, EMTALA does not provide for any exceptions. Congress rejected a case-by-case approach in determining what emergency medical treatment hospitals and physicians must provide. Affirmed.

EDITOR'S ANALYSIS: This case typifies the situation where the family asserts the patient's right to make medical decisions. When the physicians or hospital argue that treatment may be futile, the court has adopted a hands-off attitude toward social policy decisions. In this case, the infant lived for two and a half years and died in the same hospital's emergency room after being taken there for the sixth time.

QUICKNOTES

ANENCEPHALY - A physical deformity characterized by an abnormal formation of the skull and the absence of all or a portion of the brain.

EMERGENCY MEDICAL TREATMENT AND ACTIVE LABOR ACT: Prohibits hospitals with specialized capabilities or facilities from refusing appropriate transfers and requires hospitals to treat emergency medical conditions.

NOTES:

WICKLINE v. STATE

Patient (P) v. State Medicaid program (D)
Cal. App. Ct., 239 Cal. Rptr. 810 (1986).

NATURE OF CASE: Appeal of jury damage award in a suit for negligent discontinuance of Medi-Cal eligibility.

FACT SUMMARY: Wickline (P) was discharged sooner than her doctor believed appropriate due to a Medi-Cal (D) rejection of further hospitalization costs, and she suffered a blood clot in her leg, requiring amputation.

CONCISE RULE OF LAW: Since a patient's health care payor is not responsible for discharge determinations, liability will not attach to the payor for a negligent discharge.

FACTS: Wickline (P) suffered an arterial blockage in her leg. After multiple surgeries with complications, her doctor, Dr. Polonsky, determined that she should remain hospitalized for eight extra days. The doctor requested a Medi-Cal (D) approval for the extra days, but only four extra days were approved. Dr. Polonsky did not challenge this finding, though an appeal route existed. After the four days, Wickline (P) was discharged. Several physicians agreed that the discharge was reasonable given the current standard of medical practice. However, complications with Wickline's (P) leg at home eventually required amputation. Wickline (P) filed suit against Medi-Cal (D) for negligently interfering with her doctor's discretion. The jury found for Wickline (P), and Medi-Cal (D) appealed.

ISSUE: Does a patient's health care payor bear the primary responsibility for allowing a patient to be discharged from a hospital, thus incurring liability for a negligent discharge?

HOLDING AND DECISION: (Rowan, J.) No. Since a patient's health care payor is not responsible for discharge determinations, liability will not attach to the payor for a negligent discharge. A patient's physician is in a far better position to determine medically necessary procedures than is Medi-Cal (D). When an appeal route exists and is not used, then the physician cannot shift responsibility to the payor. In this case, Dr. Polonsky admitted that it was his primary responsibility to care for Wickline (P). He felt that four more days of hospitalization were needed, but he did not challenge the initial Medi-Cal (D) finding. Medi-Cal (D) based its decision on a limited set of facts which Dr. Polonsky could have questioned. Medi-Cal (D) is not liable for Wickline's (P) injuries. Reversed.

EDITOR'S ANALYSIS: The decision in this case has been substantially narrowed in subsequent cases. Outside entities that deny care can be liable for negligently reviewing medical records. Apparently there is a growing concern that cost-containment procedures are interfering with physicians' decisions.

IN RE A.C.
Hospital (P) v. Unconscious patient (D)
D.C. Ct. App., 573 A.2d 1235 (1990).

NATURE OF CASE: Appeal of order mandating Caesarian section upon a terminally ill pregnant woman.

FACT SUMMARY: A court ordered that A.C., pregnant and dying, undergo a Caesarian section to save the baby.

CONCISE RULE OF LAW: A court may not order an individual to undergo a Caesarian section to save the baby's life.

FACTS: A.C., a chronic cancer patient, became pregnant. When she was twenty-five weeks pregnant, she entered a hospital, complaining of pain. Tests revealed an inoperable tumor, and she was diagnosed as terminal. Based on conversations with doctors, she agreed to undergo a Caesarian section at twenty-eight weeks. However, her condition rapidly worsened, and by twenty-six weeks she had begun lapsing into and out of consciousness. Medical personnel believed that the only way to save the baby was an immediate C-section. However, they were not able to obtain A.C.'s consent, as she was mostly unconscious and not lucid when she was conscious. A court hearing was rapidly convened to determine what next to do. The court engaged in a balancing test between the state's interest in the fetus, the fetus' interests, and A.C.'s interests. The court ordered the C-section; unfortunately, the baby died, as did A.C. two days later. The district court of appeals reviewed the case.

ISSUE: May a court order an individual to undergo a Caesarian section to save the baby's life?

HOLDING AND DECISION: (Terry, J.) No. A court may not order an individual to undergo a Caesarian section to save the baby's life. It is a well-grounded common law rule that an individual is under no duty to take steps to save another's life. For instance, a person cannot be compelled to donate blood or an organ to save another's life. This rule applies with equal force in the context of a dying woman and her fetus: the woman cannot be compelled to undergo a procedure to save the fetus' life. Consent is required. If the woman is no longer competent, a court may hold an inquiry as to whether her consent would have been given were she competent. However, the scope of inquiry can only go so far as consent; the fetus' interests are not to be considered, nor those of the state, except perhaps in extraordinary circumstances. As the court considered those interests, it erred. Reversed.

CONCURRENCE AND DISSENT: (Belson, J.) The interests of the state and fetus are entitled to more weight than the court here gives them. In some cases, they may outweigh those of the mother.

EDITOR'S ANALYSIS: When a person is not capable of giving consent, it may be that the person had appointed a representative while they were still competent. If not, a court must try to divine what that person would have wanted. This requires an examination of all relevant circumstances, such as statements that the person might have made, as well as her value system. This inquiry is called "substituted judgment."

NOTES:

FEDERAL TRADE COMMISSION v. TENET HEALTH CARE CORP.

Federal agency (P) v. Health care corporation (D)
186 F.3d 1045 (8th Cir. 1999).

NATURE OF CASE: Appeal from an order enjoining the merger of two hospitals.

FACT SUMMARY: The district court found a substantial likelihood that the merger of of a Tenet hospital (D) with another hospital would substantially lessen competition between acute care hospitals in Poplar Bluff, Missouri.

CONCISE RULE OF LAW: Courts should refrain from intervening in a competitive situation which may upset the balance of the market in cases where there exists no evidence of barriers constraining normal operation of the market.

FACTS: Lucy Lee Hospital and Doctors' Regional Medical Center are the only two hospitals in Poplar Bluff, aside from a Veteran's Hospital. Tenet Healthcare Corporation (Tenet) (D) owns Lucy Lee Hospital, a general acute care hospital that provides primary and secondary care services in Poplar Bluff. Lucy Lee has 201 licensed beds and operates ten outpatient clinics in the surrounding counties. Doctors' Regional Medical Center in Poplar Bluff is also a general acute care hospital providing primary and secondary services. Doctors' Regional has 230 beds and also operates several rural health clinics in the area. Tenet (D) entered into an agreement to purchase Doctors' Regional for over forty million dollars, to operate it as a long-term care facility and to consolidate inpatient services at Lucy Lee. Pursuant to the Hart-Scott-Rodino Act, the hospitals filed a premerger certification with the Federal Trade Commission (FTC) (P). Shortly thereafter, the FTC (P) filed a complaint alleging that the hospitals' merger would lessen competition for primary and secondary inpatient hospitalization services in the area.

ISSUE: Should courts refrain from intervening in a competitive situation which may upset the balance of the market in cases where there exists no evidence of barriers constraining normal operation of the market?

DECISION AND HOLDING: (Beam, J.) Yes. Courts should refrain from intervening in a competitive situation which may upset the balance of the market in cases where there exists no evidence of barriers constraining normal operation of the market. A relevant market, consisting of a product market and a geographic market, must be defined before a court finds an antitrust violation. The FTC (P) in this case proposes a relevant geographic market that matches its service area. A service area and a merging firm's geographic market are not necessarily the same, however.

Because the FTC (P) failed to demonstrate a well-defined relevant market, it failed to show that the merged entity would possess market power. Patients may use hospitals outside the service area that may be closer to such residents or provide higher quality services in the patients' minds. Also, the potential efficiencies gained by the merger in this case should have been examined by the lower court to determine if this might have enhanced competition in the greater Southeast Missouri area. Reversed.

EDITOR'S ANALYSIS: The FTC has played a major role in subjecting the healthcare industry to antitrust scrutiny.

NOTES:

CHAPTER 2
THE TREATMENT RELATIONSHIP: FORMATION AND TERMINATION

QUICK REFERENCE RULES OF LAW

1. **The Duty to Accept Patients.** In obtaining the state's license to practice medicine, the state does not require, and the licensee does not engage, that he will practice at all or on other terms than he may choose to accept. (Hurley v. Eddingfield)

2. **The Duty to Accept Patients.** Liability on the part of a hospital may be predicated on the refusal of service to a patient in case of an unmistakable emergency, if the patient has relied upon a well-established custom of the hospital to render aid in such a case. (Wilmington General Hospital v. Manlove)

3. **The Duty to Accept Patients.** There is no general right to medical care or treatment provided by the state. (Wideman v. Shallowford Community Hospital)

4. **The Duty to Accept Patients.** Governmental regulation that affects a group's property interests does not constitute a taking of property where the regulated group is not required to participate in the regulated industry. (Burditt v. U.S. Department of Health and Human Services)

5. **Wrongful Reasons to Reject Patients.** Section 504 of the Rehabilitation Act of 1973 does not apply to medical treatment decisions. (United States v. University Hospital)

6. **Wrongful Reasons to Reject Patients.** In determining whether a patient is "otherwise qualified" for surgery, the possibility that reasonable accommodations might enable the patient to undergo the surgery despite the risks must be considered. (Glanz v. Vernick)

7. **Wrongful Reasons to Reject Patients.** A physician may condition care on a personal economic philosophy publicly announced to his patients. (Walker v. Pierce)

8. **Forming a Patient-Physician Relationship.** There is no rule of law that requires a physician to undertake the treatment of every patient who applies to him. (Clanton v. Von Haam)

9. **Forming a Patient-Physician Relationship.** Whether parties stand in such a relationship that the law would impose on the defendant a duty of reasonable conduct for the benefit of the plaintiff depends on the likelihood of injury, the burden of guarding against it, and the consequences of placing that burden on the defendant. (Reynolds v. Decatur Memorial Hospital)

10. **Forming a Patient-Physician Relationship.** Whether a physician-patient relationship was created is a question of fact, turning upon a determination whether the patient entrusted his treatment to the physician and the physician accepted the case. (Lyons v. Grether)

11. **Limiting the Scope of the Treatment Relationship.** A release waiving any malpractice liability of a nonprofit hospital is unenforceable. (Tunkl v. Regents of the University of California)

12. **Terminating the Treatment Relationship.** A physician may not unilaterally cease treating a patient due to lack of payment. (Ricks v. Budge)

13. **Terminating the Treatment Relationship.** A physician who abandons a patient may do so only after due notice and an ample opportunity afforded to secure the presence of other medical attendance. (Payton v. Weaver)

HURLEY v. EDDINGFIELD

Decedents heirs (P) v. Physician (D)

Ind. Sup. Ct., 59 N.E. 1058 (1901).

NATURE OF CASE: Appeal from an order granting demurrer in favor of defendant.

FACT SUMMARY: When Eddingfield (D), a physician, refused to render aid to decedent, his heirs, Hurley (P), unsuccessfully sued for wrongful death.

CONCISE RULE OF LAW: In obtaining the state's license to practice medicine, the state does not require, and the licensee does not engage, that he will practice at all or on other terms than he may choose to accept.

FACTS: Eddingfield (D) was decedent's family physician and refused to go to his aid when summoned. Although no other patients were requiring Eddingfield's (D) immediate services, and without any reason whatever, Eddingfield (D) refused the messenger's tender of a fee for his services when told of decedent's violent sickness. When death ensued, Hurley (P) sued, claiming that Eddingfield (D) wrongfully failed to meet his obligation to the public. Eddingfield's (D) demurrer to the wrongful death complaint was sustained by the court below and Hurley (P) appealed.

ISSUE: In obtaining the state's license to practice medicine, does the state require, and does the licensee engage, that he will practice at all or on other terms than he may choose to accept?

HOLDING AND DECISION: (Baker, J.) No. In obtaining the state's license to practice medicine, the state does not require, and the licensee does not engage, that he will practice at all or on other terms than he may choose to accept. Eddingfield's (D) refusal to enter into a contract of employment did not violate the law regulating the practice of medicine, which is a preventive, and not a compulsive, measure. Hurley's (P) analogies drawn from the obligations to the public on the part of innkeepers, common carriers, and the like, are beside the mark. Affirmed.

EDITOR'S ANALYSIS: The patient-healthcare provider relationship is normally a consensual one. A physician may refuse a patient for any reason, or for no reason. This freedom of contract has recently been limited by healthcare plans and insurance plans, as well as anti-discrimination laws.

QUICKNOTES

DEMURRER - The assertion that the opposing party's pleadings are insufficient and that the demurring party should not be made to answer.

NOTES:

WILMINGTON GENERAL HOSPITAL v. MANLOVE
Hospital (D) v. Deceased infant's parents (P)
Del. Sup. Ct., 174 A.2d 135 (1961).

NATURE OF CASE: Appeal from order denying summary judgment in an action brought against a hospital for refusing treatment.

FACT SUMMARY: When their infant son died after being refused treatment at Wilmington General Hospital (D), the Manloves (P) sued, contending that the Hospital (D) was liable for the death of their child.

CONCISE RULE OF LAW: Liability on the part of a hospital may be predicated on the refusal of service to a patient in case of an unmistakable emergency, if the patient has relied upon a well-established custom of the hospital to render aid in such a case.

FACTS: The Manloves' (P) infant son had been ill for several days when they took him to the emergency room at Wilmington General Hospital (D). The nurse there said that the Hospital (D) could not give any treatment because the child was under the care of a physician. She did not examine the child at all. The child died later that same day of bronchial pneumonia. The trial court found that the Hospital's (D) receipt of grants of public money and tax exemptions made it a quasi-public or a public hospital rather than a private one and concluded that liability could be imposed in an emergency case. The judge indicated that the fact that death followed in a few hours showed an emergency. When its motion for summary judgment was denied, the Hospital (D) appealed.

ISSUE: May liability on the part of a hospital be predicated on the refusal of service to a patient in case of an unmistakable emergency, if the patient has relied upon a well-established custom of the hospital to render aid in such a case?

HOLDING AND DECISION: (Southerland, J.) Yes. The Liability on the part of a hospital may be predicated on the refusal of service to a patient in case of an unmistakable emergency, if the patient has relied upon a well-established custom of the hospital to render aid in such a case. In this case, the mere recitation of the infant's symptoms was not in itself evidence of an emergency sufficient to present a question for the jury. Before such an issue could arise there would have to be evidence that an experienced nurse should have known that such symptoms constituted unmistakable evidence of an emergency. The case might turn on additional evidence not considered earlier and should go back for further proceedings. If the Manloves (P) cannot adduce evidence showing some incompetency of the nurse, or some breach of duty or some negligence, their case must fail. The order denying summary judgment is affirmed on different grounds.

EDITOR'S ANALYSIS: The court below had decided that the Hospital (D) was public and therefore could be held liable. The appellate court, however, decided that the hospital was private, but reasoned that it could still be held liable. The judge analogized to a case of negligent termination of gratuitous services, which creates a tort liability. A refusal to see a patient might result in a worsening of the condition because of the time lost in a useless attempt to obtain medical help.

QUICKNOTES
SUMMARY JUDGMENT - Judgment rendered by a court in response to a motion by one of the parties, claiming that the lack of a question of material fact in respect to an issue warrants disposition of the issue without consideration by the jury.

NOTES:

WIDEMAN v. SHALLOWFORD COMMUNITY HOSPITAL

Patient (P) v. Hospital (D)

826 F.2d 1030 (11th Cir. 1987).

NATURE OF CASE: Appeal from ruling that plaintiff's constitutional right to medical services had been violated.

FACT SUMMARY: When a county emergency vehicle took Wideman (P) to a different hospital than she had requested and she consequently gave birth prematurely, she claimed that her constitutional right to the medical care and services of her choice had been violated.

CONCISE RULE OF LAW: There is no general right to medical care or treatment provided by the state.

FACTS: When Wideman (P), who was four months pregnant, experienced abdominal pain, she called her physician, who instructed her to go immediately to Piedmont Hospital. Widener (P) then called 911 and requested an ambulance to take her to Piedmont. The DeKalb County Emergency Medical Service team refused to take Widener (P) to Piedmont, and took her against her wishes to another hospital, Shallowford Community Hospital (D). After a substantial delay, the physician at Shallowford (D) hospital spoke to Widener's (P) physician at Piedmont and had her transferred there. At that point, however, the physician was unable to stop her labor and Wideman (P) gave birth to a premature baby who survived only four hours. Wideman (P) sued Shallowford (D), alleging that the county government's policy of using its emergency vehicles only to transport patients to certain county hospitals which guaranteed the payment of the county's medical bills violated a right protected by the federal constitution. The district court assumed that the alleged policy violated a cognizable constitutional right for the provision of medical treatment and services by the county. Shallowford (D) appealed.

ISSUE: Is there a general right to medical care or treatment provided by the state?

HOLDING AND DECISION: (Hill, J.) No. There is no general right to medical care or treatment provided by the state. A state has no duty under the Fourteenth Amendment to provide protective or medical services. A constitutional duty can arise only when a state or municipality, by exercising a significant degree of custody or control over an individual, places that person in a worse situation than he would have been had the government not acted at all. In the present case, DeKalb County did not exercise a degree of coercion, dominion, or restraint over Wideman (P) sufficient to create such a special relationship. Her physical condition cannot be attributed to the county, therefore the county was under no affirmative constitutional duty to provide medical services at all. Reversed.

EDITOR'S ANALYSIS: In this case, the court held that even if the alleged policy of the county to transport patients only to certain hospitals were proved, no constitutional right would be violated. Recent Supreme Court cases dealing with access to abortions support the conclusion that the state is under no constitutional duty to provide substantive services for those within its borders. Moreover, the Constitution, according to the Supreme Court, imposes no obligation on the state to pay any of the medical expenses of indigents.

NOTES:

BURDITT v. U.S. DEPARTMENT OF HEALTH AND HUMAN SERVICES

Physician (P) v. Regulatory agency (D)
934 F.2d 1362 (5th Cir. 1991).

NATURE OF CASE: Appeal from fine assessed against a physician for alleged violation of the Emergency Medical Treatment and Active Labor Act (EMTALA).

FACT SUMMARY: When the Department of Health and Human Services (HHS) (D) fined Burditt (P), a physician, for violating EMTALA by not providing adequate emergency medical treatment, he argued that EMTALA effected a public taking of his services without just compensation in contravention of the Constitution's Fifth Amendment.

CONCISE RULE OF LAW: Governmental regulation that affects a group's property interests does not constitute a taking of property where the regulated group is not required to participate in the regulated industry.

FACTS: Burditt (P) was the physician on duty when Rivera, a patient who had received no prenatal care and had neither a regular doctor nor a means of payment, arrived at the hospital in labor and with dangerously high blood pressure. Burditt (D) refused to take care of the patient and arranged to have her transported to another hospital 170 miles away. The HHS appeals board (P) found that the hospital had properly screened the patient under EMTALA requirements and had discovered that she had an "emergency medical condition" but failed to provide stabilizing treatment, according to the evidence presented. The HHS appeals board (D) concluded that the patient was in active labor when she arrived and that Burditt (P) had not satisfied the requirements under EMTALA for a transfer before stabilization because he had not reasonably concluded that the benefits of transfer outweighed the risks and he had not arranged for the transfer with appropriate personnel and transportation. Burditt (P) appealed, alleging that EMTALA effected a public taking of his services without just compensation.

ISSUE: Does governmental regulation that affects a group's property interests constitute a taking of property where the regulated group is not required to participate in the regulated industry?

HOLDING AND DECISION: (Reavley, J.) No. Governmental regulation that affects a group's property interests does not constitute a taking of property where the regulated group is not required to participate in the regulated industry. Burditt (P) was free to negotiate with the hospital regarding his responsibilities under EMTALA. Physicians only voluntarily accept responsibilities under EMTALA if they consider it in their best interest to do so.

Accordingly, Burditt's (P) claim under the Takings Clause was without merit. Affirmed.

EDITOR'S ANALYSIS: EMTALA was passed in 1986 as part of the Omnibus Reconciliation Act. State laws had proved to be inadequate to control widespread patient dumping at hospitals. EMTALA creates two duties: a duty to screen patients and a duty to stabilize those who have been found to be in an emergency.

QUICKNOTES

EMTALA - Provides that patients in active labor be treated or transferred if the medical benefits of transfer outweigh the increased risks to the patient.

TAKING - A governmental action that substantially deprives an owner of the use and enjoyment of his or her property, requiring compensation.

NOTES:

UNITED STATES v. UNIVERSITY HOSPITAL
Federal government (P) v. Hospital (D)
729 F.2d 144 (2d Cir. 1984).

NATURE OF CASE: Appeal from ruling that a decision not to perform corrective surgery did not violate § 504 of the Rehabilitation Act.

FACT SUMMARY: When parents' decision not to have certain surgery performed on their handicapped infant was held not to be a violation of federal law, the federal government (P) appealed.

CONCISE RULE OF LAW: Section 504 of the Rehabilitation Act of 1973 does not apply to medical treatment decisions.

FACTS: When Baby Jane Doe was born with multiple birth defects, including microcephaly (an abnormally small head), the parents elected to forego the corrective surgery likely to prolong her life without improving many of her handicapping conditions. A Vermont attorney (P) unrelated to the child and her family commenced a proceeding in New York State Supreme Court seeking appointment of a guardian ad litem for the child and an order directing University Hospital (D) to perform the corrective surgery to avoid violating § 504 of the Rehabilitation Act. The Appellate Division found that the parents' informed, intelligent and reasonable decision was in the best interests of the infant and determined that there was no basis for judicial intervention. The United States (P) appealed.

ISSUE: Does § 504 of the Rehabilitation Act apply to medical treatment decisions?

HOLDING AND DECISION: (Pratt, J.) No. Section 504 of the Rehabilitation Act of 1973 does not apply to medical treatment decisions. Section 504 provides that no otherwise qualified handicapped individual in the United States shall, solely by reason of his handicap, be excluded from the participation in, be denied the benefits of, or be subjected to discrimination under any program or activity receiving federal financial assistance standard. However, a bona fide medical judgment is beyond the reach of § 504 and is to be distinguished from decisionmaking based solely on an individual's handicap. The United States' (P) argument that the infant's microcephaly, which the record indicated will result in severe mental retardation, is the handicapping condition and must be treated the same as other birth defects such as spina bifida and hydrocephalus is flawed. Discrimination against a handicapped individual is prohibited under § 504 only where the individual's handicap is unrelated to the services in question. The "otherwise qualified" criterion of § 504 cannot be meaningfully applied to a medical treatment decision. Furthermore, the legislative history indicates that Congress never intended that § 504 be used to monitor medical treatment of defective newborn infants or establish standards for

a particular quality of life. In the present case, Baby Jane Doe has been treated in an evenhanded manner in that the Hospital (D) has always been and remains willing to perform the surgeries if her parents would consent. Requiring the Hospital (D) either to undertake the surgery notwithstanding the parents' decision or alternatively, to petition the state to override the parents' decision, would impose a particularly onerous affirmative action burden upon the Hospital (D). Affirmed.

DISSENT: (Winter, J.) Since § 504 was patterned after the Civil Rights Act of 1964 prohibiting discrimination on the basis of race, Congress was persuaded that a handicapping condition is analogous to race. Although the government is not entitled to override a medical judgment, it may legitimately inquire as to whether a judgment in question was a bona fide medical judgment. A denial of medical treatment to an infant because the infant is black is not legitimated by parental consent and neither is one based on a handicapped condition.

EDITOR'S ANALYSIS: This case points out the difficulties in applying provisions of the Rehabilitation Act to medical treatment decisions. Although physicians and hospitals are free to refuse to treat patients for reasons such as the inability to pay, they may not do so for the wrong reasons. That is, they may not discriminate on the basis of a patient's race, sex, religion, disability, or other enumerated condition.

QUICKNOTES

REHABILITATION ACT OF 1973 - Provides that handicapped individuals may not be excluded from participation in any program or activities receiving federal financial assistance.

NOTES:

GLANZ v. VERNICK

HIV-positive patient (P) and decedent (P) v. Physician (D)
756 F. Supp. 632 (D. Mass. 1991).

NATURE OF CASE: Action seeking compensatory damages for pain and suffering, emotional distress, punitive damages and attorney's fees for violations of § 504 of the Rehabilitation Act.

FACT SUMMARY: Vernick (D), a physician at the Ear, Nose and Throat Clinic refused to perform surgery on Vadnais (P), Glanz's (P) decedent, after learning that Vadnais (P) was HIV-positive.

CONCISE RULE OF LAW: In determining whether a patient is "otherwise qualified" for surgery, the possibility that reasonable accommodations might enable the patient to undergo the surgery despite the risks must be considered.

FACTS: Vernick (D) treated Vadnais (P) for severe pain in the right ear and recommended surgery to repair a perforation. However, when Vernick (D) learned that Vadnais (P) was infected with HIV, he refused to perform the operation. Alleging that HIV-positive status was a "handicap" within the meaning of the Rehabilitation Act of 1973, Vadnais (P) sued for compensatory damages for the pain and suffering and emotional distress occasioned by Vernick's (D) refusal to perform the surgery.

ISSUE: In determining whether a patient is "otherwise qualified" for surgery, must the possibility that reasonable accommodations might enable the patient to undergo the surgery despite the risks be considered?

HOLDING AND DECISION: (Mazzone, J.) Yes. In determining whether a patient is "otherwise qualified" for surgery, the possibility that reasonable accommodations might enable the patient to undergo the surgery despite the risks must be considered. The "otherwise qualified" determination requires an individualized inquiry and appropriate findings of fact. Based on the evidence, facts are certainly available to warrant the conclusion that Vadnais (P) was "otherwise qualified" for surgery. Moreover, Vernick (D) has not produced any evidence that reasonable accommodations could not have been made. A strict rule of deference to a doctor's medical judgment would completely eviscerate § 504's function of preventing discrimination against the disabled in the healthcare context. Vadnais (P) must be given an opportunity to prove that the reason given by Vernick (D) that made him unqualified was a pretext or encompassed unjustified consideration of the handicap itself.

EDITOR'S ANALYSIS: This case set forth the proper evidentiary approach to be taken in § 504 cases. The plaintiff must first make out a prima facie case that he was otherwise qualified for surgery, and only then does the burden shift to the defendant to show that the plaintiff's handicap made him unqualified. Then, in order to prevail, the plaintiff must prove either that the reason given by the defendant is a pretext or that the reason encompasses unjustified consideration of the handicap itself.

NOTES:

13

WALKER v. PIERCE
Indigent patients (P) v. Physician (D)
560 F.2d 609 (4th Cir. 1977).

NATURE OF CASE: Complaint requesting damages and declaratory and injunctive relief for violation of civil rights.

FACT SUMMARY: An obstetrician's (D) policy of requesting that indigent patients having a third child voluntarily submit to sterilization following the delivery of the third child was challenged by two black female patients (P) as an incursion of their constitutional rights of privacy, due process of law and equal protection of the law, as well as discrimination on the basis of race and color.

CONCISE RULE OF LAW: A physician may condition care on a personal economic philosophy publicly announced to his patients.

FACTS: Pierce (D) was a physician who had a policy of requesting, as condition for his care, that all patients who were unable to financially support themselves voluntarily submit to sterilization following the delivery of their third child. Walker (P) was separated from her husband and receiving Aid to Families with Dependent Children and Medicaid benefits and expecting her fourth child when she refused to consent to Pierce's (D) sterilization policy. Walker (P) testified that Pierce (D) threatened to have her state assistance terminated unless she cooperated. A Department of Social Services case worker education contacted by Pierce (D) spoke with Walker (P) about the sterilization. Walker (P) later agreed to sign the consent form for sterilization. Following the delivery of her fourth child, Walker (P) signed two more consent forms and a tubal ligation was performed. Walker's (P) hospital bills and doctor's fees were order by Medicaid. Walker (P) and another patient (P) sued Pierce (D), alleging constitutional violations and race discrimination.

ISSUE: May a physician condition care on a personal economic philosophy?

HOLDING AND DECISION: (Bryan, J.) Yes. A physician may condition care on a personal economic philosophy publicly announced to his patients. There is no judicial precedent or statute inhibiting Pierce (D) from establishing and pursuing the policy he has publicly and freely announced. At no time is he shown to have forced his view upon any mother. In this case, not just one, but three formal written consents were obtained. Moreover, since Pierce (D) was not a state actor, he could not be found to have violated his patients' constitutional rights.

EDITOR'S ANALYSIS: Under the South Carolina Medicaid plan, the patient-physician relationship is one of free choice for both parties. The physician, under no contract with the state, simply submits his bill when treatment is concluded to the Medicaid insurance carrier instead of the patient. Thus he could not be found to have been a state actor for constitutional analysis purposes.

QUICKNOTES

STATE ACTOR - Term utilized in conjunction with an action brought pursuant to the Fourteenth Amendment or the Civil Rights Act, claiming that a private action that is properly attributed to the government violated the plaintiff's civil rights.

NOTES:

CLANTON v. VON HAAM
Paraplegic (P) v. Physician (D)
Ga. Ct. App., 340 S.E.2d 627 (1986).

NATURE OF CASE: Appeal from summary judgment in favor of defendant in action for professional negligence.

FACT SUMMARY: Clanton (P) claimed that Von Haam (D) was negligent because when she called him for medical advice, he refused to see her.

CONCISE RULE OF LAW: There is no rule of law that requires a physician to undertake the treatment of every patient who applies to him.

FACTS: After Clanton (P) went to the emergency room and was released, she called Von Haam (D), who had treated her earlier for a totally unrelated condition. Von Haam (D) refused to see her at that time and told her to wait until morning. Her condition deteriorated after that time until she was later admitted to the hospital and became paralyzed. Clanton (P) claimed that Von Haam (D) knew or should have known that her condition was critical and in the absence of action would result in paraplegia. Clanton (P) alleged that she was a paraplegic as a direct and proximate result of Von Haam's (D) negligent failure to recognize the need for immediate treatment. The district court granted Von Haam's (D) motion for summary judgment, based on his affidavit that no physician-patient relationship existed prior to nor was created by the phone call. Clanton (P) appealed, claiming that a jury determination was necessary to resolve the issues of whether a physician-patient relationship existed and whether Von Haam (D) was negligent.

ISSUE: Is there any rule of law that requires a physician to undertake the treatment of every patient who applies to him?

HOLDING AND DECISION: (Carley, J.) No. There is no rule of law that requires a physician to undertake the treatment of every patient who applies to him. One who has secured a medical license according to statute is not liable for damages alleged to result from the refusal to take a case. It is undisputed that Clanton (P) interpreted the phone conversation as a total refusal to render medical expertise and did not rely upon any medical advice from Von Haam (D) whatsoever. Since there was never a consensual transaction whereby Clanton (P) became Von Haam's (D) patient, no relationship was created that could give rise to any professional duty, the breach of which duty proximately caused Clanton's (P) existing condition. Affirmed.

EDITOR'S ANALYSIS: This claim for negligence was dismissed since no professional relationship could be established. Merely that the defendant was a physician and knew of the condition of the plaintiff does not create any duty of rendering medical care.

Since Clanton (P) herself never claimed to have followed the Von Haam's (D) advice, she could not hold him liable for negligence.

QUICKNOTES

NEGLIGENCE - Conduct falling below the standard of care that a reasonable person would demonstrate under similar conditions.

PROXIMATE CAUSE - The natural sequence of events without which an injury would not have been sustained.

NOTES:

REYNOLDS v. DECATUR MEMORIAL HOSPITAL

Patient's parents (P) v. Consulting doctor (D)
Ill. App. Ct., 660 N.E.2d 235 (1996).

NATURE OF CASE: Appeal from judgment for defendant in medical malpractice suit for negligence.

FACT SUMMARY: Reynolds (P) alleged that a physician-patient relationship was created when another physician (D) was contacted by the treating physician by phone for an informal consultation.

CONCISE RULE OF LAW: Whether parties stand in such a relationship that the law would impose on the defendant a duty of reasonable conduct for the benefit of the plaintiff depends on the likelihood of injury, the burden of guarding against it, and the consequences of placing that burden on the defendant.

FACTS: Reynolds (P), a two-and-a-half-year-old child, fell while jumping off a couch and was taken to the emergency room of Decatur Memorial Hospital (D). A pediatrician who examined Reynolds (P) at the hospital called Fulbright (D), another physician, to discuss Reynolds' (P) condition. When Reynolds (P) sued the Decatur Memorial Hospital (D) for negligence, he claimed that Fulbright (D) was liable. The trial court found there was no physician-patient relationship created by the telephone conversation and, therefore, no duty was owed by Fulbright (D). Reynolds (P) appealed.

ISSUE: Does the determination of whether parties stand in such a relationship that the law would impose a duty on the defendant depend on the likelihood of injury, the burden of guarding against it, and the consequences of placing that burden on the defendant?

HOLDING AND DECISION: (McCullough, J.) Yes. The relationship of physician and patient is a consensual relationship in which the patient knowingly seeks the physician's assistance and the physician knowingly accepts the person as a patient. A consensual relationship can exist where another person contacts the physician on behalf of the patient, but this is not a case where Fulbright (D) was asked to provide a service for Reynolds (P), conduct lab tests or review test results. Fulbright (D) did nothing more than answer an inquiry from a colleague. He was not contacted again and he charged no fee. A doctor who gives an informal opinion at the request of a treating physician does not owe a duty of care to the patient whose case was discussed. In a negligence action for medical malpractice, there must be a duty owed by defendant to the plaintiff, a breach of duty, an injury proximately caused by the breach, and resultant damages. The determination of whether the parties stood in such a relationship to one another that the law would impose a duty of reasonable conduct is a question of law. To find a physician-patient

relationship to result from every such informal conversation would have a chilling effect on the practice of medicine. Affirmed.

EDITOR'S ANALYSIS: The court added that a finding that informal consultations among physicians offered as a courtesy and without a fee created formal patient-physician relationships would prevent such conferences from occurring. Fulbright testified that he often received informal inquiries from other doctors asking questions and seeking suggestions. He considered this a courtesy service for which he did not bill.

NOTES:

LYONS v. GRETHER
Blind patient (P) v. Physician (D)
Va. Sup. Ct., 239 S.E.2d 103 (1977).

NATURE OF CASE: Appeal from demurrer to action for damages for pain and suffering for breach of duty to treat.

FACT SUMMARY: Grether (D), a physician, refused to treat Lyons (P), a patient who had made an appointment for treatment of a particular ailment, because she refused to remove her guide dog from his waiting room.

CONCISE RULE OF LAW: Whether a physician-patient relationship was created is a question of fact, turning upon a determination whether the patient entrusted his treatment to the physician and the physician accepted the case.

FACTS: Lyons (P), a blind person, made a medical appointment "for treatment of a vaginal infection." When she arrived at the medical office with her young son and guide dog, she was told that Grether (D), the physician, would not see her unless her guide dog was removed from the waiting room. Concerned about the safety, care, and availability of the dog, she insisted that the dog remain. Lyons (P) and her son were then "evicted" by Grether (D), who refused to treat her and failed to help her find other medical attention. Lyons (P) alleged that Grether's (D) wrongful conduct caused her great pain, suffering, and humiliation. Lyons (P) sued for damages resulting from Grether's (D) breach of his duty to treat. Grether (D) demurred.

ISSUE: Is whether a physician-patient relationship was created a question of fact, turning upon a determination whether the patient entrusted his treatment to the physician and the physician accepted the case?

HOLDING AND DECISION: (Poff, J.) Yes. Whether a physician-patient relationship was created is a question of fact, turning upon a determination whether the patient entrusted his treatment to the physician and the physician accepted the case. In this case, the facts stated in the motion for judgment and the reasonable inferences deducible therefrom were sufficient to allege the creation of a physician-patient relationship and a duty to treat. The unmistakable implication of the facts alleged in Lyons' (P) complaint was that Lyons (P) had sought and Grether (D) had granted an appointment at a designated time and place for the performance of a specific, medical service, i.e., the treatment of a particular ailment. It is immaterial that this factual allegation might have been contradicted by evidence at trial. Upon demurrer, the test of the sufficiency of a motion for judgment is whether it states the essential elements of a cause of action, not whether evidence might be adduced to defeat it. Reversed and remanded.

EDITOR'S ANALYSIS: The court also found that a factual issue arose as to whether Grether's (D) refusal to treat Lyons (P) amounted to a lawful termination of their professional relationship. A physician has no legal obligation to accept as a patient everyone who seeks his services. A physician's duty only arises upon the creation of a physician-patient relationship.

NOTES:

TUNKL v. REGENTS OF THE UNIV. OF CALIFORNIA
Patient (P) v. Hospital owners and operators (D)
Cal. Sup. Ct., 383 P.2d 441 (1963).

NATURE OF CASE: Appeal of denial of damages for malpractice.

FACT SUMMARY: Prior to admission to a nonprofit hospital, Tunkl's (P) decedent signed a release waiving any malpractice action.

CONCISE RULE OF LAW: A release waiving any malpractice liability of a nonprofit hospital is unenforceable.

FACTS: Tunkl's (P) decedent was admitted to UCLA Medical Center, a nonprofit and largely research-based medical facility, as part of a research project. Prior to admission, he signed a liability waiver. While in the hospital, he was allegedly injured due to physician malpractice. The decedent brought an action for personal injury, into which Tunkl (P) substituted as administratrix following the decedent's demise. A jury held the release valid and returned a defense verdict. The court of appeal affirmed, and the California Supreme Court granted review.

ISSUE: Is a release waiving malpractice liability of a nonprofit hospital enforceable?

HOLDING AND DECISION: (Tobriner, J.) No. A release waiving malpractice liability of a nonprofit hospital is unenforceable. Under Civil Code § 1668, a contract purporting to exculpate a party from his own negligence will not stand if it involves "the public interest." A contract will involve such interest it the party seeking exculpations engaged in performing a service of great public importance, which is often a practical necessity for some. A contract for hospital services certainly falls within this definition. Here, however, it is argued that the section should not be applied to a nonprofit charitable hospital. However, this court has already abolished charitable immunity; to the extent a charity is negligent, it may be liable. Since the basis for the jury verdict was the unenforceable contract, the matter must be retried. Reversed.

EDITOR'S ANALYSIS: Generally speaking, courts have been quite hostile to attempts by health care providers to limit their malpractice liability. General releases are almost never honored and arbitration provisions have only been partially successful. Whatever liability limitations exist do so by virtue of legislative action.

QUICKNOTES
CAL. CIVIL CODE § 1668 - Provides that all contracts which attempt to exempt anyone from responsibility for his own fraud or willful injury to the person or property of another, or violation of law, are against the policy of the law.

RICKS v. BUDGE
Patient (P) v. Physicians (D)
Utah Sup. Ct., 91 Utah 307, 64 P.2d 208 (1937).

NATURE OF CASE: Appeal of directed verdict denying award of damages for medical malpractice.

FACT SUMMARY: Dr. Budge (D) ceased treating Ricks (P) due to an unpaid account.

CONCISE RULE OF LAW: A physician may not unilaterally cease treating a patient due to lack of payment.

FACTS: From March 11 to March 15, 1935, Ricks (P) was treated by Dr. S.M. Budge (D) for an infected hand. He was released on March 15. On March 17, he again presented himself, being symptomatic. Dr. D. C. Budge (D) sent him to a hospital, where S. M. Budge (D) was on staff. Dr. S.M. Budge (D) refused to treat Ricks (P), as his account was past due. Ricks (P) went to another facility, where he was treated. Eventually, part of his hand had to be amputated. Ricks (P) sued the Budges (D) for malpractice. The trial court directed a verdict in favor of the Budges (D), and Ricks (P) appealed.

ISSUE: May a physician unilaterally cease treating a patient due to lack of payment?

HOLDING AND DECISION: (Hanson, J.) No. A physician may not unilaterally cease treating a patient due to lack of payment. A physician, upon undertaking to treat a patient, must continue to care for the patient until such time as care is no longer required. A physician can withdraw from care of a patient, but he must give the patient sufficient notice as to allow him to find alternative care. Here, the evidence was sufficient to go to a jury as to whether the Budges (D) had continued their care of Ricks (P) and then ceased to provide services without allowing him sufficient time to seek alternate care. Reversed.

EDITOR'S ANALYSIS: Many states have ethical or legal rules regarding the duty of physicians to care for those who cannot pay for services. The nature of the duty, as well as its source, varies. Clashing as they do with economic reality, these rules are usually more notable for being an aspiration than a practice.

PAYTON v. WEAVER

Disruptive patient (P) v. Clinic (D) and physician (D)
Cal. Ct. App., 182 Cal. Rptr. 225 (1982).

NATURE OF CASE: Appeal from ruling that a physician owed no duty to provide further treatment.

FACT SUMMARY: When Weaver (D), a physician, refused to treat Payton (P), she alleged violations of the Health and Safety Code, and sought a court order mandating treatment.

CONCISE RULE OF LAW: A physician who abandons a patient may do so only after due notice and an ample opportunity afforded to secure the presence of other medical attendance.

FACTS: Payton (P) required hemodialysis several times each week due to a chronic kidney condition. When Weaver (D), a physician who was treating Payton (P), sent her a letter that he would no longer treat her because of her persistent uncooperative and antisocial behavior and drug use, she filed a petition for mandate to compel Weaver (D) and the hospital to continue to provide her with outpatient dialysis services. The litigation was settled by a stipulated order which called for continued treatment provided that Payton (P) met certain conditions: keeping appointments, no alcohol or drug use, dietary restrictions, full cooperation, and counseling. The next year, Weaver (D), contending that Payton (P) had failed to fulfill any part of the bargain, again notified her that treatment would be terminated. Payton (P) initiated a second proceeding against the clinic (D) and Weaver (D). The trial court found that Payton (P) had violated each and every condition that she had accepted as part of the stipulated order and that her behavior was "knowing and intentional." Her disruptive behavior was found to affect other patients and the staff as well. The court found that, on balance, the rights and privileges of other patients endangered by Payton's (P) conduct were superior to the rights or equities which she claimed, and that Weaver (D) and the clinic (D) with which he was associated had no legal obligation to continue to provide Payton (P) with medical treatment. Payton (P) appealed.

ISSUE: May a physician who abandons a patient do so only after due notice and an ample opportunity afforded to secure the presence of other medical attendance?

HOLDING AND DECISION: (Grodin, J.) Yes. A physician who abandons a patient may do so only after due notice, and an ample opportunity afforded to secure the presence of other medical attendance. Weaver (D) gave sufficient notice to Payton (P) and discharged all obligations in that regard. It appears that Dr. Weaver (D) behaved according to the highest standards of the medical profession and that there exists no basis in law or in

equity to saddle him with a continuing obligation for Payton's (P) welfare. Health and Safety Code § 1317, requiring hospitals to provide emergency care, does not apply to Payton's (P) need for continuing treatment. Nevertheless, while disruptive behavior on the part of a patient may constitute good cause for an individual hospital to refuse further treatment, there may exist a collective responsibility on the part of providers of scarce health care resources in a community, enforceable through equity, to share the burden of difficult patients over time. This argument was not presented to the trial court, however, and the record is not adequate to support relief on that ground as a matter of law. Affirmed.

EDITOR'S ANALYSIS: The care providers in the area did ultimately agreed to share the responsibility for Payton's (P) treatment after this case was decided. Note that failure-to-treat liability, also known as abandonment liability, is analogous to breach of contract cases in that liability stems from nonmedical cessation of treatment. The action of a abandonment is distinct from an action for malpractice, which is generally grounded in cessation of treatment for medical reasons, albeit incorrect ones.

QUICKNOTES

PETITION FOR MANDATE - The communication of a decision by a reviewing court to a lower court, directing the appropriate disposition of the case.

NOTES:

3

CHAPTER 3
THE TREATMENT RELATIONSHIP:
CONFIDENTIALITY, CONSENT, AND CONFLICTS OF INTEREST

QUICK REFERENCE RULES OF LAW

1. **The Duty to Maintain Confidentiality.** Willful disclosure of confidential AIDS information does not require that the confidentiality was breached with the intent to cause injury. (Doe v. Marselle)

2. **The Duty to Breach Confidentiality.** A physician may owe a duty to a non-patient third party for injuries caused by the physician's negligence, if the injuries suffered and the manner in which they occurred were reasonably foreseeable. (Bradshaw v. Daniel)

3. **The Competing Disclosure Standards.** Prior to a medical procedure, a physician must disclose to a patient all risks which a reasonable person would consider significant in deciding whether to undergo the procedure. (Canterbury v. Spence)

4. **The Competing Disclosure Standards.** Under the medical malpractice standard in informed consent cases, physicians are required to disclose that which the reasonably careful, skillful, and prudent physician would disclose under the same or similar circumstances. (Culbertson v. Mernitz)

5. **Limiting Liability for Failure to Disclose.** In most cases, expert testimony is necessary to establish those instances where the duty to disclose arises and what disclosures a reasonable, medical practitioner would have made under the same or similar circumstances. (Rizzo v. Schiller)

6. **Fiduciary Obligations, Conflicts of Interest, and Novel Disclosure Obligations.** A physician who is seeking a patient's consent for a medical procedure must, in order to satisfy his fiduciary duty and to obtain the patient's informed consent, disclose personal interests unrelated to the patient's health, whether research or economic, that may affect his judgment. (Moore v. The Regents of the University of California)

7. **Fiduciary Obligations, Conflicts of Interest, and Novel Disclosure Obligations.** An informed consent action based upon a physician's misrepresentations regarding experience and skill may lie if the misrepresentations proximately caused a patient's injuries. (Howard v. University of Medicine & Dentistry of New Jersey)

8. **Human Experimentation and Research.** Under Maryland law, informed consent agreements in nontherapeutic research projects can constitute contracts and can constitute special relationships giving rise to duties, out of the breach of which negligence actions may lie. (Grimes v. Kennedy Krieger Institute, Inc.)

DOE v. MARSELLE

HIV-positive patient (P) v. Physician (D) and assistant (D)
Conn. Sup. Ct., 675 A.2d 835 (1996).

NATURE OF CASE: Appeal from dismissal of an action for violation of AIDS confidentiality.

FACT SUMMARY: Doe's (P) HIV status was revealed by her surgeon's assistant, Marselle (D).

CONCISE RULE OF LAW: Willful disclosure of confidential AIDS information does not require that the confidentiality was breached with the intent to cause injury.

FACTS: Doe (P) was a patient of Dr. Flores (D) and disclosed that she was infected with HIV. A surgical assistant to Flores (D), Marselle (D), discovered the information and wanted to disclose the information to her sons, who were illegal drug users and had friends in common with Doe (P). Flores (D) authorized Marselle (D) to make the disclosures provided that she not identify Doe (P) by name. When Doe (P) found out that Marselle (D) had told people in the community that she was HIV positive, she brought suit against Flores (D) and Marselle (D) for violating the AIDS confidentiality statute. The trial court ruled that the "willful" requirement of the disclosure meant that the defendants must have intended to injure Doe (P) by their disclosures. An appellate court agreed and Doe (P) petitioned to certify the question of the meaning of the word "willful" to the Connecticut Supreme Court.

ISSUE: Does willful disclosure of confidential AIDS information require that the confidentiality be breached with the intent to cause injury?

HOLDING AND DECISION: (Katz, J.) No. Willful disclosure of confidential AIDS information does not require that the confidentiality be breached with the intent to cause injury. The AIDS confidentiality statute was designed to help combat the AIDS epidemic by protecting privacy. The legislature was concerned that people would not step forward for testing and treatment if the results became public information, because AIDS victims were stigmatized. In order to accomplish this goal, disclosure of confidential HIV-related information was prohibited except in very limited and discrete circumstances. Even some health care providers are not entitled to the information. Additionally, disclosure, when authorized, is strictly limited. Given the reasons for the statute, it is difficult to find a definition of willful that would make unauthorized disclosures permissible except in the extreme situation where the person disclosing the information actually intends to injure the protected individual. This type of definition would do nothing to advance the goals of the statute. Rather, it is more logical and consistent to interpret willful to mean a knowing disclosure of confidential HIV-related information, rather than an inadvertent or nonvolitional disclosure. Accordingly, the trial court is reversed and the case is remanded.

EDITOR'S ANALYSIS: The AIDS epidemic caused states to enact confidentiality rules that were different from the rules for other diseases. This was based on the fact that the HIV virus cannot be spread through casual contact like other contagious diseases. Also, the fact that a stigma was attached to people contracting the disease was a key consideration.

QUICKNOTES

CONNECTICUT AIDS STATUTE - Prohibits disclosure of confidential HIV-related information, except in specially authorized circumstances.

NOTES:

BRADSHAW v. DANIEL
Decedent's son (P) v. Physician (D)
Tenn. Sup. Ct., 854 S.W.2d 865 (1993).

NATURE OF CASE: Appeal from summary judgment in a negligence action to recover damages for wrongful death.

FACT SUMMARY: When Mrs. Johns contracted a fatal case of Rocky Mountain Spotted Fever shortly after her husband died from the same disease, her son Bradshaw (P) brought this action against Daniel (D), Mrs. Johns' doctor, for failing to inform Mrs. Johns of the risk of exposure to the disease.

CONCISE RULE OF LAW: A physician may owe a duty to a non-patient third party for injuries caused by the physician's negligence, if the injuries suffered and the manner in which they occurred were reasonably foreseeable.

FACTS: Elmer Johns, a patient of Dr. Daniel (D), went to the hospital emergency room for treatment. Although Johns was admitted to the hospital, Daniel (D) did not see him until three days later, at which time Daniel (D) prescribed the drug of choice for Rocky Mountain Spotted Fever. He did not warn Mrs. Johns of the symptoms or the need to seek immediate treatment if she had such symptoms. Johns died the next day, and an autopsy confirmed that his death was due to Rocky Mountain Spotted Fever. Johns' wife later became ill and died from the same disease. Bradshaw (P), her son, brought this action, alleging Daniel (D) was negligent in failing to tell Johns' wife the cause of her husband's death or in failing to advise her of the risks of exposure to the disease. After a jury awarded $50,000 to Bradshaw (P), he moved for a new trial on the grounds of immediate damages, while Daniel (D) filed a motion for judgment notwithstanding the verdict on the grounds that no legal duty existed since Rocky Mountain Spotted Fever is not contagious. The court of appeals granted Daniel's (D) motion for summary judgment. This appeal followed.

ISSUE: May a physician owe a duty to a nonpatient third party for injuries caused by the physician's negligence, if the injuries suffered and the manner in which they occurred were reasonably foreseeable?

HOLDING AND DECISION: (Anderson, J.) Yes. A physician may owe a duty to a nonpatient third party for injuries caused by the physician's negligence, if the injuries suffered and the manner in which they occurred were reasonably foreseeable. Daniel (D) conceded that there is a medical duty to inform the family when there is a diagnosis of a disease like Rocky Mountain Spotted Fever, which, although not contagious, often appears in the same family through a phenomenon called clustering. Here, there was a foreseeable risk of harm to Mrs. Johns, an identifiable third party. Under these facts, Daniel (D) had a duty to warn his patient's wife of the risk to her of contracting the disease when he knew, or should have known, that his patient had the disease. Thus, the judgment of the court of appeals is reversed, and the case is remanded.

EDITOR'S ANALYSIS: As a general rule, under the common law, one person owed no affirmative duty to warn those endangered by the conduct of another. To mitigate the harshness of this rule, courts have carved out exceptions where certain special relationships exist. For example, the relationship of a physician to his patient is sufficient to support the duty to exercise reasonable care to protect third persons against risks emanating from the patient's physical or mental illness.

QUICKNOTES

JUDGMENT NOTWITHSTANDING THE VERDICT - A judgment entered by the trial judge reversing a jury verdict if the jury's determination has no basis in law or fact.

NOTES:

CANTERBURY v. SPENCE
Patient (P) v. Surgeon (D)
464 F.2d 772 (D.C.Cir.), cert. denied, 409 U.S. 1064 (1972).

NATURE OF CASE: Appeal of nonsuit dismissing medical malpractice action.

FACT SUMMARY: Canterbury (P) contended that, prior to spinal surgery, surgeon Spence (D) did not disclose the possible consequence of paralysis, which he subsequently developed.

CONCISE RULE OF LAW: Prior to a medical procedure, a physician must disclose to a patient all risks which a reasonable person would consider significant in deciding whether to undergo the procedure.

FACTS: Canterbury (P), then a minor, presented himself to orthopedist Spence (D), complaining of upper back pain. Following a diagnostic procedure, Spence (D) concluded that Canterbury (P) had a ruptured intervertebral disc, and that a laminectomy was indicated. Canterbury (P) underwent the procedure, which at first seemed successful. However, while still hospitalized, he fell out of bed, and began experiencing paralysis and incontinence thereafter, conditions which persisted. Canterbury (P) brought a malpractice action against Spence (D). One contention was that he had not been advised of the risk of paralysis. At the close of his case, the district court granted a nonsuit, as he had produced no expert testimony that advice of such risk had been required. Canterbury (P) appealed.

ISSUE: Prior to a medical procedure, must a physician disclose to a patient all risks which a reasonable person would consider significant in deciding whether to undergo the procedure?

HOLDING AND DECISION: [Judge not stated in casebook excerpt.] Yes. Prior to a medical procedure, a physician must disclose to a patient all risks which a reasonable person would consider significant in deciding whether to undergo the procedure. It is universally accepted that, prior to a surgical procedure, a patient must consent thereto. It is further accepted that such consent must be informed, as the average lay patient lacks the expertise to make unassisted judgments regarding the propriety of any particular medical treatment. The risks of a particular procedure are clearly an element that must be disclosed. However, the question arises as to what risks must be disclosed. Many courts have held, and the district court below agreed, that the key to this question is what is standard in the medical community for the type of procedure involved. This court does not agree. First, as a practical matter, no particular custom will exist on a profession-wide basis. Further, such a rule would delegate to the medical community a decision which should be made by individual physicians. Rather, the standard should be one of reasonableness: would a reasonable patient consider a particular risk significant in evaluating whether or not to undergo a procedure? This "reasonable patient" standard is consistent with the general thrust of tort and malpractice law and does not require expert testimony. Therefore, Canterbury's (P) failure to introduce such testimony was not fatal to his case. Reversed.

EDITOR'S ANALYSIS: The jurisdictions are split on the standard to be applied in this area. A majority still adopt the medical community standard; the type of standard elucidated here, remains the minority view. Consequently, in most states, expert testimony will be required in a case dealing with a lack of informed consent.

QUICKNOTES
LAMINECTOMY - A surgical procedure to remove all or a portion of a spinal vertebra.

NONSUIT - Judgment against a party who fails to make out a case.

NOTES:

CULBERTSON v. MERNITZ
Patient (P) v. Physician (D)
Ind. Sup. Ct., 602 N.E.2d 98 (1992).

NATURE OF CASE: Defendant's motion for transfer from the court of appeals' reversal of a summary judgment entered in his favor.

FACT SUMMARY: Culbertson (P) was a patient of Mernitz (D) who sued him for medical malpractice as a result of his failure to obtain an informed consent.

CONCISE RULE OF LAW: Under the medical malpractice standard in informed consent cases, physicians are required to disclose that which the reasonably careful, skillful, and prudent physician would disclose under the same or similar circumstances.

FACTS: Mernitz (D) treated Culbertson (P) for an infected cervix and recommended a surgical procedure but failed to advise her of a risk that the cervix could become adhered to the wall of the vagina. After the surgery, Culbertson's (P) cervix adhered to the wall of her vagina and she consulted another physician who later performed a total hysterectomy. Following this surgery, the Culbertsons (P) filed a proposed complaint against Mernitz (D) with the Indiana Department of Insurance. One count of the complaint alleged that Mernitz (D) failed to advise of the alternatives to surgery and the inherent risks and complications of the surgery. A medical review panel was convened and issued a written opinion that such non-disclosure did not constitute a failure to comply with the appropriate standard of care, as such complication is not considered a risk of such surgery requiring disclosure to a patient. When the Culbertsons (P) filed a civil complaint mirroring the allegations of the proposed complaint, Mernitz (D) successfully moved for summary judgment relying on the expert opinion issued by the medical review panel. The Culbertsons (P) had not filed any affidavit or other evidence in opposition, but argued at trial that the "prudent patient" standard should be utilized in evaluating informed consent claims. The court of appeals reversed. Mernitz (D) appealed.

ISSUE: Under the medical malpractice standard in informed consent cases, are physicians required to disclose that which the reasonably careful, skillful, and prudent physician would disclose under the same or similar circumstances?

HOLDING AND DECISION: (Krahulik, J.) Yes. Under the medical malpractice standard followed in Indiana's informed consent cases, physicians are required to disclose that which the reasonably careful, skillful and prudent physician would disclose under the same or similar circumstances. In general, medical expert testimony will be required to determine whether a physician has violated her duty, unless the situation is clearly within the realm of laymen's comprehension. In the present case, it cannot be said that the risk of the adherence of the cervix to the vaginal wall is a matter commonly known to lay persons. Therefore, the Culbertsons (P) needed to provide expert medical testimony to refute the unanimous opinion issued by the medical review panel in order to present a material issue of fact as to what a reasonably prudent physician would have discussed concerning the surgery. Without it, summary judgment for Mernitz (D) was appropriately granted. Reversed.

EDITOR'S ANALYSIS: Without the presentation of expert medical opinion by Culbertson (P), the trial court could only conclude that there was no general issue of material fact. Thus Mernitz's (D) summary judgment was affirmed. In some states, the majority rule that expert testimony is necessary to inform the jury as to what a reasonably prudent physician would disclose has been replaced by a "need to know" standard.

NOTES:

RIZZO v. SCHILLER
Patients of disabled child (P) v. Obstetrician (D)
Va. Sup. Ct., 445 S.E.2d 153 (1994).

NATURE OF CASE: Appeal from a verdict in favor of defendant in a medical malpractice suit for failure to obtain informed consent.

FACT SUMMARY: When Schiller (D) used forceps to deliver a baby who was permanently disabled as a result, the parents, the Rizzos (P), sued for medical malpractice in negligence and for lack of informed consent.

CONCISE RULE OF LAW: In most cases, expert testimony is necessary to establish those instances where the duty to disclose arises and what disclosures a reasonable, medical practitioner would have made under the same or similar circumstances.

FACTS: Rizzo (P) signed a blanket medical authorization form when she was admitted to the hospital in active labor. Her physician, Schiller (D), told her he would use forceps to deliver the baby and he did so. The baby suffered a trauma to the head during delivery and was permanently disabled as a result of this injury. The Rizzos (P) filed an action alleging that Schiller (D) breached the standard of care owed to them when he was negligent in the use of obstetrical forceps and that he failed to obtain Mrs. Rizzo's (P) informed consent to use the forceps. The trial court granted Dr. Schiller's (D) motion to strike the informed consent claim and the jury returned a verdict in Schiller's (D) favor on the negligence theory. The Rizzos (P) appealed, claiming that the trial court erred by striking their expert witness evidence because they had established a prima facie case that Schiller (D) had failed to obtain Mrs. Rizzo's (P) informed consent for the use of obstetrical forceps.

ISSUE: In most cases, is expert testimony necessary to establish those instances where the duty to disclose arises and what disclosures a reasonable, medical practitioner would have made under the same or similar circumstances?

HOLDING AND DECISION: (Hassell, J.) Yes. In most cases, expert testimony is necessary to establish those instances where the duty to disclose arises and what disclosures a reasonable, medical practitioner would have made under the same or similar circumstances. In this case, an expert witness testified that Mrs. Rizzo (P) was capable of making medical decisions and would have been able to deliver the baby spontaneously, without the use of forceps, had Dr. Schiller (D) simply waited. The expert testified that if forceps are used in non-emergent situations, the patient should be informed about the use and should be given the opportunity to participate in the decision whether to use forceps. The Rizzos (P) presented sufficient evidence to establish a prima facie case that Schiller (D) failed to obtain Rizzo's (P) informed consent to use the forceps. The generalized consent form Rizzo (P) signed was tantamount to no consent because it was not sufficiently informed consent. The Rizzos (P) also presented adequate evidence of proximate causation. Reversed and remanded for trial on claims of lack of informed consent.

EDITOR'S ANALYSIS: Generally, the defendant has the burden of proving that an exception to the duty to inform is present. There is no duty to obtain informed consent when the patient is incompetent and immediate treatment is necessary. If the disclosure of the risks presents a serious threat of psychological detriment to the patient, then it is considered not to be medically appropriate.

NOTES:

MOORE v. THE REGENTS OF THE UNIVERSITY OF CALIFORNIA

Patient (P) v. Physician and Medical center (D)

Cal. Sup. Ct., 793 P.2d 479 (1990), cert. denied, 499 U.S. 936 (1991).

NATURE OF CASE: Appeal from a general demurrer to a complaint asserting thirteen causes of action, including conversion, breach of fiduciary duty, fraud and deceit, unjust enrichment, intentional infliction of emotional distress, and negligent misrepresentation.

FACT SUMMARY: When Golde (D), the physician treating Moore (P) at UCLA Medical Center (D), commercially exploited cells removed from Moore's (P) spleen, Moore (P) sued, alleging that Golde's (D) failure to disclose the extent of his research and economic interests in Moore's (P) cells was a breach of fiduciary duty.

CONCISE RULE OF LAW: A physician who is seeking a patient's consent for a medical procedure must, in order to satisfy his fiduciary duty and to obtain the patient's informed consent, disclose personal interests unrelated to the patient's health, whether research or economic, that may affect his judgment.

FACTS: Moore (P) sought treatment for hairy cell leukemia at UCLA Medical Center (D) in 1976. Golde (D), the treating physician, took tests and samples and then told Moore (P) that his life was threatened and that he should have his spleen removed. Golde (D) did not tell Moore (P) his cells were unique and that access to them was of great scientific and commercial value. Moore (P) consented to treatment and to the operation, and continued treatment for seven years after. His spleen was retained for research without his knowledge or consent. Golde (D) established a cell line from Moore's (P) cells, received a patent for it, and entered into commercial agreements worth billions dollars today. Moore (P) sued Golde (D), the Regents of the University of California (D), and others, stating several causes of action including conversion, breach of fiduciary duty, fraud and deceit, unjust enrichment, intentional infliction of emotional distress, and negligent misrepresentation. The trial court sustained the Regents' (D) demurrers to the claim for conversion and held that all the other causes were also defective. Moore (P) appealed.

ISSUE: In order to satisfy his fiduciary duty and to obtain the patient's informed consent, must a physician who is seeking a patient's consent for a medical procedure, disclose personal interests unrelated to the patient's health, whether research or economic, that may affect his judgment?

HOLDING AND DECISION: (Panelli, J.) Yes. A physician who is seeking a patient's consent for a medical procedure must, in order to satisfy his fiduciary duty and to obtain the patient's informed consent, disclose personal interests unrelated to the patient's health, whether research or economic, that may affect his judgment. Moore's (P) allegations that Golde (D) failed to inform him prior to the operation of the extent of his research and economic interest in Moore's (P) cells stated a cause of action for invading a legally protected interest of his patient: either breach of fiduciary trust to disclose facts material to the patient's consent, or the performance of medical procedures without having first obtained patient's informed consent. Imposing a tort duty on scientists implicates public policy, strict liability would impede legitimate and socially useful scientific research. There is no need to impose a judicially created rule of strict liability, since enforcement of a physician's disclosure obligations will protect patients against this type of harm. Reversed.

DISSENT: (Mosk, J.) A nondisclosure cause of action is not an adequate substitute for a conversion cause of action. The remedy is largely illusory since it will be difficult to prove that no reasonably prudent person in Moore's (P) position would have given consent. A nondisclosure cause of action only resolves half the problem, it gives a patient the right to refuse consent, but no right to grant consent to commercialization if he shares in the profit. It may allow the true exploiters to escape liability.

CONCURRENCE AND DISSENT: (Broussard, J.) In the context of breach of fiduciary duty, a plaintiff should not be required to establish that he would not have proceeded with the medical treatment in question if his physician had made full disclosure, but only that the doctor's wrongful failure to disclose information proximately caused the plaintiff some type of compensable damage. In appropriate circumstances, punitive as well as compensatory damages would clearly be recoverable in such an action.

EDITOR'S ANALYSIS: The UCLA Regents, the Genetics Institute, a pharmaceutical company and one researcher were also named as defendants, but since none of them were physicians, they had no fiduciary duty to obtain Moore's (P) informed consent. They would be liable only under a theory of respondeat superior. The existence of a motivation for a medical procedure unrelated to the patient's health is a potential conflict of interest and a fact material to the patient's decision.

QUICKNOTES

CONVERSION - The act of depriving an owner of his property without permission or justification.

FIDUCIARY DUTY - A legal obligation to act for the benefit of another, including subordinating one's personal interests to that of the other person..

RESPONDEAT SUPERIOR - Rule that the principal is responsible for tortious acts committed by its agents in the scope of their agency or authority.

HOWARD v. UNIVERSITY OF MEDICINE & DENTISTRY OF NEW JERSEY

Patient (P) v. University (D)
N.J. Sup. Ct., 800 A.2d 73 (2002).

NATURE OF CASE: Appeal from the reversal of a motion to add a fraud claim to a malpractice action.

FACT SUMMARY: Howard (P) commenced a malpractice action against Dr. Heary (D) and University of Medicine & Dentistry of New Jersey. Later, Howard (P) sought leave to add a fraud claim to his complaint, which was rejected by the trial court. The appellate division reversed, and the matter was appealed to the state supreme court.

CONCISE RULE OF LAW: An informed consent action based upon a physician's misrepresentations regarding experience and skill may lie if the misrepresentations proximately caused a patient's injuries.

FACTS: Howard (P) suffered serious and progressive back injuries in an auto accident. Howard (P) decided to forgo recommended surgery and was referred to Dr. Heary (D), a professor at defendant university after he suffered additional back injuries. Dr. Heary (D) had two pre-operative consults with Howard (P), one with Howard (P) alone, and one with Howard (P) and his wife, due to the serious nature of the surgery proposed. According to Dr. Heary's (D) note of the second consult, he reiterated the risks (including the risk of paralysis), benefits and alternatives to surgery with Howard (P) and his wife. Howard (P) and his wife dispute that they were told of the risk of paralysis, and allege that they were assured by Dr. Heary (D) that he was Board Certified and had performed 60 such procedures in each of the 11 years he had been operating. Dr. Heary (D) denied making either of these assurances. Dr. Heary (D) performed the procedure on March 5, 1997, but it was unsuccessful. Howard (P) filed a malpractice action alleging he was rendered quadriplegic as a result of Dr. Heary's (D) negligence. Later, Howard (P) sought leave to add a fraud claim to his complaint, which was rejected by the trial court. The appellate division reversed, and the matter was appealed to the state supreme court.

ISSUE: May an informed consent action based upon a physician's misrepresentations regarding experience and skill lie if the misrepresentations proximately caused a patient's injuries?

DECISION AND HOLDING: (LaVecchia, J.) Yes. An informed consent action based upon a physician's misrepresentations regarding experience and skill may lie if the misrepresentations proximately caused a patient's injuries. No court has held that a claim based in fraud may lie where a physician misrepresents his skills or experience. Such a finding would circumvent the requirements for proof of causation and damages imposed in a traditional informed consent action. However, a serious misrepresentation concerning the quality or extent of a physician's professional experience can be material to the grant of intelligent and informed consent. If an objectively reasonable person could find that physician experience was material in determining the medical risk of the procedure to which plaintiff consented, and if a reasonably prudent person in plaintiff's position informed of the defendant's misrepresentations would not have consented, then a claim based on lack of informed consent may be maintained. For an informed consent action based on Dr. Heary's (D) misrepresentations to lie in addition to plaintiff's malpractice claim, Howard (P) must demonstrate that the physician's experience was material to the substantial risk of the procedure that occurred and injured Howard (P).

EDITOR'S ANALYSIS: Though the majority in *Howard* disallowed a fraud action based upon a physician's misrepresentations regarding his or her experience or professional skill, it left open the possibility that an informed consent action may lie on the same basis.

NOTES:

GRIMES v. KENNEDY KRIEGER INSTITUTE, INC.
Parents of research subjects (P) v. Research institute (D)
Md. Sup. Ct., 782 A.2d 807 (2001).

NATURE OF CASE: Appeal from the grant of summary judgment.

FACT SUMMARY: The circuit court granted summary judgment to the Kennedy Krieger Institute, Inc. (KKI) (D). Parents (P) of the children subject to the research study conducted by KKI appealed, contending that KKI owed a duty of care based on the nature of its relationship with the parents and the children participating in the study.

CONCISE RULE OF LAW: Under Maryland law, informed consent agreements in nontherapeutic research projects can constitute contracts and can constitute special relationships giving rise to duties, out of the breach of which negligence actions may lie.

FACTS: The Kennedy Krieger Institute, a prestigious research institute associated with Johns Hopkins University, created a nontherapeutic research program whereby it required certain classes of homes to have only partial lead paint abatement modifications performed. In at least some instances, including this case, the institute arranged for the landlords to receive public funding by way of grants or loans to aid in the modifications. The research institute then encouraged, and sometimes required, that the landlords rent the premises to families with young children. Children were encouraged to reside in households where the possibility of lead dust was known to the researchers to be likely, so that lead dust content of their blood could be compared with the level of lead dust in the houses at periodic intervals over a two-year period. The continuing presence of children was required in the subject houses in order for the study to be complete. The purpose of the research was to determine how effective varying degrees of lead paint abatement procedures were. The researchers acknowledged that lead paint was particularly hazardous to children, and that lead dust often remained/returned to abated houses over a period of time. The Institutional Review Board (IRB) overseeing this research abdicated its responsibility to review the potential safety and health hazard impact of this nontherapeutic study, instead advising the institute to recast the study so as to obscure such dangers. The research study was sponsored jointly by the EPA and the Maryland Department of Housing and Community Development. The parents of children with elevated blood levels of lead brought this action against KKI. KKI moved for summary judgment on the basis that no contract existed between KKI and the plaintiffs, and there was inherently no duty owed to a research subject by a researcher. The circuit court granted KKI's motion. The parents of the child subjects appealed, contending that KKI owed a duty of care based on the nature of its relationship with the parents and the children participating in the study based on a contract between the parties,

the voluntary assumption by KKI, a special relationship between the parties and federal regulation.

ISSUE: Under Maryland law, can informed consent agreements in nontherapeutic research projects constitute contracts and can the agreements constitute special relationships giving rise to duties, out of the breach of which negligence actions may lie?

DECISION AND HOLDING: (Cathell, J.) Yes. Under Maryland law, informed consent agreements in nontherapeutic research projects can constitute contracts and can constitute special relationships giving rise to duties, out of the breach of which negligence actions may lie. The very nature of nontherapeutic scientific research on human subjects can create special relationships out of which duties arise. Researchers do not have a right to place children in potentially hazardous living situations for nontherapeutic studies such as the one at issue in this case. Additionally, parents, whether improperly enticed by food stamps, money or other items, have no more right to intentionally and unnecessarily place children in potentially hazardous nontherapeutic research settings. IRBs are not designed to be objective, as they are generally internal boards tied as much to the success of a research project as to its ethical implications. This is evident in this case, where the IRB did not insure the safety of the children subjects, but encouraged researchers to misrepresent the research as therapeutic in nature. Special relationships are created between researchers and their human subjects generally. Finally, government regulations can create duties on the part of researchers toward human subjects out of which special relationships may arise. Special relationships are to be determined on a case by case basis. The circuit court erred in granting KKI's motions for summary judgment. Vacated and remanded.

CONCURRENCE: (Raker, J.) The majority correctly found that a special relationship existed between the parties giving rise to an action in tort, but went too far when it decided the duty of care was breached in this case.

EDITOR'S ANALYSIS: The court in *Grimes* denied a motion for reconsideration in this case. Judge Raker dissented, arguing that the majority's discussion of the ability of a parent or guardian to consent to the participation of a minor child in a nontherapeutic research study in the opinion was a statement of public policy, best left to the Legislature.

CHAPTER 4
MEDICAL MALPRACTICE

QUICK REFERENCE RULES OF LAW

1. **Physician Liability: The Custom-Based Standard of Care.** A conscious failure to exercise due care constitutes wilfulness sufficient to support an award of punitive damages. (McCourt v. Abernathy)

2. **Physician Liability: The Custom-Based Standard of Care.** The standard of care associated with needle choice and needle breakage is not accessible to the jury absent expert guidance. (Locke v. Pachtman)

3. **Physician Liability: Variations in the Standard of Care.** A medical practitioner has an absolute defense to a claim of malpractice when it is determined that the prescribed treatment or procedure has been approved by a considerable number of medical experts even though an alternate school of thought recommends another approach, or it is agreed among experts that alternative treatments and practices are acceptable. (Jones v. Chidester)

4. **Physician Liability: Variations in the Standard of Care.** A non-board-certified general practitioner is held to a standard of care of a reasonably competent general practitioner acting in the same or similar community in the United States in the same or similar circumstances. (Chapel v. Allison)

5. **Physician Liability: Qualification and Examination of Medical Experts.** A witness may qualify as an expert based on his knowledge, skill, experience, training, education, or a combination thereof. (Thompson v. Carter)

6. **Physician Liability: Qualification and Examination of Medical Experts.** The principal safeguard against errant expert testimony is the opportunity of opposing counsel to cross-examine, which includes the opportunity to probe bias, partisanship, or financial interest. (Trower v. Jones)

7. **Physician Liability: Qualification and Examination of Medical Experts.** When offered to prove the truth of matters asserted in them, learned writings, such as treatises, books, and articles regarding specialized areas of knowledge, are clearly hearsay. (Stang-Starr v. Byington)

8. **Res Ipsa and Negligence Per Se.** In the medical malpractice context, an event that does not ordinarily occur in the absence of negligence, standing alone, is not adequate to establish a claim under res ipsa loquitur. (Locke v. Pachtman)

9. **Ordinary Negligence.** Reasonable medical care may require more than merely following the prevailing professional standard of care. (Helling v. Carey)

10. **Breach of Contract.** There is no general rule barring damages for pain and suffering in actions for breach of contract. (Sullivan v. O'Connor)

11. **Vicarious Liability.** Where the evidence suffices to support a finding that the surgeon in fact had or exercised the right to control the details of another person's work or conduct in the operating room and the other elements of the rule are satisfied, the trier of fact may find that the surgeon was the "special employer" and is therefore liable for the negligence of the borrowed servant. (Franklin v. Gupta)

12. **Strict Liability.** Reasonable medical care may require more than merely following the prevailing professional standard of care. (Helling v. Carey)

13. **Products Liability.** A manufacturer is not strictly liable for injuries caused by a prescription drug so long as the drug was properly prepared and accompanied by warnings of its dangerous propensities. (Brown v. Superior Court)

14. Causation. A plaintiff in a wrongful death/malpractice action need not prove that the decedent more likely than not would have survived absent the alleged malpractice. (Herskovits v. Group Health Cooperative of Puget Sound)

15. Statutes of Limitations. A medical malpractice plaintiff is not barred by the statute of repose if she can demonstrate that there was an ongoing course of continuous negligent medical treatment. (Cunningham v. Huffman)

16. Affirmative Defenses. Except as public policy proscribes an agreement limiting liability, the pure comparative negligence statute adopted in New York in 1975 does not foreclose a complete defense that by express consent of the injured party no duty exists and, therefore, no recovery may be had. (Schneider v. Revici)

17. Arbitration and Waiver of Liability. An agent or representative, contracting for medical services on behalf of a group of employees, has implied authority to agree to arbitration of malpractice claims of enrolled employees arising under the contract. (Madden v. Kaiser Foundation Hospital)

18. Damages and Settlement. Recovery of damages is appropriate if the award is based on the loss of future earnings a plaintiff is likely to suffer because of inability to work for as long a period of time in the future as he could have done had he not sustained the accident. (Fein v. Permanente Medical Group)

19. Damages and Settlement. The West Virginia Wrongful Death Statute specifically sets forth the losses for which damages can be recovered. (Roberts v. Stevens Clinic Hospital)

20. Damages and Settlement. Although judicial deference must be given to the decision of an insurance company to settle a claim within the policy limits, a claim for bad faith may, in limited circumstances, be asserted against the insurance company notwithstanding a "deems expedient" provision. (Bleday v. OUM Group)

21. Hospital Liability. A hospital that is maintained as a charitable institution is not liable for the negligence of its physicians and nurses in the treatment of patients. (Schloendorff v. Society of New York Hospital)

22. Hospital Liability. A "holding out" or representation may arise when the hospital acts or omits to act in some way which leads the patient to a reasonable belief he is being treated by the hospital by one of its employees. (Adamski v. Tacoma General Hospital)

23. Hospital Liability. A hospital may be liable for the negligence of its staff. (Darling v. Charleston Community Memorial Hospital)

24. Hospital Liability. A hospital has a duty to exercise due care in the selection of its medical staff. (Johnson v. Misericordia Community Hospital)

25. Managed Care Liability. A health maintenance organization may be liable for the malpractice of its doctors. (Boyd v. Albert Einstein Medical Center)

26. Managed Care Liability. Since a patient's health care payor is not responsible for discharge determinations, liability will not attach to the payor for a negligent discharge. (Wickline v. State)

27. Managed Care Liability. ERISA does not preempt a plaintiff's vicarious liability claim of malpractice against a health maintenance organization. (Dukes v. U.S. Healthcare, Inc.)

28. Medical Malpractice Reform. So long as a measure limiting damages in medical malpractice actions is rationally related to a legitimate state interest, policy determinations as to the need for, and the desirability of, such an enactment are for the legislature to determine. (Fein v. Permanente Medical Group)

McCOURT v. ABERNATHY

Decedent's survivor (P) v. Treating physicians (D)
S.C. Sup. Ct., 457 S.E.2d 603 (1995).

NATURE OF CASE: Appeal from award of actual and punitive damages in a medical malpractice suit.

FACT SUMMARY: When McCourt (P) went to the hospital complaining of chest pain following an accident while working with horses, Dr. Abernathy (D) repeatedly treated her but failed to appreciate the seriousness of her condition and failed to order observation or request consultation intervention.

CONCISE RULE OF LAW: A conscious failure to exercise due care constitutes wilfulness sufficient to support an award of punitive damages.

FACTS: McCourt (P) worked with horses and had pricked her finger with a pin. She later went to the hospital following an accident when a horse had bolted and she had dislocated her shoulder. When the finger became swollen and McCourt (P) returned to the emergency room, she was released. The next day she became significantly worse and she was admitted to the hospital where she died several days later from beta strep septicemia. A jury awarded $3,550,000 in actual and punitive damages against Drs. Abernathy (D) and Clyde (D). They appealed, claiming that the trial judge had erred in failing to charge several jury instructions relating to mistake in diagnosis or error in judgment.

ISSUE: Does a conscious failure to exercise due care constitute wilfulness?

HOLDING AND DECISION: (Shaw, J.) Yes. A conscious failure to exercise due care constitutes wilfulness sufficient to support an award of punitive damages. In order for a plaintiff to recover punitive damages, there must be evidence that the defendant's conduct was wilful, wanton, or in reckless disregard of the plaintiff's rights. Abernathy (D) failed to exercise due care in treating McCourt (P). The jury instructions given as a whole clearly intimated that a mere mistake in diagnosis or error in judgment alone is insufficient to support a finding of malpractice. The jury's determination of damages is entitled to substantial deference. The record contained sufficient evidence of conduct to support the awards of punitive damages. Affirmed.

EDITOR'S ANALYSIS: The court enumerated the various instances when the doctors (D) failed to exercise due care. They failed to diagnose and treat McCourt (P) on three separate occasions, they failed to order timely diagnostic tests, they failed to appreciate the seriousness of her deteriorating condition in the face of highly abnormal blood work, they failed to aggressively monitor her deteriorating condition, and they failed to promptly seek the immediate aid of a specialist. Therefore the court found that the doctors (D) had consciously failed to exercise due care.

NOTES:

LOCKE v. PACHTMAN
Patient (P) v. Surgeon (D)
Mich. Sup. Ct., 521 N.W.2d 786 (1994).

NATURE OF CASE: Appeal from directed verdict for defendant in a medical malpractice action affirmed on appeal.

FACT SUMMARY: When a needle broke during an operation and could not be located by the operating physicians, Locke (P) sued for negligence but failed to make a prima facie showing regarding the standard of care.

CONCISE RULE OF LAW: The standard of care associated with needle choice and needle breakage is not accessible to the jury absent expert guidance.

FACTS: Following surgery in which a needle broke off in her body and could not be located, Locke (P) filed a negligence action against the surgeon, Pachtman (D). Locke (P) alleged that she suffered great pain and disfigurement as a result of Pachtman's (D) negligence. Her husband filed a derivative claim. In testimony presented at trial, Locke's (P) expert witness could not identify any negligent conduct. The expert testimony was confused and not sufficient to establish a standard of care with regard to any "incorrect technique" which may have led to the needle breakage. Locke (P) also introduced evidence to the effect that Pachtman (D) had made statements following the surgery admitting that she had used a needle that was too small and apologizing for her mistake. The trial judge granted Pachtman's (D) motion for a directed verdict, the appellate court affirmed, and Locke (P) appealed.

ISSUE: Is the standard of care associated with needle choice and needle breakage not accessible to the jury absent expert guidance?

HOLDING AND DECISION: (Mallett, J.) Yes. The standard of care associated with needle choice and needle breakage is not accessible to the jury absent expert guidance. Proof of a medical malpractice claim requires the demonstration of the applicable standard of care, breach of that standard of care by the defendant, injury, and proximate causation. To survive a motion for directed verdict, the plaintiff must make a prima facie showing regarding each of the above elements. In this case, Locke's (P) expert witness never explained what a reasonably prudent surgeon would do, in keeping with the standards of professional practice, that might not have been done by Pachtman (D). The jury should not be left to speculate in this regard. While the statements made by Pachtman (D) may have indicated that she thought she had made a mistake, a jury could not reasonably infer from those statements alone that Pachtman's (D) actions did not conform to the standard of professional practice for the community as a whole. Affirmed.

DISSENT: (Levin, J.) The statements Pachtman (D) made refer neither to a personal nor a general standard of care. The statements can reasonably be read either way, and a jury should decide the meaning of Pachtman's (D) statements. Pachtman's (D) statements satisfied Locke's (P) burden of presenting prima facie evidence of the standard of care and breach.

EDITOR'S ANALYSIS: The plaintiff in this case also alleged negligent supervision based on the fact that Dr. Roberts (D), the attending physician, attended another operation in the middle of Locke's (P) surgery. Testimony was presented that it was not unusual for an attending physician at the University of Michigan Hospital to leave a resident alone during portions of a procedure. Since no breach of the standard of care could be inferred, that claim was also dismissed.

QUICKNOTES

DIRECTED VERDICT - A verdict ordered by the court in a jury trial.

PRIMA FACIE SHOWING - An action in which the plaintiff introduces sufficient evidence to submit an issue to the judge or jury for determination.

PROXIMATE CAUSE - The natural sequence of events without which an injury would not have been sustained.

NOTES:

JONES v. CHIDESTER

Patient (P) v. Orthopedic surgeon (D)
Pa. Sup. Ct., 610 A.2d 964 (1992).

NATURE OF CASE: Review of medical malpractice verdict in favor of defendant.

FACT SUMMARY: When Chidester (D) was accused of medical malpractice, he contended that he had a perfect defense under the "two schools" doctrine.

CONCISE RULE OF LAW: A medical practitioner has an absolute defense to a claim of malpractice when it is determined that the prescribed treatment or procedure has been approved by a considerable number of medical experts even though an alternate school of thought recommends another approach, or it is agreed among experts that alternative treatments and practices are acceptable.

FACTS: Chidester (D) performed orthopedic surgery on Jones (P), who was later treated by a neurosurgeon for resulting nerve injury to his leg. It was confirmed by other doctors that Jones (P) had suffered a "drop foot" as a result of the nerve injury. Jones (P) filed a medical malpractice lawsuit. At trial, Jones (P) alleged that his nerve injury was the result of Chidester's (D) use of a tourniquet. Both sides presented testimony by medical experts supporting their positions. Chidester's (D) experts testified that his technique was medically acceptable, while Jones' (P) experts insisted that it constituted unacceptable practice. At the close of the evidence, the court gave the jury an instruction on the "two schools" doctrine, stating that Chidester (D) would not be held liable merely for exercising his judgment in applying a course of treatment supported by a reputable and respected body of medical experts. The jury returned a verdict in favor of Chidester (D). On appeal, Jones (P) argued that under Pennsylvania law the test for the doctrine was a "considerable number" of physicians rather than "reputable and respected" physicians as the court had charged the jury.

ISSUE: Does a medical practitioner have an absolute defense to a claim of malpractice when it is determined that the prescribed treatment or procedure has been approved by a considerable number of medical experts even though an alternate school of thought recommends another approach, or it is agreed among experts that alternative treatments and practices are acceptable?

HOLDING AND DECISION: (Papadakos, J.) Yes. A practitioner has an absolute defense to a claim of malpractice when it is determined that the prescribed treatment or procedure has been approved by a considerable number of medical experts even though an alternate school of thought recommends another approach, or it is agreed among experts that alternative treatments and practices are acceptable. The jury are not to judge by determining which school, in their judgment, is the best. There

is confusion and contradiction in the use of the standards for the jury charge. It is insufficient to show there exists a "small minority" of physicians who agree with Chidester's (D) questioned practice. A school of thought should be adopted not only by "reputable and respected physicians" in order to insure quality but also by a "considerable number" of medical practitioners. The burden of showing that there are two schools of thought falls to Chidester (D), whose expert witnesses should state the factual reasons to support his claim that there is a considerable number of professionals who agree with the treatment employed by him. Reversed and remanded.

CONCURRENCE: (McDermott, J.) A doctor cannot be faulted if he properly administers the methods which to his knowledge and experience seems the better of two, so long as the group advocating the method is comprised of a sufficient number of reputable and respected members.

CONCURRENCE: (Zappala, J.) I disagree with the majority that the existence of two schools of medical thought may ever be a question of fact to be submitted to a jury. It is a question of law for the judge to determine in the first instance whether there are two schools of medical thought.

EDITOR'S ANALYSIS: This case clarified the proper jury charge. The court said that it would not attempt to place a numerical certainty on what constitutes a "considerable number." After the defendant's witness establishes that there are two schools of thought, it is up to the jury to determine whether they believe the defendant should be insulated from liability as a result.

NOTES:

CHAPEL v. ALLISON
Patient (P) v. General practitioner (D)
Mont. Sup. Ct., 785 P.2d 204 (1990).

NATURE OF CASE: Appeal from motion for a directed verdict in favor of defendant in a medical malpractice action.

FACT SUMMARY: When an expert witness in a medical malpractice case applied the "same locality" rule, comparing Allison's (D) standard of care with that of a licensed general practitioner in the same or similar communities within Montana, Chapel (P) claimed that such a rule was no longer acceptable, given the increased accessibility of medical literature and modern communications.

CONCISE RULE OF LAW: A non-board-certified general practitioner is held to a standard of care of a reasonably competent general practitioner acting in the same or similar community in the United States in the same or similar circumstances.

FACTS: Chapel (P) was injured when he was kicked by a horse and was treated by Allison (D), who applied a leg cast. When the cast was removed, the leg exhibited a varus deformity (bow-leggedness) which required surgery to correct. Chapel (P) had been Allison's (D) patient for nearly twenty years. Chapel (P) sued Allison (D), a general practitioner, for medical malpractice. Chapel's (P) expert witness testified that a general practitioner would not normally handle that type of injury. The district court said that the competency of the expert witness was very shaky and the court granted Allison's (D) motion for a directed verdict. During pretrial procedures, Chapel (P) had made a motion in limine that the "same locality rule" was not applicable to this case, but the court denied the motion. Chapel (P) claimed that recent cases have ruled that the same locality rule was outdated. Board certified specialists in Montana have been held to be subject to a national standard of care. Chapel (P) alleged that a doctor in general practice is under a legal duty to seek consultation with or refer a patient to a specialist when the doctor knows or should know in the exercise of reasonable care that the services of a specialist are indicated. Allison (D) claimed that restricting the degree of care to the same or similar communities in Montana was proper and that it would be impracticable to require a general practitioner to be held to the standard of care of whatever area of expertise in which his treatment might fall. An amicus brief filed by the Montana Trial Lawyers Association contended that there was a trend away from the locality rule. An amicus brief from the Montana Medical Association recommended the adoption of the "same or similar locality" standard, without geographical limitations, for general practitioners, but the application of a "national" specialist standard to any physician who holds himself out to be a specialist.

ISSUE: Is a non-board-certified general practitioner held to a standard of care of a reasonably competent general practitioner acting in the same or similar community in the United States in the same or similar circumstances?

HOLDING AND DECISION: (Sheehy, J.) Yes. A non-board-certified general practitioner is held to a standard of care of a reasonably competent general practitioner acting in the same or similar community in the United States in the same or similar circumstances. The same locality rule, which was limited to Montana communities, is abandoned. A similar circumstances rule permits consideration by the trier of fact of legitimate local factors. This opinion applies only to general practitioners. Reversed and remanded.

EDITOR'S ANALYSIS: The court in this case adopted the standard suggested by the Montana Medical Association in its amicus brief. It chose a middle ground, balancing the rights of negligently injured patients with those of doctors for due process and a fair hearing. Rural doctors are scarce and very valuable and it was unsuccessfully contended that the similar locality rule was needed to keep physicians there providing essential health services.

QUICKNOTES

AMICUS BRIEF - A brief submitted by a third party, not a party to the action, that contains information for the court's consideration in conformity with its position.

MOTION IN LIMINE - Motion by one party brought prior to trial to exclude the potential introduction of highly prejudicial evidence.

NOTES:

THOMPSON v. CARTER
Patient (P) v. Physician (D)
Miss. Sup. Ct., 518 So.2d 609 (1987).

NATURE OF CASE: Appeal from a directed verdict in favor of defendant in an action for medical malpractice.

FACT SUMMARY: When her expert witness was not permitted to testify concerning the standard of care to which physicians were required to conform with respect to the administration of certain drugs because he lacked a medical degree, Thompson (P) appealed.

CONCISE RULE OF LAW: A witness may qualify as an expert based on his knowledge, skill, experience, training, education, or a combination thereof.

FACTS: Thompson (P) contended that she developed Stevens Johnson Syndrome as a result of Carter's (D) negligent prescribing of a drug. Hughes, a pharmacologist and toxicologist, testified on the issues of liability and causation. The trial court found that Hughes was qualified to testify as an expert witness as to causation but was not qualified to testify concerning the standard of care to which physicians are required to conform with respect to the use and administration of drugs. Thompson (P) had no other expert witness and a proffer of Hughes' testimony was made which, if admitted, would have made a prima facie case. The trial court granted Carter's (D) motion for a directed verdict on the grounds that Thompson (P) had failed to establish the standard of care by an expert possessing a medical degree. Thompson (P) appealed, alleging that a medical degree was not necessary; what was necessary was that the witness possessed medical knowledge, however obtained.

ISSUE: May a witness qualify as an expert based on his knowledge, skill, experience, training, education, or a combination thereof?

HOLDING AND DECISION: (Prather, J.) Yes. A witness may qualify as an expert based on his knowledge, skill, experience, training, education, or a combination thereof. Qualification as an expert does not necessarily rest upon the educational or professional degree a witness possesses. As a pharmacologist/toxicologist, Hughes was an expert in the area in which his testimony was offered. Therefore, he was qualified to deliver expert testimony, notwithstanding his lack of a medical degree, on the issue of a physician's standard of care in the use and administration of a drug. Reversed and remanded.

EDITOR'S ANALYSIS: The court mentioned that other jurisdictions had held likewise. If a witness otherwise has sufficient scientific and practical experience, he or she may be held competent to testify despite the lack of a medical degree. In this case, Hughes taught medical students and advised and counseled physicians as to drug use and administration.

NOTES:

TROWER v. JONES
Patient (P) v. Physician (D)
Ill. Sup. Ct., 520 N.E.2d 297 (1988).

NATURE OF CASE: Appeal from defense verdict in medical malpractice action.

FACT SUMMARY: When Trower's (P) expert witness was questioned on cross-examination as to his previous experience and compensation for testifying, Trower (P) argued that the impeachment questions were unwarranted.

CONCISE RULE OF LAW: The principal safeguard against errant expert testimony is the opportunity of opposing counsel to cross-examine, which includes the opportunity to probe bias, partisanship, or financial interest.

FACTS: Jones (D) misdiagnosed Trower's (P) abdominal pains and her fallopian tubes and ovary had to be removed later, as a result. Since her illness, Trower (P) has been unable to conceive and she brought this action against Jones (D) for medical malpractice. Trower (P) called upon an expert witness who was a fellow of the American Board of Medical Legal Consultants to testify on direct as to the proper standard of care. On cross-examination, the witness acknowledged that the Board was a for-profit organization and that its purpose was to review cases involving suspected malpractice and to furnish expert testimony. The court found in favor of Jones (D). Trower (P) alleged, on appeal, that the circuit court improperly permitted questioning on cross-examination of the expert witness as to his income, the frequency of his rendering expert testimony, and whether he testified only for plaintiffs.

ISSUE: Is the principal safeguard against errant expert testimony the opportunity of opposing counsel to cross-examine, which includes the opportunity to probe bias, partisanship, or financial interest?

HOLDING AND DECISION: (Cunningham, J.) Yes. The principal safeguard against errant expert testimony is the opportunity of opposing counsel to cross-examine, which includes the opportunity to probe bias, partisanship, or financial interest. Although in earlier cases it was held to be error to permit questioning a witness as to how many times he had testified and what compensation he received for doing so, the difficulty and the importance of thorough, comprehensive cross-examination of experts has increased markedly since that time. Cross-examination has become more difficult in part because of the increased latitude given experts when rendering their opinions. For example, experts can now render opinions without prior disclosure of the underlying facts or data upon which those opinions are based, and can render opinions based on certain inadmissible evidence. The questions regarding the expert witness's income in this case were permissible. The circuit court properly permitted counsel to inquire, on cross-examination, as to the frequency with which the witness testified for plaintiffs. Affirmed.

EDITOR'S ANALYSIS: This case reflects the modern trend in impeaching expert witnesses as "hired guns." Earlier, such questioning was considered to be irrelevant or prejudicial. Some states have enacted legislation regulating the qualifications of expert witnesses.

QUICKNOTES

HARMLESS ERROR - An error taking place during trial that does not require the reviewing court to overturn or modify the trial court's judgment in that it did not affect the appellant's substantial rights or the disposition of the action.

IMPEACHMENT - The discrediting of a witness by offering evidence to show that the witness lacks credibility.

NOTES:

STANG-STARR v. BYINGTON

Patient (P) v. Doctor (D)

Neb. Sup. Ct., 532 N.W.2d 26 (1995).

NATURE OF CASE: Appeal from medical malpractice verdict in favor of the defendant.

FACT SUMMARY: When Stang-Starr's (P) expert medical witness was not allowed to have entered into evidence the texts on which he had relied in forming his medical opinion, and all of Byington's (D) hearsay objections were sustained by the court, she appealed.

CONCISE RULE OF LAW: When offered to prove the truth of matters asserted in them, learned writings, such as treatises, books, and articles regarding specialized areas of knowledge, are clearly hearsay.

FACTS: Stang-Starr (P) alleged that Byington (D) had negligently failed to diagnose and treat abnormalities in her cervix, resulting in a diagnosis of stage IV cervical cancer. Byington (D) disputed whether a correct diagnosis would have made a difference. Stang-Starr (P) called on a physician who testified that based on his knowledge and information obtained from textbooks, medical literature, and personal experience, he had formed an opinion, to a reasonable medical probability, as to the standard of care required of a board-certified obstetrician in May 1986 in Lincoln or similar communities. The court sustained Byington's (D) objections that all texts, medical bulletins and other writings on which the expert had relied were hearsay and could not be introduced as evidence. The jury found in favor of Byington (D). Stang-Starr (P) appealed, alleging that the district court erred by refusing to permit her to question her medical experts regarding medical texts and treatises upon which they relied in their testimony.

ISSUE: Are learned writings, such as treatises, books, and articles regarding specialized areas of knowledge, hearsay when offered to prove the truth of matters asserted in them?

HOLDING AND DECISION: (Caporale, J.) Yes. When offered to prove the truth of matters asserted in them, learned writings, such as treatises, books, and articles regarding specialized areas of knowledge, are clearly hearsay. When Stang-Starr (P) attempted to elicit testimony from her witness concerning what a particular authority had reported about an issue, she was attempting to use her witness to recite the opinion of each authority cited, instead of eliciting her witness' expert opinion derived from the witness's own knowledge and experience. The witness was merely seeking to act as a conduit for inadmissible hearsay. The district court did not err in sustaining Byington's (D) objections to the proffered evidence or the offers of proof made in regard to the evidence. Affirmed.

EDITOR'S ANALYSIS: The emerging modern approach allows testimony from learned treatises, guidelines or other similar authoritative sources that the expert acknowledges to be reliable. The Federal Rules of Evidence 803 (18) adopted this approach. Package inserts for prescription drugs are regularly admitted as independent evidence on the standard of care under the hearsay exception for tabulations, lists and directories generally relied on by persons in particular occupations.

QUICKNOTES

HEARSAY - An out-of-court statement made by a person other than the witness testifying at trial that is offered in order to prove the truth of the matter asserted.

NOTES:

LOCKE v. PACHTMAN
Patient (P) v. Surgeon (D)
Mich. Sup. Ct., 521 N.W.2d 786 (1994).

NATURE OF CASE: Appeal from directed verdict for defendant in a medical malpractice action affirmed on appeal.

FACT SUMMARY: When the court held there was insufficient expert testimony for the case to go to the jury, Locke (P) alleged that needle breakage does not ordinarily occur in the absence of someone's negligence and that the case should go to the jury under a theory of res ipsa loquitur.

CONCISE RULE OF LAW: In the medical malpractice context, an event that does not ordinarily occur in the absence of negligence, standing alone, is not adequate to establish a claim under res ipsa loquitur.

FACTS: When a needle broke off in Locke's (P) body during an operation and could not be located by the operating physicians, Locke (P) sued for negligence but failed to make a prima facie showing regarding the standard of care. Locke (P) then alleged that even if expert testimony was insufficient to establish the proper standard of care, the case should have proceeded to the jury on a theory of res ipsa loquitur. The lower courts rejected this argument. Locke (P) appealed.

ISSUE: In the medical malpractice context, is an event that does not ordinarily occur in the absence of negligence, standing alone, adequate to establish a claim under res ipsa loquitur?

HOLDING AND DECISION: (Mallett, J.) No. In the medical malpractice context, an event that does not ordinarily occur in the absence of negligence, standing alone, is not adequate to establish a claim under res ipsa loquitur. Something more is required, be it the common knowledge that the injury does not ordinarily occur without negligence or expert testimony to that effect. Neither standard was met here. Even Locke's (P) own expert witness acknowledged that needle breakage is one of the many risks of surgery, suggesting that faulty equipment might be a cause of breakage. Affirmed.

EDITOR'S ANALYSIS: This case is typical of certain recurring situations in medical malpractice litigation where many courts allow a case to go to the jury without expert testimony. Leaving sponges and other foreign objects behind is another common scenario. In addition to res ipsa loquitur, such cases may be tried on a basis of negligence per se, obvious negligence, or the "common knowledge" rule.

QUICKNOTES

NEGLIGENCE PER SE - Conduct amounting to negligence as a matter of law because it is either so contrary to ordinary prudence or it is in violation of statute.

RES IPSA LOQUITUR - A rule of law giving rise to an inference of negligence where the instrument inflicting the injury is in the exclusive control of the defendant and where such harm could not ordinarily result in the absence of negligence.

NOTES:

HELLING v. CAREY

Blind patient (P) v. Ophthalmologists (D)
Wash. Sup. Ct., 519 P.2d 981 (1974).

NATURE OF CASE: Appeal from judgment in favor of the defendant in a medical malpractice case.

FACT SUMMARY: When Carey (D), an ophthalmologist, failed to give a glaucoma test to Helling (P), a patient under forty, Helling (P) contended that his negligence proximately resulted in her blindness.

CONCISE RULE OF LAW: Reasonable medical care may require more than merely following the prevailing professional standard of care.

FACTS: Helling (P) was Carey's (D) patient. Carey (D) was an ophthalmologist who had fitted Helling (P) with contact lenses but had not administered any test for glaucoma in the ten years he had been treating her. By the time Carey (D) finally administered the test for glaucoma and discovered that Helling (P) was suffering from this disease, she had essentially lost her peripheral vision and her central vision had been reduced. Helling (P) then filed a complaint against Carey (D) and his partner (D) alleging that she had suffered severe and permanent damage to her eyes as a result of their negligence. The testimony of medical experts during the trial established the fact that the standards of the profession did not require routine pressure tests to patients under the age of forty because the disease occurred so rarely in that age group. However, the standard of the profession did require such tests if the patient's complaints and symptoms indicated to the physician that glaucoma should be suspected. The trial court entered judgment for Carey (D) following the jury verdict. Helling (P) appealed.

ISSUE: May reasonable medical care require more than merely following the prevailing professional standard of care?

HOLDING AND DECISION: (Hunter, J.) Yes. Reasonable medical care may require more than merely following the prevailing professional standard of care. It is the duty of the courts to say what is required to protect patients under forty from the damaging results of glaucoma. The reasonable standard that should have been followed under the undisputed facts of this case was the timely giving of this simple, harmless pressure test to Helling (P). In failing to do so, Carey (D) was negligent, which proximately resulted in the blindness sustained by Helling (P) for which Carey (D) is liable. Reversed and remanded on the issue of damages only.

EDITOR'S ANALYSIS: This case was unusual in that liability was imposed despite the medical custom or standard practice of the profession. The judge quoted Justice Holmes' famous statement that "what usually is done may be evidence of what ought to be done, but what ought to be done is fixed by a standard of reasonable prudence, whether it usually is complied with or not," to support his position. He also quoted Justice Hand who stated that "courts may in the end say what is required; there are precautions so imperative that even their universal disregard will not excuse their omission."

NOTES:

SULLIVAN v. O'CONNOR
Disfigured patient (P) v. Plastic surgeon (D)
Mass. Sup. Ct., 296 N.E.2d 183 (1973).

NATURE OF CASE: Appeal from damages awarded plaintiff for breach of a contract to perform plastic surgery.

FACT SUMMARY: When O'Connor (D) was found liable for breach of contract for having disfigured his patient, Sullivan (P), he objected to the damages awarded for pain and suffering and mental distress.

CONCISE RULE OF LAW: There is no general rule barring damages for pain and suffering in actions for breach of contract.

FACTS: Sullivan (P), a professional entertainer, had entered into a contract with O'Connor (D), a surgeon, wherein he promised to perform plastic surgery on Sullivan's (P) nose and thereby enhance her beauty and improve her appearance. Sullivan (P) sued for breach of contract because the result of the surgery was to disfigure and deform her nose and to cause her pain in body and mind. Sullivan (P) also sued for medical malpractice, charging that O'Connor (D) had been negligent in performing the surgery. The jury returned a verdict for Sullivan (P) on the contract count, and for O'Connor (D) on the negligence count. When the jury awarded damages for the worsening of Sullivan's (P) condition, pain and suffering, and mental anguish, O'Connor (D) appealed, claiming that Sullivan's (P) damages should have been limited to the recovery of her out-of-pocket expenses.

ISSUE: Is there any general rule barring damages for pain and suffering in actions for breach of contract?

HOLDING AND DECISION: (Kaplan, J.) No. There is no general rule barring damages for pain and suffering in actions for breach of contract. Where, as in this case, the doctor has been absolved of negligence by the trier, an expectancy measure may be thought harsh. But when the contract calls for an operation on the person of a plaintiff, psychological as well as physical injury may be expected to figure somewhere in the recovery. Sullivan (P) should not be confined to her out-of-pocket expenses; she was entitled to recover for the worsening of her condition, and for the pain and suffering and mental distress involved. Affirmed.

EDITOR'S ANALYSIS: This case was unusual since contract theory is rarely the basis of a medical malpractice suit. Clear proof is required in such actions. The advantages of using a contract theory for recovery are that no expert witnesses are needed, there is usually a longer statute of limitations, and statutory restrictions can be avoided.

NOTES:

FRANKLIN v. GUPTA
Patient (P) v. Surgeon (D), nurse (D), and hospital (D)
Md. App. Ct., 567 A.2d 524 (1990).

NATURE OF CASE: Appeal from judgment for the defendant in a medical malpractice suit.

FACT SUMMARY: When Franklin (P), a patient, sought damages for injuries sustained during an operation, he sued the surgeon and unsuccessfully requested a jury instruction holding Gupta (D) liable under a vicarious liability theory.

CONCISE RULE OF LAW: Where the evidence suffices to support a finding that the surgeon in fact had or exercised the right to control the details of another person's work or conduct in the operating room and the other elements of the rule are satisfied, the trier of fact may find that the surgeon was the "special employer" and is therefore liable for the negligence of the borrowed servant.

FACTS: Gupta (D), a general surgeon, had recommended surgical treatment for Franklin's (P) carpal tunnel syndrome. Franklin (P) suffered from various disorders and was considered a "high risk patient for anesthesia" by the anesthesiologist. When attempting to administer local anesthesia, the nurse anesthetist (D) noticed that Franklin (P) was losing oxygen. He had to be resuscitated when his heart stopped beating entirely. The anesthesiologist (D) then asked Gupta (D) to cancel the surgery. Franklin (P) never had the surgery on his wrist and sued the doctors (D), nurse (D), and the hospital (D), claiming that the anesthesia was ineffective and had caused him physical and emotional trauma. The Health Claims Arbitration Office appointed a panel that found no liability on the part of any of the defendants. Franklin (P) rejected the decision and sought damages in the Circuit Court for Baltimore City. Franklin (P) unsuccessfully requested that a jury instruction be given alleging that Gupta (D), in his capacity as the surgeon, could be held liable under the "captain of the ship" doctrine. After a de novo trial, the jury agreed that there was no liability on the part of Gupta (D), but it concluded that the other defendants were culpable. The trial court granted the losing defendants' motions for a new trial or remittitur. Franklin (P) appealed.

ISSUE: Where the evidence suffices to support a finding that the surgeon in fact had or exercised the right to control the details of another person's work or conduct in the operating room and the other elements of the rule are satisfied, may the trier of fact find that the surgeon was the "special employer" and is therefore liable for the negligence of the borrowed servant?

HOLDING AND DECISION: (Wilner, J.) Yes. Where the evidence suffices to support a finding that the surgeon in fact had or exercised the right to control the details of another person's work or conduct in the operating room and the other elements of the rule are satisfied, the trier of fact may find that the surgeon was the "special employer" and is therefore liable for the negligence of the borrowed servant. The "captain of the ship" theory of liability is inappropriate and has been rejected modernly. Furthermore, since there was no evidence that Gupta (D) in any way supervised or controlled, attempted to supervise or control, or had the right or power to supervise or control, the conduct and decisions of the anesthesiologist (D) or the nurse (D), he cannot be held liable under the traditional "borrowed servant" rule either. The proposed instruction was properly rejected. Affirmed.

EDITOR'S ANALYSIS: The two theories of liability mentioned in this case — the captain of the principle ship and the borrowed servant principle — may also be used by hospitals in their own defense. Hospitals may show that they were not vicariously liable for the conduct of the nurses because they had lent their "servant" to the doctor. Hospitals generally enjoyed a charitable or governmental immunity from liability until recently.

QUICKNOTES
"CAPTAIN OF THE SHIP" DOCTRINE - Theory of liability whereby the operating surgeon is held responsible for those working under him without any showing of actual control.

REMITTITUR - The authority of the court to reduce the amount of damages awarded by the jury.

NOTES:

HELLING v. CAREY

Blind patient (P) v. Ophtholmologists (D)

Wash. Sup. Ct., 519 P.2d 981 (1974).

NATURE OF CASE: Appeal from judgment in favor of the defendant in a medical malpractice case.

FACT SUMMARY: When Carey (D), an ophtholmologist, failed to give glaucoma test to a patient under forty, he was found to have been negligent.

CONCISE RULE OF LAW: Reasonable medical may require more than merely following the prevailing professional standard of care.

FACTS: Helling (P) was Carey's (D) patient. Carey (D) was an ophthalmologist who had fitted Helling (P) with contact lenses but had not administered any test for glaucoma in the ten years he had been treating her. By the time Carey (D) finally administered the test for glaucoma and discovered that Helling (P) was suffering from this disease, she had essentially lost her peripheral vision and her central vision had been reduced. Helling (P) then filed a complaint against Carey (D) and his partner (D) alleging that she had suffered severe and permanent damage to her eyes as a result of their negligence. The testimony of medical experts during the trial established the fact that the standards of the profession did not require routine pressure tests to patients under the age of forty because the disease occurred so rarely in that age group. However, the standard of the profession did require such tests if the patient's complaints and symptoms indicated to the physician that glaucoma should be suspected. The trial court entered judgment for Carey (D) following the jury verdict. Helling (P) appealed.

ISSUE: May reasonable medical care require more than merely following the prevailing professional standard of care?

HOLDING AND DECISION: (Hunter, J.) Reasonable medical may require more than merely following the prevailing professional standard of care.

CONCURRENCE: (Utter, J.) A greater duty of care should be imposed on Carey (D) and his partner than was established by their profession. The duty could be imposed when a disease, such as glaucoma, can be detected by a simple, well-known, harmless test whose results are definitive and the disease can be successfully arrested by early detection, but where the effects of the disease are irreversible if undetected over a substantial period of time. In choosing between an innocent plaintiff and a doctor who acted reasonably according to his specialty, but who could have prevented the full effects of this disease by administering a simple, harmless test and treatment, the plaintiff should not have to bear the risk of loss. As such, imposition of liability approaches that of strict liability. If the standard of a reasonably prudent specialist is, in fact, inadequate to offer reasonable protection to the plaintiff, then liability can be imposed without fault.

EDITOR'S ANALYSIS: This position has not been adopted by any jurisdiction. Rather, there has been a movement to restrict strict liability to products liability cases. Many no-fault government programs are designed to copy the basic structure of Workers Compensation.

NOTES:

BROWN v. SUPERIOR COURT
DES children (P) v. Court (D)
Cal. Sup. Ct., 751 P.2d 470 (1988).

NATURE OF CASE: Review of medical products liability case brought under theories of strict liability, breach of express and implied warranty, fraud, and negligence.

FACT SUMMARY: Brown (P) and a number of other plaintiffs alleged that numerous drug manufacturers which produced diethylstilbestrol (DES), a substance they alleged had been used by their mothers to prevent miscarriage, were liable because the drug was defective and had caused them injury when their mothers had ingested it.

CONCISE RULE OF LAW: A manufacturer is not strictly liable for injuries caused by a prescription drug so long as the drug was properly prepared and accompanied by warnings of its dangerous propensities.

FACTS: Brown (P) and other plaintiffs contended that they had been injured as a result of their mothers' ingestion of DES, a drug that they claimed was unsafe for use in preventing miscarriages. Brown (P) alleged that the drug manufacturers knew that the drug contained a cancer-causing substance, yet they failed to warn users or their physicians. The drug manufacturers claimed that if they were subject to strict liability, they might be reluctant to undertake research programs to develop new and beneficial pharmaceuticals.

ISSUE: Is a manufacturer strictly liable for injuries caused by a prescription drug so long as the drug was properly prepared and accompanied by warnings of its dangerous propensities?

HOLDING AND DECISION: (Mosk, J.) No. A manufacturer is not strictly liable for injuries caused by a prescription drug so long as the drug was properly prepared and accompanied by warnings of its dangerous propensities. The negligence standard set forth in comment k to § 402A of the Restatement Second of Torts should be applied to this case, since the drug may be classified as an unavoidably unsafe product. Comment k states that liability attaches only if a manufacturer fails to warn of dangerous propensities of which it was or should have been aware.

EDITOR'S ANALYSIS: The court in this case discussed the various options available in the area of medical products liability. It agreed with the manufacturers that strict liability would deter drug manufacturers from conducting new research. The development and availability of new products was found to be in the public interest.

QUICKNOTES

STRICT LIABILITY - Liability for all injuries proximately caused by a party's conducting of certain inherently dangerous activities without regard to negligence or fault.

NOTES:

HERSKOVITS v. GROUP HEALTH COOPERATIVE OF PUGET SOUND

Estate representative (P) v. Hospital owner (D)
Wash. Sup. Ct., 99 Wash. d. 609, 664 P.2d 474 (1983).

NATURE OF CASE: Appeal from summary judgment dismissing wrongful death/malpractice action.

FACT SUMMARY: A trial court dismissed Herskovits' (P) malpractice action when she failed to show that her decedent would probably have survived absent the alleged malpractice.

CONCISE RULE OF LAW: A plaintiff in a wrongful death/malpractice action need not prove that the decedent more likely than not would have survived absent the alleged malpractice.

FACTS: Herskovits' (P) decedent presented himself to Group Health Cooperative of Puget Sound (D), complaining of coughs and chest pain. Group Health (D) failed to diagnose lung cancer, which was diagnosed by another facility one year later. The decedent's lung was removed, but the decedent died 20 months later. Herskovits (P) sued Group Health for negligent failure to diagnose. Group Heath (D) moved for summary judgment, contending that the decedent suffered from a probability of dying even if it had promptly diagnosed the cancer. At best, the decedent had a 39% chance of recovery; the hospital's (D) alleged negligence reduced it to 25%. The trial court granted summary judgment, and Herskovits (P) appealed.

ISSUE: Must a plaintiff in a wrongful death/malpractice action prove that the decedent more likely than not would have survived absent the alleged malpractice?

HOLDING AND DECISION: (Dore, J.) No. A plaintiff in a wrongful death/malpractice action need not prove that the decedent more likely than not would have survived absent the alleged malpractice. To hold otherwise would have the practical effect of shielding medical providers from liability anytime a decedent did not have a greater than 50% chance of living, no matter how egregious its negligence. This is not a proper result. Analytically, the issue boils down to proximate cause, a jury question. Using this case as an example, the question is whether a diminution in chances of survival from 39% to 25% could be considered a substantial factor in bringing about injury. This, as noted before, is a jury question, and not properly resolvable at the summary judgment level. The trial court was therefore in error in so granting. Reversed.

CONCURRENCE: (Pearson, J.) All that is required to be shown is that a substantial reduction in chance of survival was caused by the alleged malpractice.

DISSENT: (Brachtenbach, J.) The basic question is whether the doctor's malpractice caused the patient's death. When the patient probably would have died anyway, this cannot be so.

EDITOR'S ANALYSIS: The opinion was concerned with liability only. However, damages recoverable would be an issue in the context of this case. One possible measure of damages would be to make them commensurate with the lessening of the decedent's chance of survival due to the malpractice. In this case, Herskovits (P) would get 14% of full recovery under the measure.

NOTES:

CUNNINGHAM v. HUFFMAN
Patient (P) v. Physician (D) and clinic (D)
Ill. Sup. Ct., 609 N.E.2d 321 (1993).

NATURE OF CASE: Appeal from appellate judgment reinstating medical malpractice case against the defendant's clinic.

FACT SUMMARY: When Cunningham (P) had continuing problems as the result of Huffman's (D) treatment of her at Carle Clinic (D), she alleged that the statute of repose could not bar her medical malpractice claims because there was an ongoing course of treatment which tolled the statute.

CONCISE RULE OF LAW: A medical malpractice plaintiff is not barred by the statute of repose if she can demonstrate that there was an ongoing course of continuous negligent medical treatment.

FACTS: Huffman (D), a specialist and a member of the Carle Clinic Association (Carle) (D), had inserted an intrauterine device (IUD) into Cunningham (P) in 1977. Cunningham (P) subsequently had pain and another IUD was inserted in 1980 and removed in 1981. Another physician operated to remove another IUD in 1988. When Cunningham (P) brought a medical malpractice suit against Huffman (D) and Carle (D) in 1989, the circuit court dismissed it with prejudice because it was time-barred. Cunningham (P) appealed, arguing that the continuous course of treatment doctrine tolled the running of the statute of repose until the end of the patient/physician relationship. On appeal, the dismissal was affirmed as to Huffman (D), but the appellate court held that the trial court erred in dismissing the counts as to Carle (D), the clinic, without leave to amend. The appellate court stated that in medical malpractice actions, the statute of repose is triggered only on the last day of treatment, and if the treatment is for the same condition, there is no requirement that the negligence be continuous throughout the treatment. Carle (D) appealed, alleging that the continuous course of treatment doctrine did not apply to a multispecialty health care institution.

ISSUE: Is a medical malpractice plaintiff barred by the statute of repose if she can demonstrate that there was an ongoing course of continuous negligent medical treatment?

HOLDING AND DECISION: (Heiple, J.) No. A plaintiff is not barred by the statute of repose if she can demonstrate that there was an ongoing course of continuous negligent medical treatment. Once treatment by the negligent physician is discontinued, the statute of repose begins to run, regardless of whether or not the patient is aware of the negligence. This is so because the statute of repose is triggered by the act or omission or occurrence causing an injury, rather than by the patient's discovery of the injury, as is the case for statutes of limitations. The tort of continuing negligent treatment applies to a multispecialty clinic when several doctors negligently treat a patient for a specific problem over a finite time span. To the extent that a party brings an action against the clinic as an entity in and of itself, rather than on a theory of vicarious liability, she can state a cause of action against a multispecialty clinic. Affirmed.

EDITOR'S ANALYSIS: This case dealt with the tolling of the statute of limitations in medical malpractice cases. In this case, continuing negligent treatment tolled the statute. In other cases, fraudulent concealment and the discovery rule may be applied to toll the statute as well.

QUICKNOTES

STATUTE OF REPOSE - A law prescribing the period of time in which an action can be commenced that begins to run upon the delivery of goods or the completion of performance.

TOLL - A fee imposed in order to use another's property; the expiration of a statute of limitations period, terminating the right to commence a lawsuit.

NOTES:

SCHNEIDER v. REVICI
Breast cancer patient (P) v. Physician (D)
817 F.2d 987 (2d. Cir. 1987).

NATURE OF CASE: Appeal from a judgment for the plaintiff and award of damages for medical malpractice.

FACT SUMMARY: When the district court refused to charge the jury with respect to the affirmative defense of an alleged covenant not to sue and express assumption of risk at the close of Scheider's (P) malpractice trial, Revici (D) appealed.

CONCISE RULE OF LAW: Except as public policy proscribes an agreement limiting liability, the pure comparative negligence statute adopted in New York in 1975 does not foreclose a complete defense that by express consent of the injured party no duty exists and, therefore, no recovery may be had.

FACTS: When a lump was discovered in Schneider's (P) breast, she was advised to undergo a biopsy and possible partial mastectomy. She refused and instead consulted Dr. Revici (D), a physician with a novel noninvasive treatment for cancer. After fourteen months of Revici's (D) treatment, when the lump had increased in size and the cancer had spread, Schneider (P) had to undergo a bilateral mastectomy at a hospital. Schneider (P) then sued Revici (D) for fraud, premised on his alleged promise to cure Schneider (P) of breast cancer, and for medical malpractice. Over Revici's (D) objections, the district judge refused to charge the jury on the affirmative defense of express assumption of risk. The jury subsequently found that Revici (D) was not liable on the claim of common law fraud but was liable on the medical malpractice claim. Revici (D) appealed, challenging the district court's refusal to charge with respect to an alleged covenant not to sue and express assumption of risk. Schneider (P) argued that it was against public policy for one expressly to assume to risk of medical malpractice and thereby dissolve the physician's duty to treat a patient according to medical community standards.

ISSUE: Except as public policy proscribes an agreement limiting liability, does the pure comparative negligence statute adopted in New York in 1975 foreclose a complete defense that by express consent of the injured party no duty exists and, therefore, no recovery may be had?

HOLDING AND DECISION: (Miner, J.) No. Except as public policy proscribes an agreement limiting liability, the pure comparative negligence statute adopted in New York in 1975 does not foreclose a complete defense that by express consent of the injured party no duty exists and, therefore, no recovery may be had. An informed decision to avoid surgery and conventional chemotherapy is within the patient's right to determine what shall be done with her own body. There existed sufficient evidence—in the language of the Consent for Medical Care form that Schneider (P) had signed, and in testimony presented—to allow the jury to consider express assumption of risk as an affirmative defense that would totally bar recovery. It was therefore error for the district court to deny Revici's (D) request for a jury charge on the issue. Reversed and remanded.

EDITOR'S ANALYSIS: The court also discussed the history of New York state tort law. Although assumption of risk was a defense to an action for the recovery of damages for personal injuries prior to the adoption of the comparative negligence statute in 1975, it was predicated on a contract theory. In 1985 the Court of Appeals of New York held that express assumption of risk could still provide a complete defense, while implied assumption of risk was subsumed by the comparative negligence statute.

QUICKNOTES

PURE COMPARATIVE NEGLIGENCE STATUTE - Eliminates contributory negligence as a total bar to recovery.

NOTES:

MADDEN v. KAISER FOUNDATION HOSPITAL

State employee/patient (P) Medical healthcare plan (D)
Cal. Sup. Ct., 552 P.2d 1178 (1976).

NATURE OF CASE: Appeal from an order denying enforcement of an arbitration provision in a medical services contract.

FACT SUMMARY: Madden (P) successfully moved to stay Kaiser's (D) motion to compel arbitration because she was not aware of its provisions at the time of the negligent injury.

CONCISE RULE OF LAW: An agent or representative, contracting for medical services on behalf of a group of employees, has implied authority to agree to arbitration of malpractice claims of enrolled employees arising under the contract.

FACTS: When Madden (P), a state employee, enrolled under the Kaiser Plan (D) in 1965, it did not contain an arbitration provision. In 1971, the Kaiser Foundation Health Plan (D) and the Board of Administration of the State Employees Retirement System amended their contract to include a provision for binding arbitration of any claims arising from the violation of a legal duty incident to the Agreement. Madden (P) underwent a hysterectomy at the Kaiser Hospital in Los Angeles in 1971 during which her bladder was perforated, blood transfusions were required, and she contracted serum hepatitis. Madden (P) filed a malpractice lawsuit against Kaiser (D) and the blood banks. Kaiser (D) moved to stay the action and compel arbitration. Opposing the motion, Madden (P) filed a declaration stating that because of her absence from work by reason of illness, she had not received the notice about the arbitration agreement and thus had no knowledge that the Kaiser Plan (D), at the time of her operation, required arbitration of malpractice claims. The trial court denied the motion to stay the action and compel arbitration. Kaiser (D) appealed.

ISSUE: Does an agent or representative, contracting for medical services on behalf of a group of employees, have implied authority to agree to arbitration of malpractice claims of enrolled employees arising under the contract?

HOLDING AND DECISION: (Tobriner, J.) Yes. An agent or representative, contracting for medical services on behalf of a group of employees, has implied authority to agree to arbitration of malpractice claims of enrolled employees arising under the contract. The principles of adhesion contracts do not bar enforcement of terms of a negotiated contract that neither limit the liability of the stronger party nor bear oppressively on the weaker. Such principles do not bar enforcement of the arbitration amendment against Madden (P). The trial court erred in denying Kaiser's (D) motion to compel arbitration and in refusing to stay the action against Kaiser (D). Reversed.

DISSENT: (Mosk, J.) Had the original master contract executed by the Board and Kaiser (D) provided for arbitration, Madden (P) might have been bound thereby when she signed a written enrollment in the program. But six years after enrollment by Madden (P), an amendment providing for abdication of fundamental rights can be effective only if Madden (P) consents thereto in writing.

EDITOR'S ANALYSIS: The court found in this case that the Board, as agent for the employees, had implied authority to provide for arbitration for malpractice claims. Enforcement of the arbitration provision was also found not to violate constitutional or statutory protections of the right to trial by jury. Courts regularly enforce arbitration agreements that do not contain express waivers of jury trial.

NOTES:

FEIN v. PERMANENTE MEDICAL GROUP
Heart attack victim (P) v. Medical plan (D)
Cal. Sup. Ct., 695 P.2d 665 (1985).

NATURE OF CASE: Cross-appeals from a judgment awarding plaintiff damages in a medical malpractice action.

FACT SUMMARY: When damages were awarded in a medical malpractice action, Fein (P) appealed, arguing that the state law limiting noneconomic damages and modifying the collateral source rule was unconstitutional. Permanente Medical Group (D) also appealed, claiming that the trial court committed reversible error in permitting the jury to award damages for the loss of earnings attributable to Fein's so-called lost years and in failing to order that the bulk of the damages award be paid periodically rather than in a lump sum.

CONCISE RULE OF LAW: Recovery of damages is appropriate if the award is based on the loss of future earnings a plaintiff is likely to suffer because of inability to work for as long a period of time in the future as he could have done had he not sustained the accident.

FACTS: Fein (P) was thirty-four years old when he felt chest pain and went to Permanente Medical Group (D). The pain was treated as a muscle spasm, but it turned out to be a heart attack and Fein (P) was later hospitalized and operated on. Fein (P) sued Permanente (D), alleging that his heart condition should have been diagnosed earlier and that treatment should have been given either to prevent the heart attack or lessen its residual effects. Medical testimony at trial established that if Fein (P) had been properly treated, his future life expectancy would have been decreased by only ten to fifteen percent, rather than by half as it was now. The jury awarded damages for past lost wages, future medical expenses, and for wages lost in the future as a result of the reduction in Fein's life expectancy, as well as noneconomic damages to compensate for pain and suffering and other intangibles. Both parties appealed.

ISSUE: Is recovery of damages appropriate if the award is based on the loss of future earnings a plaintiff is likely to suffer because of inability to work for as long a period of time in the future as he could have done had he not sustained the accident?

HOLDING AND DECISION: (Kaus, J.) Yes. Recovery of damages is appropriate if the award is based on the loss of future earnings a plaintiff is likely to suffer because of inability to work for as long a period of time in the future as he could have done had he not sustained the accident. Because Permanente (D) failed to raise the issue of periodic payment earlier, the trial court judgment cannot be reversed on that ground. As for the limit on noneconomic damages challenged by Fein (P), the legislature did not act irrationally in choosing to modify the collateral source rule as one means of lowering the costs of malpractice litigation. The Medical Injury Compensation Reform Act of 1975 is not unconstitutional. Affirmed.

EDITOR'S ANALYSIS: The Medical Injury Compensation Reform Act modified California's common law collateral source rule. A medical malpractice defendant is now permitted to introduce evidence of collateral source benefits received by or payable to a plaintiff, but the plaintiff is also permitted to introduce evidence of the amounts he has paid to secure the benefits. The source of the collateral benefits is prohibited from obtaining subrogation, so that there can be no "double deduction" for any tort recovery.

QUICKNOTES

MEDICAL INJURY COMPENSATION REFORM ACT - California law limiting noneconomic damages in medical malpractice cases to #250,000 and modifying the "collateral source" rule.

NOTES:

ROBERTS v. STEVENS CLINIC HOSPITAL
Decedent's parents (P) v. Hospital (D)
W. Va. Sup. Ct., 345 S.E.2d 791 (1986).

NATURE OF CASE: Appeal from jury award of compensatory damages in a wrongful death action.

FACT SUMMARY: When their child died as a result of Stevens Clinic's (D) malpractice, the Robertses (P) successfully sued for compensatory damages.

CONCISE RULE OF LAW: The West Virginia Wrongful Death Statute specifically sets forth the losses for which damages can be recovered.

FACTS: Michael Roberts died as a result of medical malpractice and the jury awarded compensatory damages to his family (P). The Stevens Clinic Hospital (D) alleged that the "home movie" introduced at trial by the Robertses (P) inaccurately highlighted certain aspects of Michael's life. The closing argument of the Robertses' (P) attorney improperly implied that the duty of the jury was to place a value on Michael's (P) life, although opposing counsel failed to object. The jury awarded $10,000,000 in damages and Stevens Clinic (D) appealed, requesting remittitur to a lower amount.

ISSUE: Does the West Virginia Wrongful Death Statute specifically set forth the losses for which damages can be recovered?

HOLDING AND DECISION: (Neely, J.) Yes. The West Virginia Wrongful Death Statute specifically sets forth the losses for which damages can be recovered. The district court's decision as to the admissibility of evidence is reversible only when the record shows a clear abuse of discretion. Therefore the admission of the home video as evidence will be left intact since the video was neither inflammatory nor prejudicial. However, the jury's award must be reduced from $10,000,000 to $3,000,000 because the Robertses' (P) attorney invited the jury to place a value on Michael's life. If that were the measure of damages, no jury verdict would be excessive since no amount of money can compensate for the death of a child. It is important to consider what jury award in a case of this type will establish the proper climate for out-of-court settlements. Reversed and remanded.

DISSENT: (McHugh, J.) Damages in a wrongful death case for nonpecuniary losses, such as mental anguish, should not be reduced to present value. Whether an award for solatium is excessive is not properly determined by calculating its annual yield. The insurance companies coldly asserted that this case was not "worth" $10,000,000 and maintained that reduction to a more "reasonable" figure was appropriate.

EDITOR'S ANALYSIS: This case illustrates the general rule that the loss of life is not compensated. Compensable noneconomic damages such as sorrow, mental anguish, and solace are specifically set out in the state statute. Since the other members of the family had not suffered any personal injuries, the court ruled that the jury's award was excessive in this case.

QUICKNOTES
SOLATIUM - Damages awarded to a plaintiff in order to provide solace to the victim or to otherwise compensate for emotional injury.

WEST VIRGINIA WRONGFUL DEATH STATUTE - Law limiting malpractice damages to compensation for mental anguish, loss of income and services of the decedent, hospital expenses, and funeral expenses.

NOTES:

BLEDAY v. OUM GROUP
Podiatrist (P) v. Insurer (D)
Pa. Super. Ct., 645 A.2d 1358 (1994).

NATURE OF CASE: Appeal from grant of defendants' motion to dismiss action for damages for breach of duty to defend malpractice lawsuits.

FACT SUMMARY: When his insurer, OUM Group (D), settled a malpractice claim without his approval, Bleday (P) filed a complaint alleging breach of the duty of good faith and sought damages for increased insurance premiums, loss of earnings, and harm to his professional reputation.

CONCISE RULE OF LAW: Although judicial deference must be given to the decision of an insurance company to settle a claim within the policy limits, a claim for bad faith may, in limited circumstances, be asserted against the insurance company notwithstanding a "deems expedient" provision.

FACTS: Bleday (P), a podiatrist, secured malpractice insurance from the OUM Group (D). The policy provided that OUM (D) could settle any claim or suit as it deemed expedient. Over Bleday's (P) objections, OUM (D) settled a malpractice claim made by a patient. When Bleday's (P) complaint alleging that the OUM Group (D) had breached their duty of good faith in settling without his consent was dismissed, Bleday (P) appealed, claiming that the OUM Group (D), despite the policy language "deems expedient," had the duty to act in good faith in the handling of its claims.

ISSUE: Although judicial deference must be given to the decision of an insurance company to settle a claim within the policy limits, may a claim for bad faith, in limited circumstances, be asserted against the insurance company notwithstanding a "deems expedient" provision?

HOLDING AND DECISION: (Hudock, J.) Yes. Although judicial deference must be given to the decision of an insurance company to settle a claim within the policy limits, a claim for bad faith may, in limited circumstances, be asserted against the insurance company notwithstanding a "deems expedient" provision. In this case, however, Bleday (P) did not sufficiently plead a cause of action in bad faith against OUM (D) and the trial court properly granted OUM's (D) preliminary objections. Something more is required to maintain a cause of action for bad faith when a claim is settled within the policy limits. Affirmed.

EDITOR'S ANALYSIS: In other cases, the "deems expedient" provision has been interpreted as granting the insurer the discretion to settle cases for amounts within the policy limits, regardless of whether the claim is frivolous or not. Every contract that is entered into requires the good faith performance of its provisions, however. Thus, the "deems expedient" provision is not absolute.

NOTES:

SCHLOENDORFF v. SOCIETY OF NEW YORK HOSPITAL

Patient (P) v. Hospital (D)
N.Y. Sup. Ct., 105 N.E. 92 (1914).

NATURE OF CASE: Appeal from a directed verdict in favor of the defendant.

FACT SUMMARY: When Schloendorff (P), a patient, was operated on without her consent and later developed gangrene, she unsuccessfully sued the Hospital (D).

CONCISE RULE OF LAW: A hospital that is maintained as a charitable institution is not liable for the negligence of its physicians and nurses in the treatment of patients.

FACTS: Schloendorff (P) went to the Society of New York Hospital (D), a charitable institution, complaining of a stomach disorder. When a physician discovered a lump, Schloendorff (P) allegedly agreed to an ether examination but not to an operation. Schloendorff (P) alleged she was operated on without her consent or knowledge. Following the operation, gangrene developed in her left arm and some of her fingers had to be amputated. She then sued the Hospital (D) for the wrong. When the court directed a verdict for the Hospital (D), Schloendorff (P) appealed.

ISSUE: Is a hospital that is maintained as a charitable institution liable for the negligence of its physicians and nurses in the treatment of patients?

HOLDING AND DECISION: (Cardozo, J.) No. A hospital that is maintained as a charitable institution is not liable for the negligence of its physicians and nurses in the treatment of patients. The relation between a Hospital (D) and its physicians is not that of master and servant. The hospital does not undertake to act through them, but merely to procure them to act upon their own responsibility. The wrong was not that of the Hospital (D), it was that of physicians. The trial judge did not err in his direction of a verdict. A ruling would, indeed, be an unfortunate one that might constrain charitable institutions, as a measure of self-protection, to limit their activities. Affirmed.

EDITOR'S ANALYSIS: The court in this case also found that nurses were not servants of the hospital, but rather delegates of the surgeon to whose orders they were subject. The physician was considered to be an independent contractor, liable for his own wrongs, but involving the Hospital (D) in no liability, if due care had been taken in his selection. The court also ruled that an operation without the patient's permission would constitute a trespass, and not mere negligence. This case was later overruled.

QUICKNOTES

TRESPASS - Unlawful interference with, or damage to, the real or personal property of another.

NOTES:

ADAMSKI v. TACOMA GENERAL HOSPITAL

Patient (P) v. Hospital (D), physician (D), and nurses (D)
Wash. Ct. App., 579 P.2d 970 (1978).

NATURE OF CASE: Appeal from summary judgment in favor of defendant in action for damages alleging negligent diagnosis and treatment.

FACT SUMMARY: When an emergency room physician (D) was negligent in his diagnosis and treatment, the patient Adamski (P), also sued the Hospital (D) on a theory of respondeat superior.

CONCISE RULE OF LAW: A "holding out" or representation may arise when the hospital acts or omits to act in some way which leads the patient to a reasonable belief he is being treated by the hospital by one of its employees.

FACTS: Adamski (P) broke his finger while playing basketball. When he went to the emergency room at Tacoma General Hospital (D), the physician in charge, Dr. Tsoi, (D) treated him. The wound had to be reopened and cleaned three days later because Dr. Tsoi (D) had not adequately treated the wound for a deep infection. Adamski (P) sued Dr. Tsoi (D) and the nurse-employees and the Hospital (D) alleging that Dr. Tsoi (D) was negligent and that he was acting as the Hospital's (D) agent. Tacoma General's (D) motion for summary judgment was granted because the trial court concluded that Dr. Tsoi (D) was an independent contractor and not an employee of the Hospital (D). Therefore the court refused to hold the Hospital (D) liable on a respondeat superior theory. Adamski (P) appealed, alleging that a substantial and genuine issue arose as to whether the relationship between Tacoma General (D) and its emergency room physician was that of principal and agent.

ISSUE: May a "holding out" or representation arise when the hospital acts or omits to act in some way which leads the patient to a reasonable belief he is being treated by the hospital by one of its employees?

HOLDING AND DECISION: (Reed, J.) Yes. A "holding out" or representation may arise when the hospital acts or omits to act in some way which leads the patient to a reasonable belief he is being treated by the hospital by one of its employees. A jury could find that Tacoma General (D) held itself out as providing emergency care services to the public and that Adamski (P) reasonably believed Dr. Tsoi (D) was employed by the Hospital (D) to deliver that emergency room service. Clearly, when the facts before the trial court and the fair inferences therefrom are viewed in a light most favorable to Adamski (P), a jury could find that the emergency room personnel were "held out" as employees of the Hospital (D). Since Dr. Tsoi (D) was performing an inherent function of the Hospital (D), a substantial issue also arises as to whether the relationship between the emergency room physician (D) and the Hospital (D) was that of principal and agent. It was error to resolve this issue by summary judgment. Reversed.

EDITOR'S ANALYSIS: The court in this case points out that there has been a recent expansion of hospital liability for negligent medical acts committed on its premises. Present-day hospitals do much more than furnish facilities for treatment, according to one decision. Although many cases preserved the distinction between the liability of an employee and the immunity of a physician who was considered to be an independent contractor, this distinction was considered to be artificial where the physician was employed for an extended period of time and performed a service which was an "inherent function of the hospital."

QUICKNOTES

RESPONDEAT SUPERIOR - Rule that the principal is responsible for tortious acts committed by its agents in the scope of their agency or authority.

NOTES:

DARLING v. CHARLESTON COMMUNITY MEMORIAL HOSPITAL

Patient (P) v. Hospital (D)

Ill. Sup. Ct., 33 Ill. 2d 326, 211 N.E.2d 253 (1965),
cert. denied, 383 U.S. 946 (1966).

NATURE OF CASE: Appeal from award of damages for medical malpractice.

FACT SUMMARY: Darling (P) sought to hold Charleston Community Memorial Hospital (D) liable for the alleged negligence of its staff.

CONCISE RULE OF LAW: A hospital may be liable for the negligence of its staff.

FACTS: When Darling (P) broke his leg, he was taken to the emergency room at Charleston Community Memorial Hospital (D). The attending physician, Alexander (D), set the break and put the leg in a cast. The next day, Darling's (P) toes turned dark and cold. The cast was removed, but much of the tissue in the leg had become necrotic as a result of the constriction caused by the cast. The lower leg eventually had to be amputated. Darling (P) sued Alexander (D) and Charleston (D). After settling with Alexander (D), Darling (P) tried the case against Charleston (D). The jury returned a verdict of $150,000. This was affirmed by the state court of appeals, and the state supreme court granted review on the issue of whether a hospital could be held liable for the negligence of its staff.

ISSUE: May a hospital be liable for the negligence of its staff?

HOLDING AND DECISION: (Schaefer, J.) Yes. A hospital may be liable for the negligence of its staff. The notion that a hospital only provides facilities and does not purport to act through its staff physicians and nurses does not reflect reality. Modern hospitals do much more than provide facilities. They employ a large staff of doctors, nurses, administrators, and other workers, and do not hesitate to collect fees for services performed at the hospital. A person availing himself of a hospital reasonably expects the hospital as an entity to treat him. Consequently, no legitimate basis for not holding a hospital vicariously responsible for the torts of its staff exists. Here, the jury found both Alexander (D) negligent in the procedures he utilized, and the nursing staff negligent in its postprocedure followups. This was amply supported by the evidence. Affirmed.

EDITOR'S ANALYSIS: Traditionally, doctors have been viewed as independent contractors by their hospitals. Under the common law "independent contractor" rule, one employing a contractor as opposed to an employee will not be vicariously responsible therefor. Just as the rule has been weakened in recent times in society in general, so it has in medicine.

JOHNSON v. MISERICORDIA COMMUNITY HOSPITAL
Patient (P) v. Hospital (D)
Wis. Sup. Ct., 301 N.W.2d 156 (1981).

NATURE OF CASE: Review of a damage award in a medical malpractice suit.

FACT SUMMARY: Misericordia Community Hospital (D) was found to have been liable for its negligence in the selection of its medical staff.

CONCISE RULE OF LAW: A hospital has a duty to exercise due care in the selection of its medical staff.

FACTS: Johnson (P) was treated at Misericordia (D) by a physician (D) who unsuccessfully attempted to remove a pin fragment from Johnson's (P) right hip and damaged his nerve, causing a permanent paralytic condition. The physician (D), who was found to have negligently performed the surgical procedure, had been hired by Misericordia (D) at a time when it did not have a functioning credentials committee. At trial, evidence was presented that the physician's (D) competence as an orthopedic surgeon was suspect and that his privileges had been denied and restricted at other hospitals. No investigation had been made by anyone at Misericordia (D) of the statements recited in the physician's (D) application there. The trial court instructed the jury that the Hospital (D) was required to exercise reasonable care in the granting of medical staff privileges. Expert testimony was necessary to establish the degree of care, skill, and judgment usually exercised under like or similar circumstances by the average hospital. There was evidence presented that a hospital, exercising ordinary care, would not have appointed that physician (D) to its medical staff. The jury found the physician (D) was negligent in the treatment he afforded Johnson (P) and attributed 20% of the causal negligence to him and 80% to the Hospital (D). Misericordia (D) appealed.

ISSUE: Does a hospital have a duty to exercise due care in the selection of its medical staff?

HOLDING AND DECISION: (Coffey, J.) Yes. A hospital has a duty to exercise due care in the selection of its medical staff. The jury's finding of negligence on the part of Misericordia (D) must be upheld, as there was credible evidence which reasonably supported this finding. A hospital should, at a minimum, require completion of the application and verify the accuracy of the applicant's statements, especially with regard to his medical education, training, and experience. This is not to say that hospitals are insurers of the competence of their medical staff, for a hospital will not be negligent if it exercises the noted standard of care in selecting its staff. Affirmed.

EDITOR'S ANALYSIS: This case demonstrates the modern view. Hospital liability has been expanded to include a direct responsibility for the maintenance of an acceptable standard of care. Two forms of hospital negligence with respect to physicians have been identified: negligent selection and retention, and negligent supervision.

NOTES:

BOYD v. ALBERT EINSTEIN MEDICAL CENTER
Patient (P) v. Health maintenance organization (D)
Pa. Super. Ct., 377 Pa. Super. 609, 547 A.2d 1229 (1988).

NATURE OF CASE: Appeal of summary judgment dismissing wrongful death/malpractice action.

FACT SUMMARY: Boyd (P) sought to hold a health maintenance organization liable for the malpractice of its doctors.

CONCISE RULE OF LAW: A health maintenance organization may be liable for the malpractice of its doctors.

FACTS: Health maintenance organization of Pennsylvania (D) (HMO) operated a health care provider system wherein members would be referred to primary care physicians approved by HMO (D), who in turn could refer them to specialists. Certain hospitals were also members of HMO (D). Boyd's (P) decedent underwent a breast biopsy by HMO (D) physician Cohen (D). During the procedure, Cohen (D) inadvertently perforated her chest wall. The decedent subsequently died as a result of complications arising therefrom. Boyd (P) sued, among others, HMO (D). HMO (D) successfully moved for summary judgment on the grounds that its participating doctors were independent contractors. Boyd (P) appealed.

ISSUE: May a health maintenance organization be liable for the malpractice of its doctors?

HOLDING AND DECISION: (Olszewski, J.) Yes. A health maintenance organization may be liable for the malpractice of its doctors. A health maintenance organization generally covenants with its members to provide quality health care. It screens its participating physicians and limits the choice of its members as to with whom they may consult. Further, participating doctors must comply with various regulations. Under such a scenario, a triable issue of fact is raised as to whether the participating doctors are ostensible agents of the health maintenance organization. Here, HMO (D) fell into the typical pattern for health maintenance organizations generally, as described above, and therefore may be liable on an ostensible agency theory. Summary judgment was therefore inappropriate. Reversed.

CONCURRENCE: (McEwen, J.) Whether HMO (D) "guaranteed" the quality of care provided to its subscribers is a factual issue that should not be resolved by summary judgment.

EDITOR'S ANALYSIS: Health maintenance organizations are a relatively new phenomenon. Like hospitals, their member doctors tend to be contractors rather then employees. Also like hospitals, courts are becoming increasingly receptive to various theories of liability for the torts of their doctors.

NOTES:

WICKLINE v. STATE

Patient (P) v. State Medicaid program (D)
Cal. App. Ct., 239 Cal. Rptr. 810 (1986).

NATURE OF CASE: Appeal of jury damage award in a suit for negligent discontinuance of Medi-Cal eligibility.

FACT SUMMARY: Wickline (P) was discharged sooner than her doctor believed appropriate due to a Medi-Cal (D) rejection of further hospitalization costs, and she suffered a blood clot in her leg, requiring amputation.

CONCISE RULE OF LAW: Since a patient's health care payor is not responsible for discharge determinations, liability will not attach to the payor for a negligent discharge.

FACTS: Wickline (P) suffered an arterial blockage in her leg. After multiple surgeries with complications, her doctor, Dr. Polonsky, determined that she should remain hospitalized for eight extra days. The doctor requested a Medi-Cal (D) approval for the extra days, but only four extra days were approved. Dr. Polonsky did not challenge this finding, though an appeal route existed. After the four days, Wickline (P) was discharged. Several physicians agreed that the discharge was reasonable given the current standard of medical practice. However, complications with Wickline's (P) leg at home eventually required amputation. Wickline (P) filed suit against Medi-Cal (D) for negligently interfering with her doctor's discretion. The jury found for Wickline (P), and Medi-Cal (D) appealed.

ISSUE: Does a patient's health care payor bear the primary responsibility for allowing a patient to be discharged from a hospital, thus incurring liability for a negligent discharge?

HOLDING AND DECISION: (Rowan, J.) No. Since a patient's health care payor is not responsible for discharge determinations, liability will not attach to the payor for a negligent discharge. A patient's physician is in a far better position to determine medically necessary procedures than is Medi-Cal (D). When an appeal route exists and is not used, then the physician cannot shift responsibility to the payor. In this case, Dr. Polonsky admitted that it was his primary responsibility to care for Wickline (P). He felt that four more days of hospitalization were needed, but he did not challenge the initial Medi-Cal (D) finding. Medi-Cal (D) based its decision on a limited set of facts which Dr. Polonsky could have questioned. Medi-Cal (D) is not liable for Wickline's (P) injuries. Reversed.

EDITOR'S ANALYSIS: The decision in *Wickline v. State* has been substantially narrowed in subsequent cases. Outside entities that deny care can be liable for negligently reviewing medical records. Apparently there is a growing concern that cost-containment procedures are interfering with physicians' decisions.

NOTES:

DUKES v. U.S. HEALTHCARE, INC.
Decedents' survivors (P) v. HMO organizor (D)
57 F.3d 350 (3d Cir. 1995).

NATURE OF CASE: Appeal from dismissal after removal of state medical malpractice suits to federal court by defendant.

FACT SUMMARY: U.S. Healthcare (D) contended that the federal statute governing pension plans preempted two state tort actions for medical malpractice, the Dukes' (P) and the Viscontis' (P).

CONCISE RULE OF LAW: ERISA does not preempt a plaintiff's vicarious liability claim of malpractice against a health maintenance organization.

FACTS: David Dukes died after his hospital refused to perform routine blood tests following surgery. The Viscontis' (P) baby was stillborn when the doctors failed to diagnose preeclampsia. Mrs. Dukes (P) and the Viscontis (P) filed separate medical malpractice actions in state court against health maintenance organizations (HMOs) (D) organized by U.S. Healthcare (D). U.S. Healthcare (D) removed the cases to federal court on preemption grounds, arguing that the injured patients had obtained medical care as a benefit from a welfare-benefit plan governed by the Employee Retirement Income Security Act of 1974 (ERISA). The court then granted U.S. Healthcare's (D) motion to dismiss. Dukes (P) claimed that removal was improper because the suits were tort actions, and appealed.

ISSUE: Does ERISA preempt a plaintiff's vicarious liability claim of malpractice against an HMO?

HOLDING AND DECISION: (Stapleton, J.) No. ERISA does not preempt a plaintiff's vicarious liability claim of malpractice against a health maintenance organization. On the other hand, patients who sue for health insurance benefits under ordinary contract law must pursue their case in federal court under ERISA if their insurance is provided by a private employer. In this case, Dukes (P) attacked the low quality of the medical treatment her husband received, not that the HMO (D) erroneously withheld benefits due under the plan. She argued that U.S. Healthcare HMO (D) should be held liable under agency and negligence principles, and not under contract principles. Healthcare's (D) argument that the employer and the HMOs (D) had impliedly contracted that the health care services provided would be of acceptable quality cannot be determined at this time since no documents reflecting such an agreement were available to the court. Nothing in this record suggests an agreement to displace the otherwise applicable state laws of agency and tort. Reversed and remanded.

EDITOR'S ANALYSIS: This case left open the possibility that an employer and an HMO could agree that a quality of health care standard articulated in their contract would replace the standard that would otherwise be supplied by the applicable state law of tort. HMOs would much prefer to have malpractice claims be governed by ERISA, because it contains certain provisions that favor the defense. Under ERISA, no compensatory damages for pain and suffering or wrongful death are available. Punitive damages also are not available under ERISA.

QUICKNOTES
ERISA: Federal statute regulating employer-sponsored pension plans. Also covers fringe benefits such as health insurance.

NOTES:

FEIN v. PERMANENTE MEDICAL GROUP
Injured patient (P) v. Medical group (D)
Cal. Sup. Ct., 695 P.2d 665 (1985).

NATURE OF CASE: Cross-appeals from judgment awarding plaintiff one million dollars in medical malpractice damages.

FACT SUMMARY: Fein (P) appealed from the trial court's application of the Medical Injury Compensation Reform Act of 1975 (MICRA) to limit damages, alleging that it was unconstitutional.

CONCISE RULE OF LAW: So long as a measure limiting damages in medical malpractice actions is rationally related to a legitimate state interest, policy determinations as to the need for, and the desirability of, such an enactment are for the legislature to determine.

FACTS: On account of Permanente Medical Group's (D) failure to diagnose Fein's (P) heart condition, the jury awarded $500,000 for "noneconomic damages" to compensate for pain and suffering and other intangible damages sustained by Fein (P) from the time of his injury until his death. The trial court reduced the noneconomic damages to $250,000. Fein (P) claimed that the trial court erred in applying the provisions of MICRA, a California state law limiting noneconomic damages and modifying the traditional collateral source rule in medical malpractice cases. Fein (P) claimed that § 3333.2, which limited noneconomic damages to $250,000, denied due process and violated equal protection and was therefore unconstitutional, and appealed.

ISSUE: So long as a measure is rationally related to a legitimate state interest, are policy determinations as to the need for, and the desirability of, an enactment for the legislature to determine?

HOLDING AND DECISION: (Kaus, J.) Yes. So long as a measure limiting damages in medical malpractice action is rationally related to a legitimate state interest, policy determinations as to the need for, and the desirability of, an enactment are for the legislature to determine. Fein (P) had no vested property right in a particular measure of damages and the legislature possessed broad authority to modify the scope and nature of such damages. The constitutionality of measures affecting such economic rights under the Due Process Clause does not depend on judicial assessment of the justifications for the act or the wisdom or fairness of the enactment. The California legislature limited the application of § 3333.2 to medical malpractice cases because it was responding to an insurance "crisis" in that particular area and the statute is rationally related to the legislative purpose. Affirmed.

DISSENT: (Bird, J.) In order to provide special relief to negligent healthcare providers and their insurers, MICRA arbitrarily singles out a few injured patients to be stripped of important and well-established protections against negligently inflicted harm. Crisis or no crisis, this court is duty bound to apply the constitutional guarantee against irrational and invidious classifications.

EDITOR'S ANALYSIS: This case deals with the limitations that MICRA imposed on medical malpractice suits. Relief is limited by that statute. Lawyer's contingency fees in medical malpractice cases are limited to: 40% of the first $50,000, 33% of the next $50,000, 25% of the next $100,000, and 10% of any amounts above $200,000.

QUICKNOTES
MICRA: California statute limiting malpractice damages for noneconomic injuries to $250,000.

NOTES:

CHAPTER 5
THE RIGHT AND "DUTY" TO DIE

QUICK REFERENCE RULES OF LAW

1. **Refusal of Life-Sustaining Treatment: The Competent Patient.** The state's interest weakens and the individual's right to privacy grows as the degree of bodily invasion increases and the prognosis dims. (In the Matter of Karen Quinlan)

2. **Refusal of Life-Sustaining Treatment: The Competent Patient.** The patient's ability to control his bodily integrity through informed consent also encompasses a right to informed refusal. (In re Conroy)

3. **Refusal of Life-Sustaining Treatment: The Competent Patient.** There is a general liberty interest in refusing medical treatment. (Cruzan v. Director, Missouri Department of Health)

4. **The Patient Whose Competence is Uncertain.** A confused or forgetful patient whose confusion or forgetfulness does not interfere with her ability to decide about surgery is competent to refuse treatment. (Lane v. Candura)

5. **The Patient Whose Competence Is Uncertain.** A patient must appreciate the nature of her medical condition and must be able to make a rational choice about living in order to be competent to accept or refuse treatment. (Department of Human Services v. Northern)

6. **The Incompetent Patient.** The right of an adult who was once competent to determine the course of her medical treatment remains intact even when she is no longer able to assert that right or to appreciate its effectuation. (In re Conroy)

7. **The Incompetent Patient.** The right of a patient in an irreversibly vegetative state to determine whether to refuse life-sustaining medical treatment may be exercised by the patient's family or close friend. (In re Jobes)

8. **The Incompetent Patient.** A state may apply a clear and convincing evidence standard in proceedings where a guardian seeks to discontinue nutrition and hydration of a person diagnosed to be in a persistent vegetative state. (Cruzan v. Director, Missouri Department of Health)

9. **Physician-Assisted Suicide.** A state prohibition against causing or aiding a suicide does not offend the Fourteenth Amendment. (Washington v. Glucksberg)

10. **Physician-Assisted Suicide.** The distinction between refusing lifesaving medical treatment and assisted suicide is not arbitrary or irrational. (Vacco v. Quill)

11. **Futility.** Once an individual has been diagnosed as presenting an emergency medical condition, the hospital must provide that treatment necessary to prevent the material deterioration of the individual's condition or provide for an appropriate transfer. (In re Baby K)

12. **Futility.** A damages action based upon the discontinuance of life-sustaining treatment falls under a state medical malpractice statute. (Causey v. St. Francis Medical Center)

IN THE MATTER OF KAREN QUINLAN
Patient's father (P) v. Hospital (D)
N.J. Sup. Ct., 355 A.2d 647 (1976).

NATURE OF CASE: Appeal from denial of an injunction and of request of a father to be appointed guardian of his moribund daughter.

FACT SUMMARY: Although Karen Quinlan was in a chronic persistent vegetative state, her father was not permitted to act as her guardian and order the discontinuance of all extraordinary medical procedures.

CONCISE RULE OF LAW: The state's interest weakens and the individual's right to privacy grows as the degree of bodily invasion increases and the prognosis dims.

FACTS: Karen Quinlan was taken to a hospital after being unconscious for fifteen minutes. She remained in a chronic persistent vegetative state, debilitated and moribund, her life sustained by a respirator and tubal feeding. Karen's father asked the superior court to appoint him guardian of his daughter and give him express power to authorize the discontinuance of all extraordinary medical procedures sustaining his daughter's life. The court denied his request. Karen's father appealed, claiming that prevailing medical standards must be reconsidered in a case of forced sustaining by cardio-respiratory processes of an irrevocably doomed patient.

ISSUE: Does the state's interest weaken and the individual's right to privacy grow as the degree of bodily invasion increases and the prognosis dims?

HOLDING AND DECISION: (Hughes, J.) Yes. The state's interest weakens and the individual's right to privacy grows as the degree of bodily invasion increases and the prognosis dims. A right of personal privacy exists and certain areas of privacy have been found to be guaranteed under the Constitution. The unwritten constitutional right of privacy was found to exist in the penumbra of specific guarantees of the Bill of Rights and is broad enough to encompass a patient's decision to decline medical treatment under certain circumstances. The claimed interests of the state in this case are essentially the preservation and sanctity of human life and defense of a physician's right to administer medical treatment according to his best judgment. Since the medical treatment involved serves only a maintenance function and no cure or improvement of her condition is possible, the individual's right to privacy overcomes the state interest. Prevailing medical standards which could be considered "ordinary" in the context of the possibly curable patient are "extraordinary" in the context of the forced sustaining by cardio-respiratory processes of an irrevocably doomed patient. Reversed.

EDITOR'S ANALYSIS: The court stated that if Karen Quinlan herself were competent to make the decision, her choice would be vindicated by the law. Her prognosis was extremely poor—she would never resume cognitive life. In such a case, the interests of the patient must be evaluated by the court as predominant.

QUICKNOTES

PENUMBRA - A doctrine whereby authority of the federal government is implied pursuant to the Necessary and Proper Clause; one implied power may be inferred from the conferring of another implied power.

NOTES:

IN RE CONROY
Nephew (P) v. Guardian ad litem (D)
N.J. Sup. Ct., 486 A.2d 1209 (1985).

NATURE OF CASE: Review of the reversal of lower court's decision that a guardian could discontinue life-sustaining treatment of an incompetent patient.

FACT SUMMARY: Conroy's nephew and guardian requested the court's permission to have the feeding-tube removed from his elderly aunt because she was incompetent.

CONCISE RULE OF LAW: The patient's ability to control his bodily integrity through informed consent also encompasses a right to informed refusal.

FACTS: Conroy, who was suffering from an organic brain syndrome, was adjudicated to be incompetent and her nephew was appointed to be her guardian. The nephew petitioned the court for permission to discontinue Conroy's feeding tube, which kept her alive in a hospital while suffering from various serious conditions. The guardian ad litem opposed the petition, but the trial court granted the petition. The intermediate court of appeals reversed. While the case was before the intermediate court, Conroy died with her feeding tube still in place. The N.J. Supreme Court nevertheless heard the case because it involved a matter of substantial importance capable of repetition but evading review.

ISSUE: Does the patient's ability to control his bodily integrity through informed consent also encompasses a right to informed refusal?

HOLDING AND DECISION: (Schreiber, J.) Yes. The patient's ability to control his bodily integrity through informed consent also encompasses a right to informed refusal. A competent adult person generally has the right to decline to have any medical treatment initiated or continued. The right to make certain decisions concerning one's body is also protected by the federal Constitutional right of privacy. The right to life-sustaining medical treatment is not absolute. There is no doubt that Ms. Conroy, if competent to make the decision and if resolute in her decision, could have chosen to have her nasogastric tube withdrawn. Her interest in freedom from nonconsensual invasion of her bodily integrity would outweigh any state interest in preserving life or in safeguarding the integrity of the medical profession. Rejecting her artificial means of feeding would not constitute attempted suicide and would not constitute a public health or safety hazard, nor would any third persons be harmed therefrom. A competent person's common law and constitutional rights do not depend on the quality or value of her life. Reversed.

EDITOR'S ANALYSIS: This case set forth the four state interests that may limit a person's right to refuse medical treatment. The state's interest in preserving life is commonly considered the most important. The others are to prevent suicide, to safeguard the integrity of the medical profession, and to protect innocent parties. In cases that do not involve the protection of the actual or potential life of someone other than the decision maker, the state's interest and abstract interest in preserving the life of the competent person generally gives way to the patient's much stronger personal interest in directing the course of his own life.

NOTES:

CRUZAN v. DIRECTOR, MISSOURI DEPARTMENT OF HEALTH

Comatose patient's parents (P) v. State (D)

497 U.S. 261 (1990).

NATURE OF CASE: Review of reversal of state court authorization to terminate life-sustaining treatment.

FACT SUMMARY: When Nancy Cruzan's parents (P) requested that hospital employees terminate the artificial nutrition and hydration procedures keeping her alive, they were told they needed judicial approval.

CONCISE RULE OF LAW: There is a general liberty interest in refusing medical treatment.

FACTS: Cruzan was injured in an automobile accident and never recovered consciousness. She lived in a persistent vegetative state in a state hospital. Her parents (P) successfully obtained state trial court approval for the termination of the artificial nutrition and hydration procedures keeping her alive. When the state Supreme Court reversed, the Cruzans (P) appealed, alleging that Nancy had a right under the federal Constitution which would require the hospital to withdraw life-sustaining treatment from her under these circumstances.

ISSUE: Is there a general liberty interest in refusing medical treatment?

HOLDING AND DECISION: (Rehnquist, C. J.) Yes. There is a general liberty interest in refusing medical treatment. With the advance of medical technology capable of sustaining life well past the point where natural forces would have brought certain death in earlier times, cases involving the right to refuse life-sustaining treatment have burgeoned. Decisions prior to the incorporation of the Fourth Amendment into the Fourteenth Amendment analyzed searches and seizures involving the body under the Due Process Clause and were thought to implicate substantial liberty interests. For purposes of this case, this court assumes that the United States Constitution would grant a competent person a constitutionally protected right to refuse lifesaving hydration and nutrition. However, since Missouri (D) has adopted a reasonable procedural standard for deciding when an incompetent person's right to refuse treatment should be invoked, Missouri (D) may impose treatment if its standard so warrants. Affirmed.

CONCURRENCE: (Scalia, J.) The federal courts have no business in this field. American law has always accorded the state the power to prevent, by force if necessary, suicide—including suicide by refusing to take appropriate measures necessary to preserve one's life. The point at which life becomes "worthless" and the point at which the means necessary to preserve it become "extraordinary" or inappropriate are neither set forth in the Constitution nor known to the nine Justices of this Court any better than they are known to nine people picked at random from the Kansas City telephone directory.

EDITOR'S ANALYSIS: This case articulated the concept that citizens have a constitutional "right to die." The facts of the case, however, led to a holding in favor of the State (D). Since due procedural standards had been established by the State of Missouri, (D) Nancy Cruzan's parents (P) were not successful in their efforts to have life-sustaining treatment terminated.

NOTES:

LANE v. CANDURA
Physician (P) v. Gangrene patient (D)
Mass. App. Ct., 376 N.E.2d 1232 (1978).

NATURE OF CASE: Challenge to patient's competency to refuse medical treatment.

FACT SUMMARY: Rosaria Candura (D) refused the amputation of her right foot and lower leg after originally agreeing to the surgery. Her physicians (P) challenged her competency to make this decision.

CONCISE RULE OF LAW: A confused or forgetful patient whose confusion or forgetfulness does not interfere with her ability to decide about surgery is competent to refuse treatment.

FACTS: Rosaria Candura (D) was a 77-year-old woman with gangrene in her right foot and lower leg. Diagnosing her condition, Candura's physicians (P) recommended immediate amputation. Candura (D) originally agreed to this course of action, but later refused. In support of her decision, Candura (D) stated that she had been unhappy since her husband's passing, that she did not wish to be a burden to her children, that she did not believe the operation would cure her, that she did not wish to live as an invalid in a nursing home and that she did not fear death, but welcomed it. Two prior amputative surgeries, one depriving Candura (D) of her toe and the other depriving her of part of her foot, had failed to halt the spread of gangrene in her right foot and leg. Candura's physicians (P) describe her as irascible, defensive and sometimes confused.

ISSUE: Is a confused or forgetful patient whose confusion or forgetfulness does not interfere with her ability to decide about surgery competent to refuse treatment?

DECISION AND HOLDING: (Per curiam) Yes. A confused or forgetful patient whose confusion or forgetfulness does not interfere with her ability to decide about surgery is competent to refuse treatment. In this case, Candura (D) cites several reasons for refusing treatment. On this point, she seems to be quite lucid. Further, she appreciates the consequences of her decision, citing the possibility of death. Thus, her confusion as to other issues did not cloud her refusal to amputative treatment.

EDITOR'S ANALYSIS: Whether a patient is competent to refuse treatment is judged in part on the rationality of the patient's reasoning, rather than simply upon the patient's capacity for reasoning or understanding generally.

DEPARTMENT OF HUMAN SERVICES v. NORTHERN
State (P) v. Incompetent patient (D)
Tenn. Ct. App., 563 S.W.2d 197 (1978).

NATURE OF CASE: Appeal from court ruling of incompetence.

FACT SUMMARY: Northern (D) insisted that her feet were black because of soot or dirt, when in fact they were gangrenous.

CONCISE RULE OF LAW: A patient must appreciate the nature of her medical condition and must be able to make a rational choice about living in order to be competent to accept or refuse treatment.

FACTS: Northern (D) was a 72-year-old patient with gangrene of both feet who refused her physician's recommendation of amputative surgery of the feet to prevent her death. The physician testified that Northern (D) failed to appreciate the dangers to her life and that if she had appreciated the seriousness of her condition, heard her physician's opinions, and concluded against an operation, then he would believe that she had understood and could decide for herself. But he stated, she was functioning on a psychotic level with respect to her gangrenous feet. The Department of Human Services (P) successfully sought to have her declared incompetent. Northern (D) appealed.

ISSUE: Must a patient appreciate the nature of her medical condition and must she be able to make a rational choice about living in order to be competent to accept or refuse treatment?

HOLDING AND DECISION: (Todd, J.) Yes. A patient must appreciate the nature of her medical condition and must be able to make a rational choice about living in order to be competent to accept or refuse treatment. In this case, Northern (D) cannot or will not comprehend the facts. If she gave evidence of a comprehension of the facts of her condition then her decision, however unreasonable to others, would be honored by the courts. Affirmed.

EDITOR'S ANALYSIS: This case sets out one possible test for a patient's competence. Other states have tests involving a person's ability to appreciate the nature and consequences of her act. In New Jersey, a patient must have a clear understanding of the nature of her illness and prognosis, and of the risks and benefits of the proposed treatment, and have the capacity to reason and make judgments about that information.

IN RE CONROY
Nephew (P) v. Guardian ad litem (D)
N.J. Sup. Ct., 486 A.2d 1209 (1985).

NATURE OF CASE: Review of the reversal of lower court's decision that a guardian could discontinue life-sustaining treatment of an incompetent patient.

FACT SUMMARY: Conroy's nephew and guardian requested the court's permission to have the feeding-tube removed from his elderly aunt because she was incompetent.

CONCISE RULE OF LAW: The patient's ability to control his bodily integrity through informed consent also encompasses a right to informed refusal.

FACTS: Conroy, who was suffering from an organic brain syndrome, was adjudicated to be incompetent and her nephew was appointed to be her guardian. The nephew petitioned the court for permission to discontinue Conroy's feeding tube, which kept her alive in a hospital while suffering from various serious conditions. The guardian ad litem opposed the petition, but the trial court granted the petition. The intermediate court of appeals reversed. While the case was before the intermediate court, Conroy died with her feeding tube still in place. The N.J. Supreme Court nevertheless heard the case because it involved a matter of substantial importance capable of repetition but evading review.

ISSUE: Does the patient's ability to control his bodily integrity through informed consent also encompasses a right to informed refusal?

HOLDING AND DECISION: (Schreiber, J.) Yes. The patient's ability to control his bodily integrity through informed consent also encompasses a right to informed refusal. A competent adult person generally has the right to decline to have any medical treatment initiated or continued. The right to make certain decisions concerning one's body is also protected by the federal Constitutional right of privacy. The right to life-sustaining medical treatment is not absolute. There is no doubt that Ms. Conroy, if competent to make the decision and if resolute in her decision, could have chosen to have her nasogastric tube withdrawn. Her interest in freedom from nonconsensual invasion of her bodily integrity would outweigh any state interest in preserving life or in safeguarding the integrity of the medical profession. Rejecting her artificial means of feeding would not constitute attempted suicide and would not constitute a public health or safety hazard, nor would any third persons be harmed therefrom. A competent person's common law and constitutional rights do not depend on the quality or value of her life. Reversed.

EDITOR'S ANALYSIS: This case set forth the four state interests that may limit a person's right to refuse medical treatment. The state's interest in preserving life is commonly considered the most important. The others are to prevent suicide, to safeguard the integrity of the medical profession, and to protect innocent parties. In cases that do not involve the protection of the actual or potential life of someone other than the decision maker, the state's interest and abstract interest in preserving the life of the competent person generally gives way to the patient's much stronger personal interest in directing the course of his own life.

NOTES:

IN RE JOBES

Comatose patient's husband (P) v. Nursing home (D)

N.J. Sup. Ct., 529 A.2d 434 (1987).

NATURE OF CASE: Appeal from judicial authorization to terminate life-sustaining treatment.

FACT SUMMARY: When Jobes' parents and husband unsuccessfully requested that the nursing home remove her feeding tube, they sought judicial authorization to do so.

CONCISE RULE OF LAW: The right of a patient in an irreversibly vegetative state to determine whether to refuse life-sustaining medical treatment may be exercised by the patient's family or close friend.

FACTS: Jobes was injured in a traffic accident and never recovered consciousness after an operation to remove her dead fetus. At trial, evidence was introduced as to her prior statements that she would not wish life-sustaining procedures undertaken. The trial court granted the family's substituted medical judgment and approved the authorization to terminate the treatment. An appeal followed.

ISSUE: May the right of a patient in an irreversibly vegetative state to determine whether to refuse life-sustaining medical treatment be exercised by the patient's family or close friend?

HOLDING AND DECISION: (Garibaldi, J.) Yes. The right of a patient in an irreversibly vegetative state to determine whether to refuse life-sustaining medical treatment may be exercised by the patient's family or close friend. For non-elderly, non-hospitalized patients in a persistent vegetative state like Jobes, the surrogate decisionmaker who declined life-sustaining medical treatment must secure statements from at least two independent physicians knowledgeable in neurology that the patient was in a persistent vegetative state and that there was no reasonable possibility that the patient would ever recover to a cognitive, sapient state. Affirmed.

EDITOR'S ANALYSIS: The court stated that since there were close and caring family members willing to make the decision in Jobes' case, there was no need to have a guardian appointed. The court did require, however, that the responsible relatives comply with the medical confirmation procedures established. If there is disagreement among the family members or evidence of improper motives or practice, then judicial intervention would be called for.

NOTES:

QUICKNOTES

SAPIENT - Intelligent; judicious.

CRUZAN v. DIRECTOR, MISSOURI DEPARTMENT OF HEALTH

Comatose patient's parents (P) v. State (D)
497 U.S. 261 (1990).

NATURE OF CASE: Review of a decision by the Missouri Supreme Court that clear and convincing evidence must be presented of an incompetent patient's wishes to be effective.

FACT SUMMARY: When Cruzan's family (P) sought the court's permission to withdraw her life support system, the State (D) argued that statements Cruzan had made previously in favor of discontinued medical treatment were insufficient evidence of her true wishes.

CONCISE RULE OF LAW: A state may apply a clear and convincing evidence standard in proceedings where a guardian seeks to discontinue nutrition and hydration of a person diagnosed to be in a persistent vegetative state.

FACTS: Cruzan suffered severe brain damage from an automobile accident that left her in a persistent vegetative state. A few years later, her parents (P) sought to have her feeding tube discontinued. The Missouri supreme court found that there was insufficient evidence that Cruzan would want the treatment withdrawn. Missouri law required that proof of the incompetent's wishes as to the withdrawal of treatment be established by clear and convincing evidence. The U.S. Supreme Court granted certiorari.

ISSUE: May a state apply a clear and convincing evidence standard in proceedings where a guardian seeks to discontinue nutrition and hydration of a person diagnosed to be in a persistent vegetative state?

HOLDING AND DECISION: (Rehnquist, C. J.) Yes. A state may apply a clear and convincing evidence standard in proceedings where a guardian seeks to discontinue nutrition and hydration of a person diagnosed to be in a persistent vegetative state. An intermediate standard of proof, i.e., clear and convincing evidence, may be mandated when the individual interests at stake in a state proceeding are both particularly important and more substantial than mere loss of money. The Due Process Clause requires that the state repose judgment on these matters with the patient herself and not with the substituted judgment of her family members. A state may choose to defer only to the patient's wishes and it may require clear and convincing evidence of such a patient's wishes. Affirmed.

CONCURRENCE: (O'Connor, J.) Today's decision does not preclude a future determination that the Constitution requires the states to implement the decisions of a patient's duly appointed surrogate. Nor does it prevent states from developing other approaches for protecting an incompetent individual's liberty interest in refusing medical treatment. No national consensus has yet emerged on the best solution for this difficult and sensitive problem.

DISSENT: (Brennan, J.) Missouri may constitutionally impose only those procedural requirements that serve to enhance the accuracy of a determination of Cruzan's wishes. The Missouri "safeguard" that the Court upholds today does not meet that standard. A state generally must either repose the choice of a treatment with the person whom the patient himself would have chosen as proxy or leave that decision to the patient's family.

EDITOR'S ANALYSIS: This was a landmark case. Following this decision, the family (P) returned to state court with new evidence of Cruzan's wishes and the court ruled in favor of the family (P). The feeding tube was withdrawn. Cruzan died a few months after the U.S. Supreme Court issued the above decision.

NOTES:

WASHINGTON v. GLUCKSBERG
Physicians and gravely ill patients (P) v. State (D)
521 U.S. 702 (1997).

NATURE OF CASE: Review of holding that a state statute banning assisted suicide was unconstitutional.

FACT SUMMARY: Washington State's (D) van on assisted suicide was challenged as unconstitutional.

CONCISE RULE OF LAW: A state prohibition against causing or aiding a suicide doe snot offend the Fourteenth Amendment.

FACTS: Washington State (D) passed a law making the promotion of a suicide attempt a felony. Glucksberg (P), three other physicians (P) and three gravely ill patients sued the State of Washington (D) in federal court, seeking a declaration that Washington's (D) statute banning assisted suicide was, on its face, unconstitutional. Glucksberg (P) asserted the existence of a liberty interest protected by the Fourteenth Amendment which extended to a personal choice by a mentally competent, terminally ill adult to commit physician-assisted suicide. The district court agreed and concluded that the statute was unconstitutional because it placed an undue burden on the exercise of that constitutionally protected interest. A panel of the court of appeals for the Ninth Circuit reversed. The Ninth Circuit then reheard the case en banc, reversed the panel's decision and affirmed the district court. The court decided that the statute was unconstitutional as applied to terminally ill competent adults who wished to hasten their deaths with medication prescribed by their physicians. The Supreme Court granted certiorari.

ISSUE: Does a state prohibition against causing or aiding a suicide offend the Fourteenth Amendment?

HOLDING AND DECISION: (Rehnquist, C.J.) No. A state prohibition against causing or aiding a suicide doe snot offend the Fourteenth Amendment. The Fourteenth Amendment prohibits the government from infringing any fundamental liberty interests, unless the infringement is narrowly tailored to serve a compelling state interest. But merely because many of the rights and liberties protected by the Due Process Clause sound in personal autonomy does not warrant the sweeping conclusion that any and all important, intimate, and personal decisions are so protected. The history of the law's treatment of assisted suicides in this country has been and continues to be one of the rejection of nearly all efforts to permit it. The asserted "right" to assistance in committing suicide is not a fundamental liberty interest protected by the Due Process Clause. Therefore a less stringent standard of review applies. Since Washington's (D) assisted suicide statute implicates a number of state interests, it is rationally related to legitimate government interests. The Washington statute does not violate the Fourteenth Amendment, either on its face or as applied to competent, terminally ill adults who wish to hasten their deaths by obtaining medication prescribed by their doctors. Reversed and remanded.

EDITOR'S ANALYSIS: Although the Supreme Court decided in *Cruzan v. Director, Mo. Dept. of Health,* 497 U.S. 261 (1990), that the Constitution granted competent persons a constitutionally protected right to refuse lifesaving hydration and nutrition, no general "right to die" exists. Although the Netherlands has recently permitted the practice of euthanasia, no reliable statistics are yet available to evaluate the results. The Court noted that the right to physician-assisted suicide would in effect lead to a much broader license would could prove extremely difficult to police and contain.

NOTES:

VACCO v. QUILL

State attorney general (D) v. Physicians (P)
521 U.S. 793 (1997).

NATURE OF CASE: Review of appellate decision that New York's statute prohibiting assisted suicide was unconstitutional.

FACT SUMMARY: A state statute forbidding assisted suicide was challenged as unconstitutional under the Equal Protection Clause of the Fourteenth Amendment since competent patients could permissibly refuse lifesaving treatment.

CONCISE RULE OF LAW: The distinction between refusing lifesaving medical treatment and assisted suicide is not arbitrary or irrational.

FACTS: Quill (P) and other physicians (P) practicing in New York (D) asserted that although it would be consistent with the standards of their medical practice to prescribe lethal medication for mentally competent, terminally ill patients, they were deterred from doing so by New York's (D) ban on assisted suicide. They urged that because New York permitted a competent person to refuse life-sustaining medical treatment, and because the refusal of such treatment was essentially the same thing as physician-assisted suicide, New York's (D) ban violated the Equal Protection Clause. The district court disagreed, but the court of appeals for the Second Circuit reversed, finding that those in the final stages of fatal illness who were on life-support systems were allowed to hasten their deaths by directing the removal of such systems; but those who were similarly situated, except for the previous attachment of life-sustaining equipment, are not allowed to hasten death by self-administering prescribed drugs. The Supreme Court granted certiorari.

ISSUE: Is the distinction between refusing lifesaving medical treatment and assisted suicide arbitrary or irrational?

HOLDING AND DECISION: (Rehnquist, C.J.) No. The distinction between refusing lifesaving medical treatment and assisted suicide is not arbitrary or irrational. Logic and contemporary practice support New York's (D) judgment that the two acts are different, and New York (D) may therefore, consistent with the Constitution, treat them differently. A doctor who assists a suicide must, necessarily and indubitably, intend primarily that the patient be made dead. The law has long used actors' intent or purpose to distinguish between two acts that may have the same result. Many courts and legislatures have drawn clear lines between assisted suicide and withdrawing or permitting the refusal of unwanted lifesaving medical treatment by prohibiting the former but permitting the latter. New York's (D) statutes outlawing assisted suicide neither infringe fundamental rights nor involve suspect classifications, and are therefore entitled to a strong presumption of validity. On their faces, neither New York's (D) ban on assisted suicide nor its statutes permitting patients to refuse medical treatment treat anyone differently than anyone else or draw any distinctions between persons. Reversed.

CONCURRENCE: (O'Connor, J.) The state's interests in protecting those who are not truly competent or facing imminent death, or those whose decisions to hasten death would not truly be voluntary, are sufficiently weighty to justify a prohibition against physician-assisted suicide.

CONCURRENCE: (Stevens, J.) Although in general the state's interest in the contributions each person may make to society outweighs the person's interest in ending her life, this interest does not have the same force for a terminally ill patient faced not with the choice of whether to live, only of how to die. Allowing the individual, rather than the state, to make judgments about the quality of life that a particular individual may enjoy does not mean that the lives of the terminally ill, disabled people have less value. Rather, it gives proper recognition to the individual's interest in choosing a final chapter that accords with her life story.

EDITOR'S ANALYSIS: Physicians assisting in their patients' suicides are usually not convicted by juries. Dr. Jack Kevorkian, for example, has been prosecuted but never convicted pf assisted suicide. Assisted suicide and euthanasia are officially prohibited, but physicians are rarely criminally prosecuted for either.

NOTES:

IN RE BABY K

Hospital (P) v. Parents of anencephalic infant (D)
16 F.3d 590 (4th Cir. 1994).

NATURE OF CASE: Appeal from declaratory judgment that hospitals must provide stabilizing care to any individual presenting an emergency medical condition.

FACT SUMMARY: When an anencephalic infant was born at a hospital and the mother did not agree with doctors as to the appropriate level of care, the hospital sought a declaratory judgment that it was not required to provide respiratory support or other aggressive treatments for the infant.

CONCISE RULE OF LAW: Once an individual has been diagnosed as presenting an emergency medical condition, the hospital must provide that treatment necessary to prevent the material deterioration of the individual's condition or provide for an appropriate transfer.

FACTS: Baby K was born with anencephaly, a congenital malformation that rendered her permanently unconscious. The physicians recommended that, since most such infants die within a few days of birth due to breathing difficulties, only supportive care in the form of nutrition, hydration, and warmth be provided. Baby K's mother insisted that mechanical breathing assistance also be provided whenever the infant developed difficulty breathing, which the physicians opposed. As a result of this disagreement with the physicians, the hospital unsuccessfully sought to have the infant transferred to another hospital. The infant was later transferred to a nursing home but returned to the hospital's emergency room three times due to breathing difficulties. The hospital filed an action to resolve the issue of whether it was obligated to provide emergency medical treatment that it deemed medically and ethically inappropriate. The district court found that under the Emergency Medical Treatment and Active Labor Act (EMTALA) the hospital, like all hospitals that have entered into Medicare provider agreements, had a duty to screen for emergency medical conditions and to provide such treatment as may be necessary or transfer the patient. The hospital appealed.

ISSUE: Once an individual has been diagnosed as presenting an emergency medical condition, must the hospital provide that treatment necessary to prevent the material deterioration of the individual's condition or provide for an appropriate transfer?

HOLDING AND DECISION: (Wilkins, J.) Yes. Once an individual has been diagnosed as presenting an emergency medical condition, the hospital must provide that treatment necessary to prevent the material deterioration of the individual's condition or provide for an appropriate transfer. Since Baby K's breathing difficulty qualifies as an emergency medical condition and transfer was not an option since the mother had not requested it,

the hospital was required to provide stabilizing care. Although the prevailing standard of medical care for infants with anencephaly is to provide only warmth, nutrition, and hydration, due to their extremely limited life expectancy, EMTALA does not provide for any exceptions. Congress rejected a case-by-case approach in determining what emergency medical treatment hospitals and physicians must provide. Affirmed.

EDITOR'S ANALYSIS: This case typifies the situation where the family asserts the patient's right to make medical decisions. When the physicians or hospital argue that treatment may be futile, the court has adopted a hands-off attitude toward social policy decisions. In this case, the infant lived for two and a half years and died in the same hospital's emergency room after being taken there for the sixth time.

QUICKNOTES

ANENCEPHALY - A physical deformity characterized by an abnormal formation of the skull and the absence of all or a portion of the brain.

EMERGENCY MEDICAL TREATMENT AND ACTIVE LABOR ACT: Prohibits hospitals with specialized capabilities or facilities from refusing appropriate transfers and requires hospitals to treat emergency medical conditions.

NOTES:

CAUSEY v. ST. FRANCIS MEDICAL CENTER

Family of comatose patient (P) v. Hospital (D)

La. Ct. App., 719 So.2d 1072 (1998).

NATURE OF CASE: Petition for damages against a hospital for failure decision to discontinue dialysis.

FACT SUMMARY: Sonya Causey died when her physician at St. Francis Medical Center (D) discontinued her dialysis treatment. Causey's family (P) brought this action against the medical center (D) for discontinuing life-saving treatment. The medical center (D) filed a motion of prematurity, asserting that this action is covered under Louisiana's Medical Malpractice Act.

CONCISE RULE OF LAW: A damages action based upon the discontinuance of life-sustaining treatment falls under a state medical malpractice statute.

FACTS: Sonya Causey was a 31-year-old, quadriplegic, end-stage renal failure, comatose patient who was transferred to St. Francis Medical Center (St. Francis) (D) from a nursing home when she suffered cardiorespiratory arrest. Dr. Herschel Harter (D), Causey's treating physician at St. Francis (D), believed that continuing dialysis would have no benefit. Causey's family (P), however, demanded aggressive life-sustaining care. Dr. Harter attempted to transfer Causey to another medical center willing to provide such care. He (D) was unsuccessful. Dr. Harter (D) then appealed to the St Francis' Morals and Ethics Board. The Board agreed with Dr. Harter's (D) decision to discontinue dialysis, life-support procedures, and to enter a "no-code" status (do not resuscitate). Causey was taken off a feeding tube and other similar devices. The day the ventilator was removed, Mrs. Causey died of respiratory and cardiac failure. Causey's husband, mother and father (P) brought this petition for damages against St. Francis (D) and Dr. Harter (D). St. Francis (D) and Dr. Harter (D) filed an exception of prematurity asserting that this action was covered under Louisiana's Medical Malpractice Act.

ISSUE: Does a damages action based upon the discontinuance of life-sustaining treatment fall under a state medical malpractice statute?

HOLDING AND DECISION: (Brown, J.) Yes. A damages action based upon the discontinuance of life-sustaining treatment falls under a state medical malpractice statute. Medical professionals are licensed by society to make certain decisions concerning life-prolonging technology. Standards of medical malpractice require a physician to act with a degree of skill and care ordinarily possessed by those in the same medical specialty acting under the same or similar conditions. In this case, we are asked to examine the appropriateness of Dr. Harter's (D) decision to discontinue dialysis. This requires an examination of what other physicians might do in the same or similar circumstances. The Medical Malpractice Act is thus applicable and this matter should be first submitted to a medical review panel.

EDITOR'S ANALYSIS: *Causey* also addresses the issue of medical futility. There are two types of medical futility, qualitative and quantitative. Qualitative medical futility exists where medical treatment cannot provide a sufficient benefit to justify its use, whereas quantitative futility exists where there is too low a likelihood that medical treatment will have its desired effect.

NOTES:

6

CHAPTER 6
ORGAN TRANSPLANTATION:
THE CONTROL, USE, AND ALLOCATION OF BODY PARTS

QUICK REFERENCE RULES OF LAW

1. **Incompetent Organ "Donors."** A court of equity may permit that a kidney be removed from an incompetent ward of the state upon petition of the ward's mother. (Strunk v. Strunk)

2. **Incompetent Organ "Donors."** A guardian of the person has the care of the ward's person and must look to the latter's health, education, and support. (In re Pescinski)

3. **Redefining Death.** An anencephalic newborn is not "dead" for purposes of organ donation solely by reason of its congenital deformity. (In re T.A.C.P.)

4. **Mandates or Incentives for Organ Donation.** The next of kin have no property right in the remains of a decedent other than a limited right to possess the body for burial purposes. (State v. Powell)

5. **Mandates or Incentives for Organ Donation.** Although the existence of an interest may be a matter of state law, whether that interest rises to the level of a "legitimate claim of entitlement" protected by the Due Process Clause is determined by federal law. (Brotherton v. Cleveland)

6. **Mandates or Incentives for Organ Donation.** One human being is under no legal compulsion to give aid or to take action to save another human being or to rescue. (McFall v. Shimp)

7. **Ownership of Human Tissue.** A patient may not maintain a conversion action for the unauthorized use of his excised organ or cells. (Moore v. The Regents of the University of California)

STRUNK v. STRUNK

Incompetent's mother (P) v. Incompetent's guardian ad litem (D)

Ky. Ct. App., 445 S.W.2d 145 (1969).

NATURE OF CASE: Appeal from the county court's authorization of a kidney transplant.

FACT SUMMARY: The chancery court granted Strunk's (P) petition to authorize a kidney transplant with her incompetent son acting as a donor to his brother, suffering from kidney disease. The incompetent's guardian ad litem (D) appeals.

CONCISE RULE OF LAW: A court of equity may permit that a kidney be removed from an incompetent ward of the state upon petition of the ward's mother.

FACTS: Arthur Strunk and Ava Strunk (P) have two sons, Tommy and Jerry. Tommy Strunk is 28 years old, married, an employee, part-time student and patient suffering from a fatal kidney disease. Jerry Strunk is 27 years old, incompetent and committed to a state institution maintained for the feebleminded. When it was determined that Tommy would need a kidney transplant to survive, his entire family, mother, father and collateral relatives were tested. The only medically acceptable potential donor was Jerry, who was tested as a last resort. Ava (P) then petitioned the chancery court to authorize the transplant on behalf of Jerry. The Department of Mental Health entered the case as amicus curiae and asserted that the operation was in Jerry's best interest, due to his emotional reliance on Tommy and the potential effects Tommy's death would have on him. The chancery court granted Ava's (P) petition and Jerry's guardian ad litem (D) appeals here.

ISSUE: Does a court of equity have the power to permit a kidney to be removed from the incompetent ward of the state upon petition of his mother, for the purpose of being transplanted into the body of his brother, who is dying of kidney disease?

HOLDING AND DECISION: (Osbourne, J.) Yes. A court of equity may permit that a kidney be removed from an incompetent ward of the state upon petition of the ward's mother. In this case, all immediate family members have recommended the transplant. The Department of Mental Health also recommends that the transplant is in Jerry's best interest. The renal transplant is quickly becoming the most common of all organ transplants, and can currently be performed with minimal danger to both the donor and the donee. The chancery court based its decision upon substantive evidence and has an inherent authority to make the decision it did.

DISSENT: (Steinfeld, J.) There exists too much uncertainty in this case to authorize such an intrusion upon the incompetent's person. The operation authorized in this case is not without danger to Jerry and its success for Tommy is not guaranteed. Furthermore, the evidence presented that the transplant will provide a psychological benefit to Jerry who would otherwise be unable to deal with his brother's death is tenuous at best.

EDITOR'S ANALYSIS: In the field of organ transplantation, there is some concern regarding abuse. Persons might favor or value the lives of a competent potential donee over that of an incompetent potential donor.

NOTES:

IN RE PESCINSKI
Guardian (P) v. Incompetent brother (D)
Wis. Sup. Ct., 226 N.W.2d 180 (1975).

NATURE OF CASE: Appeal from a holding that a county court does not have the power to order an operation on an incompetent ward without permission.

FACT SUMMARY: In dire need of a kidney transplant, a sister petitioned the court for an order to have a kidney removed from her brother who was incompetent and a state mental patient.

CONCISE RULE OF LAW: A guardian of the person has the care of the ward's person and must look to the latter's health, education, and support.

FACTS: The sister of Pescinski, an incompetent mental patient, was on a dialysis machine after the removal of both kidneys. Tests had established that her brother was a suitable kidney donor. Another sister of Pescinski, who was his guardian, sought his guardian ad litem's permission to have her brother's kidney removed and transplanted. When the guardian ad litem refused consent, the county court held that it did not have the power to give consent for the operation. The sister appealed.

ISSUE: Does a guardian of the person have the care of the ward's person and must he look to the latter's health, education and support?

HOLDING AND DECISION: (Wilkie, J.) Yes. A guardian of the person has the care of the ward's person and must look to the latter's health, education and support. The guardian must act, if at all, loyally in the best interests of his ward. There is absolutely no evidence here that any interests of the ward will be served by the transplant. The doctrine of substituted judgment should not be adopted in this state. Affirmed.

DISSENT: (Day, J.) To avoid the concerns expressed by the guardian ad litem, there are certain definite standards which could and should be imposed in such cases. A strong showing that without the kidney transplant the proposed donee stands to suffer death should be made. Then, a showing should be made that reasonable steps were taken to acquire the kidney from other sources and that the incompetent proposed donor is closely related by blood. With these guidelines the fear expressed that institutions for the mentally ill will merely become storehouses for spare parts for people on the outside is completely unjustified.

EDITOR'S ANALYSIS: The United States permits the use of minors or mentally incompetent persons as organ donors. This is not permitted in many other countries. The Council of Europe has recommended that organ donation not be allowed except in cases where the ward donor has the capacity to understand and has given his consent.

QUICKNOTES

SUBSTITUTION OF JUDGMENT DOCTRINE - Doctrine prevailing in certain jurisdictions authorizing the court to sanction an estate plan that decreases tax payments upon the petition of the guardian of an incompetent.

NOTES:

IN RE T.A.C.P.

Parents of brain-dead infant (P) v. Health care providers (D)
Fla. Sup. Ct., 609 So.2d 588 (1992).

NATURE OF CASE: Review of order certified by the appellate court.

FACT SUMMARY: The parents of an anencephalic child sought to have their child declared dead so that her organs could be donated.

CONCISE RULE OF LAW: An anencephalic newborn is not "dead" for purposes of organ donation solely by reason of its congenital deformity.

FACTS: The parents of the child T.A.C.P. were informed that their child would be born without an upper brain, or anencephalic. The parents, hoping to offer some benefit to others in the face of their loss, sought a declaration that the child was "dead," so that her organs could be donated. The health care providers refused out of fear of liability. The parents then sought a legal ruling on the matter. The question of the definition of death was certified by the appellate court and forwarded to the Supreme Court of Florida.

ISSUE: Is an anencephalic newborn considered "dead" for purposes of organ donation solely by reason of its congenital deformity?

HOLDING AND DECISION: (Kogan, J.) No. An anencephalic newborn is not "dead" for purposes of organ donation solely by reason of its congenital deformity. Florida generally defines death as cardiopulmonary failure. An exception exists for whole-brain death when the heart is kept operable by artificial means. In this case, the anencephalic infant fits neither of these definitions. Though lacking an upper brain, the child's heart will operate for a short time, and some primordial brain function exists. While this is a policy issue of tremendous import, there is no sufficiently sound reason under the current law to extend the definition of death to include anencephaly. No organ donation would have been legal.

EDITOR'S ANALYSIS: There is no hope for the survival of an anencephalic infant. They are not conscious and most likely do not have any pain response. The need for infant organs makes it very difficult to avoid considering anencephalic infants as a source for these organs. A medical council concluded in 1995 that it was ethical to use organs from an anencephalic infant who was not yet dead so long as parental consent was obtained, along with other precautionary measures.

NOTES:

STATE v. POWELL
Decedents' parents (P) v. State (D)
Fla. Sup. Ct., 497 So.2d 1188 (1986).

NATURE OF CASE: Review of a circuit court order finding a state statute allowing corneal transplants unconstitutional.

FACT SUMMARY: Parents (P) of two deceased sons challenged a state statute permitting the use of corneas from deceased persons without the knowledge of consent of the next of kin as unconstitutional.

CONCISE RULE OF LAW: The next of kin have no property right in the remains of a decedent other than a limited right to possess the body for burial purposes.

FACTS: A Florida statute authorized the removal of corneal tissue during autopsies for use in transplants. No removal could occur if the next of kin objected, but the statue did not require that they be notified. The corneas of two men who died in accidents were removed for transplanting without giving notice to or obtaining consent from their parents (P). The Powells (P) and the Whites (P) brought an action claiming damages for the alleged wrongful removal of their sons' corneas and seeking a judgment declaring the state statute unconstitutional. The trial court granted the Powells' (P) motion for summary judgment and the case was certified for review by the Florida Supreme Court.

ISSUE: Do the next of kin have a property right in the remains of a decedent?

HOLDING AND DECISION: (Overton, J.) No. The next of kin have no property right in the remains of a decedent other than a limited right to possess the body for burial purposes. Fundamental rights of personal liberty which must be subjected to strict scrutiny concern freedom of choice in personal matters involved in existing, ongoing relationships among living persons. The right of the next of kin to bring a tort claim for interference with burial does not rise to the constitutional dimension of a fundamental right traditionally protected under either the federal or state Constitution. The record contains no evidence that the Powells' (P) or the Whites' (P) objections to the removal of corneal tissues for human transplants are based on any fundamental tenets of their religious beliefs. The statute is constitutional because it rationally promotes the permissible state objective of restoring sight to the blind. Reversed.

EDITOR'S ANALYSIS: The court explained that a person's constitutional rights terminate at death. If any rights do exist, they belong to the decedent's next of kin. A legislative act carries with it the presumption of validity and the party challenging a statute's constitutionality must carry the burden of establishing that the statute bears no reasonable relationship to a permissible legislative objective.

QUICKNOTES

FLORIDA STATUTE § 732.9185: Provides for corneal removal in any case where a decedent is under the jurisdiction of the coroner, there is no known objection by the next of kin, and the removal will not interfere with the autopsy.

NOTES:

BROTHERTON v. CLEVELAND
Decedent's widow (P) v. Municipality (D)
923 F.2d 477 (6th Cir. 1991).

NATURE OF CASE: Appeal from dismissal of a § 1983 claim for wrongful corneal removal.

FACT SUMMARY: Brotherton (P), the widow of a decedent whose corneas had been removed and used as anatomical gifts, contended that she had a property interest in the decedent's dead body protected by the Constitution.

CONCISE RULE OF LAW: Although the existence of an interest may be a matter of state law, whether that interest rises to the level of a "legitimate claim of entitlement" protected by the Due Process Clause is determined by federal law.

FACTS: When Steven Brotherton was found pulseless in a car and taken to a hospital, he was pronounced dead on arrival. His wife, Deborah Brotherton (P) declined to consider making an anatomical gift of his organs. Nevertheless, after an autopsy at the county coroner's office, his corneas were removed and sent to an eye bank. Deborah (P) did not know of the removal until she read the autopsy report. Deborah Brotherton (P) then filed suit on her own behalf and on behalf of a purported class of similarly situated plaintiffs, under 42 U.S.C. § 1983, alleging that her husband's corneas were removed without due process of law and in violation of the Equal Protection Clause. She also asserted state law claims for emotional distress. The district court dismissed the case and Brotherton (P) appealed.

ISSUE: Although the existence of an interest may be a matter of state law, does federal law determine whether that interest rises to the level of a "legitimate claim of entitlement" protected by the Due Process Clause?

HOLDING AND DECISION: (Martin, J.) Yes. Although the existence of an interest may be a matter of state law, whether that interest rises to the level of a "legitimate claim of entitlement" protected by the Due Process Clause is determined by federal law. The aggregate of rights granted by the State of Ohio to Steven's widow (P) rises to the level of a "legitimate claim of entitlement" in her husband's body, including his corneas, protected by the Due Process Clause of the Fourteenth Amendment. The removal of the corneas was caused by established state procedures. However, Ohio failed to provide the necessary predeprivation process. A property interest may not be destroyed without a hearing. The deprivation of property resulting from an established state procedure can only satisfy due process if there is a predeprivation hearing. The only governmental interest enhanced by the removal of the corneas is the interest implementing the organ/tissue donation program; this interest is not substantial enough to allow the state to consciously disregard

those property rights which it has granted. The policy and custom of the county coroner's office is an established state procedure necessitating predeprivation process. Reversed.

EDITOR'S ANALYSIS: This case concerns an Ohio statute which was part of the Uniform Anatomical Gift Act governing gifts of organs and tissues for research or transplants. The statute granted a right to the spouse to control the body of the decedent. A claim for disturbance of the body may also be brought by the surviving spouse.

QUICKNOTES
42 U.S.C. § 1983: Civil rights remedial statute for violation of federal rights created elsewhere.

UNIFORM ANATOMICAL GIFT ACT: Govern gifts of organs and tissues for research or transplants; permits a coroner to remove the corneas of autopsy subjects without consent, provided the coroner has no knowledge of an objection.

NOTES:

McFALL v. SHIMP
Bone marrow disease victim (P) v. Reluctant donor (D)
10 Pa. D. & C.3d 90 (1978).

NATURE OF CASE: Request for a preliminary injunction to compel an organ donation.

FACT SUMMARY: When McFall (P) determined that Shimp (D) would be a suitable bone marrow donor, he sought a court order compelling Shimp (D) to submit to further tests and, eventually, the bone marrow transplant.

CONCISE RULE OF LAW: One human being is under no legal compulsion to give aid or to take action to save another human being or to rescue.

FACTS: McFall (P), who suffered from a rare bone marrow disease, learned that only Shimp (D), his first cousin, was suitable as a donor for a bone marrow transplant which was necessary for McFall (P) to live. When Shimp (D) refused, McFall (P) sought an injunction to compel him to undergo further tests and the transplant. McFall (P) argued that a court of equity may apply an ancient statute that in order to save the life of one of its members by the only means available, society may infringe upon one's absolute right to his "bodily security."

ISSUE: Is one human being under a legal compulsion to give aid or to take action to save another human being or to rescue?

HOLDING AND DECISION: (Flaherty, J.) No. One human being is under no legal compulsion to give aid or to take action to save another human being or to rescue. For our law to compel Shimp (D) to submit to an intrusion of his body would change every concept and principle upon which our society is founded. To do so would defeat the sanctity of the individual, and would impose a rule which would know no limits, and one could not imagine where the line would be drawn. The requested equitable relief is denied.

EDITOR'S ANALYSIS: McFall (P) died two weeks after the court's decision. The court referred to the horrors of the Holocaust and the Inquisition in its discussion. Forcible extraction of living body tissue was said to cause revulsion to the judicial mind.

NOTES:

MOORE v. THE REGENTS OF THE UNIVERSITY OF CALIFORNIA

Patient (P) v. Physician and Medical center (D)
Cal. Sup. Ct., 793 P.2d 479 (1990).

NATURE OF CASE: Appeal from the reversal of a general demurrer to a complaint asserting conversion of body cells.

FACT SUMMARY: After holding that Moore (P) had a right of informed consent when a physician (D) profited from studying and using his cells without permission, the court discussed whether his property rights were violated when his cells were used without his permission.

CONCISE RULE OF LAW: A patient may not maintain a conversion action for the unauthorized use of his excised organ or cells.

FACTS: Moore (P) sought treatment for hairy cell leukemia at UCLA Medical Center (D) in 1976. Golde (D), the treating physician, took tests and samples and then told Moore (P) that his life was threatened and that he should have his spleen removed. Golde (D) did not tell Moore (P) his cells were unique and that access to them was of great scientific and commercial value. Moore (P) consented to treatment and to the operation, and continued treatment for seven years after. His spleen was retained for research without his knowledge or consent. Golde (D) established a cell line from Moore's (P) cells, received a patent for it, and entered into commercial agreements worth billions dollars today. Moore (P) sued Golde (D), the Regents of the University of California (D), and others, stating several causes of action including conversion, breach of fiduciary duty, fraud and deceit, unjust enrichment, intentional infliction of emotional distress, and negligent misrepresentation. The trial court sustained the Regents' (D) demurrers to the claim for conversion and held that all the other causes were also defective. Moore (P) appealed. The court of appeals reversed the lower court, concluding that a patient must have the ultimate power to control what becomes of his or her tissues, and permitting the action for conversion. UCLA (D) appealed.

ISSUE: May a patient maintain a conversion action for the unauthorized use of his excised organ or cells?

HOLDING AND DECISION: (Panelli, J.) No. A patient may not maintain a conversion action for the unauthorized use of his excised organ or cells. It is not necessary to force the round pegs of "privacy" and "dignity" into the square hole of "property" in order to protect the patient, since the fiduciary duty and informed-consent theories protect these interests directly by requiring full disclosure. The subject matter of the Regents' (D) patent—the patented cell line and the products derived from it—cannot be Moore's (P) property. The patented cell line is both factually and legally distinct from the cells taken from Moore's (P) body. Patent

law rewards the inventive effort, not the discovery of naturally occurring raw materials. Research on human cells plays a critical role in medical research. The free exchange of cell lines among researchers will surely be compromised if each cell sample becomes the potential subject matter of a lawsuit. Because liability for conversion is predicated on a continuing ownership interest, companies would be unlikely to invest in developing or marketing a product when uncertainty about clear title exists. Reversed and remanded.

CONCURRENCE AND DISSENT: (Broussard, J.) The pertinent inquiry is not whether a patient generally retains an ownership interest in a body part after its removal from the body, but rather whether a patient has a right to determine, before a body part is removed, the use to which the part will be put after its removal. Although the Uniform Anatomical Gift Act applies only to anatomical gifts that take effect on or after the death of the donor, the general principle of "donor control" which the act embodies is clearly not limited to that setting. If the physician (D) had informed Moore (P), prior to removal, of the possible uses to which his body part could be put and Moore (P) had authorized one particular use, it is clear that he and the Regents (D) would be liable for conversion if they disregarded Moore's (P) decision and used the body part in an unauthorized manner for their own economic benefit.

DISSENT: (Mosk, J.) For present purposes, no distinction can be made between Moore's (P) cells and the Mo cell line. But for the cells of Moore's (P) body taken by the physician (D), there would have been no Mo cell line. There is no authority to support the majority's conclusion that the patent cut office all of Moore's (P) rights to share in the proceeds of the Regents' (D) commercial exploitation of the cell line derived from his own body tissue. A nondisclosure cause of action is not an adequate substitute for a conversion cause of action. An informed consent claim would only be valid against a physician and not against the hospital or other researchers involved who benefited from the patient's cells.

EDITOR'S ANALYSIS: On remand, a settlement was reached. Researchers later found a way to produce large amounts of lymphokines without using Moore's (P) cell line. Moore (P) may have lost because there was no bodily invasion since the cells were already outside of his body.

QUICK NOTES

FIDUCIARY DUTY - A legal obligation to act for the benefit of another, including subordinating one's personal interests to that of the other person..

CONVERSION - The act of depriving an owner of his property without permission or justification.

INFORMED CONSENT - A person's agreement to allow something to happen that is based on a full disclosure of facts needed to make an intelligent decision.

CHAPTER 7
REPRODUCTIVE RIGHTS AND GENETIC TECHNOLOGIES

QUICK REFERENCE RULES OF LAW

1. **A Right to Procreate?** It is better for all the world, if instead of waiting to execute degenerate offspring for crime, or to let them starve for their imbecility, society can prevent those who are manifestly unfit from continuing their kind. (Buck v. Bell)

2. **A Right to Procreate?** Legislation mandating the sterilization of certain criminals runs afoul of the Equal Protection Clause. (Skinner v. Oklahoma)

3. **A Right to Avoid Procreation? Contraception.** A governmental purpose to control or prevent activities constitutionally subject to state regulation may not be achieved by means which sweep unnecessarily broadly and thereby invade the area of protected freedoms. (Griswold v. Connecticut)

4. **A Right to Avoid Procreation? Abortion.** A state may not, consistent with the Constitution, absolutely prohibit elective abortions. (Roe v. Wade)

5. **A Right to Avoid Procreation? Abortion.** A state may regulate abortion only where such regulation does not place an undue burden on a woman's ability to make a decision to terminate her pregnancy before viability. (Planned Parenthood of Southeastern Pennsylvania v. Casey)

6. **A Right to Avoid Procreation? Abortion.** A statute criminalizing partial birth abortions violates the Constitution where it places a substantial obstacle in the path of a woman seeking an abortion of a nonviable fetus. (Stenberg v. Carhart)

7. **State or Federal Recognition of Fetal Interests: Pregnant Women and Forced Medical Treatment.** A court may not order an individual to undergo a Caesarian section to save the baby's life. (In re A.C.)

8. **State or Federal Recognition of Fetal Interests: Pregnant Women and Drug Use.** The word "child" as used in South Carolina's child abuse and endangerment statute includes viable fetuses. (Whitner v. South Carolina)

9. **State or Federal Recognition of Fetal Interests: Pregnant Women and Drug Use.** A state hospital's performance of a diagnostic test to obtain evidence of a patient's criminal conduct for law enforcement purposes is an unreasonable search if the patient has not consented to the procedure. (Ferguson v. City of Charleston)

10. **Using Reproductive Technologies to Create New Families: In Vitro Fertilization and Frozen Embryos.** A court must only enforce agreements entered into at the time in vitro fertilization is begun, subject to the right of either party to change his or her mind about disposition up to the point of use or destruction of any preembryos. (J.B. v. M.B. & C.C.)

11. **Using Reproductive Technologies to Create New Families: Womb and Ovum Donors.** Where compensation beyond pregnancy-related expenses is paid to a surrogate mother and the mother consents to the father's custody of the child before a suitable period has passed following the child's birth, a surrogacy agreement may not be upheld. (R.R. v. M.H.)

12. **Using Reproductive Technologies to Create New Families: Womb and Ovum Donors.** A district court has authority to issue a prebirth order of parentage where the plaintiffs are the sole genetic sources of the child in question, the gestational carrier agrees to the order sought, the proposed order is uncontested, and where the plaintiffs have waived any contradictory provisions in the contract. (Culliton v. Beth Israel Deaconess Medical Center)

BUCK v. BELL
Sterilized patient (P) v. State school official (P)
274 U.S. 200 (1927).

NATURE OF CASE: Review of an order upholding state statute permitting sterilization of the feeble-minded.

FACT SUMMARY: A Virginia state statute permitting the sterilization of Buck (D), a feeble-minded woman, was challenged as unconstitutional.

CONCISE RULE OF LAW: It is better for all the world, if instead of waiting to execute degenerate offspring for crime, or to let them starve for their imbecility, society can prevent those who are manifestly unfit from continuing their kind.

FACTS: Bell (P), the superintendent of the State Colony for Epileptics and Feeble-Minded, was ordered to perform an operation on Buck (D) cutting her Fallopian tubes so she could never have children. Buck (D), an 18-year-old feeble-minded woman committed to the State Colony, appealed, alleging that in no circumstances could such an order be justified. The state supreme court affirmed the order, and the U.S. Supreme Court granted review.

ISSUE: Is it better for all the world, if instead of waiting to execute degenerate offspring for crime, or to let them starve for their imbecility, society can prevent those who are manifestly unfit from continuing their kind?

HOLDING AND DECISION: (Holmes, J.) Yes. It is better for all the world, if instead of waiting to execute degenerate offspring for crime, or to let them starve for their imbecility, society can prevent those who are manifestly unfit from continuing their kind. The principle that sustains compulsory vaccination is broad enough to cover cutting the Fallopian tubes. There can be no doubt that so far as procedure is concerned, the rights of the patient are most carefully considered under the statute. Affirmed.

EDITOR'S ANALYSIS: This case asserts that government entities can have an interest in controlling the reproductive capacity of certain individuals or groups. The public welfare may call upon the best citizens for their lives. Therefore it would be strange if it could not call upon those who already sap the strength of the state for these lesser sacrifices, according to this Court.

NOTES:

SKINNER v. OKLAHOMA

Habitual criminal (D) v. State attorney general (P)

316 U.S. 535 (1942).

NATURE OF CASE: Review of a judgment directing the involuntary sterilization of a habitual criminal.

FACT SUMMARY: A state statute permitting sterilization of habitual criminals was challenged by Skinner (D), a convicted felon, as unconstitutional.

CONCISE RULE OF LAW: Legislation mandating the sterilization of certain criminals runs afoul of the Equal Protection Clause.

FACTS: Skinner (D) was convicted of robbery three times. Proceedings were subsequently instituted against him under a state law permitting the State Attorney General (P) to commence proceedings against a habitual criminal, defined as one who is convicted of three or more felonies, for a judgment that such person be rendered sexually sterile. A jury found that the operation of vasectomy could be performed on Skinner (D) without detriment to his general health. A judgment directing the operation be performed was affirmed by the Supreme Court of Oklahoma. Skinner (D) appealed, alleging that Oklahoma's Habitual Criminal Sterilization Act was unconstitutional by reason of the Fourteenth Amendment. Since the difference between a felony and a non-felony depended on when the felonious intent arose and not on the intrinsic quality of the act, Skinner (D) argued that invidiously discriminated against a group.

ISSUE: Does legislation mandating the sterilization of certain criminals run afoul of the Equal Protection Clause?

HOLDING AND DECISION: (Douglas, J.) Yes. Legislation mandating the sterilization of certain criminals runs afoul of the Equal Protection Clause. Strict scrutiny of the classification which a state makes in a sterilization law is essential, lest unwittingly or otherwise invidious discriminations are made against groups or types of individuals in violation of the constitutional guarantee of just and equal laws. When the law lays an unequal hand on those who have committed intrinsically the same offense and sterilizes one but not the other, it has made an invidious discrimination. Sterilization of those who have thrice committed grand larceny with immunity for those who are embezzlers is a clear, pointed, unmistakable discrimination. The Act violates the equal protection clause of the Fourteenth Amendment. We are dealing here with legislation which involves one of the basic civil rights of man. Marriage and procreation are fundamental to the very existence and survival of the race. The guarantee of equal protection of the laws is a pledge of the protection of equal laws. Reversed.

CONCURRENCE: (Stone, C.J.) The real question in this case is not one of equal protection, but whether the wholesale condemnation of a class to such an invasion of personal liberty, without opportunity to any individual to show that his is not the type of case which would justify resort to it, satisfies the demands of due process.

EDITOR'S ANALYSIS: This case hints that there may be a "fundamental" right to procreate. Conversely, tort claims may also be brought in cases where sterilization fails. For example, wrongful conception claims may be brought by parents when a negligently performed sterilization results in the birth of a healthy child.

NOTES:

GRISWOLD v. CONNECTICUT
State (P) v. Physician (D)
381 U.S. 479 (1965).

NATURE OF CASE: Review of conviction for violation of a state law forbidding the use of contraceptives.

FACT SUMMARY: Griswold (D) was convicted as an accessory under a statute prohibiting the use of contraceptives.

CONCISE RULE OF LAW: A governmental purpose to control or prevent activities constitutionally subject to state regulation may not be achieved by means which sweep unnecessarily broadly and thereby invade the area of protected freedoms.

FACTS: Griswold (D) was a physician who prescribed contraceptives to married persons and was found guilty as an accessory under a state statute banning the sale of contraceptives to anyone. He appealed, alleging that the statute was unconstitutional.

ISSUE: May a governmental purpose to control or prevent activities constitutionally subject to state regulation be achieved by means which sweep unnecessarily broadly and thereby invade the area of protected freedoms?

HOLDING AND DECISION: (Douglas, J.) No. A governmental purpose to control or prevent activities constitutionally subject to state regulation may not be achieved by means which sweep unnecessarily broadly and thereby invade the area of protected freedoms. Specific guarantees in the Bill of Rights have penumbras, formed by emanations from those guarantees that help give them life and substance. Various guarantees create zones of privacy. The present case concerns relationships lying within the zone of privacy created by several fundamental constitutional guarantees. And it concerns a law which, in forbidding the use of contraceptives rather than regulating their manufacture or sale, seeks to achieve its goals by means having a maximum destructive impact upon that relationship. Reversed.

CONCURRENCE: (Goldberg, J.) The concept of liberty protects those personal rights that are fundamental and is not confined to the specific terms of the Bill of Rights. The language and history of the Ninth Amendment supports the right of marital privacy.

CONCURRENCE: (Harlan, J.) The proper constitutional inquiry in this case is whether this Connecticut statute infringes the Due Process Clause of the Fourteenth Amendment because the enactment violates basic values "implicit in the concept of ordered liberty."

CONCURRENCE: (White, J.) There is nothing in this record justifying the sweeping scope of this statute, with its telling effect on the freedoms of married persons; therefore it deprives such persons of liberty without due process of law.

DISSENT: (Stewart, J.) Therefore, there is no general right of privacy to be found in the Bill of Rights, in any other part of the Constitution, or in any case ever before decided by this Court. If the law before us does not reflect the standard of the people of Connecticut, the people of Connecticut can freely exercise their true Ninth and Tenth Amendment rights to persuade their elected representatives to repeal it.

EDITOR'S ANALYSIS: This case seems to create another constitutional right to avoid procreation. However, the case did not resolve the issue of whether the right to use contraceptives applied only to married couples. Stewart's dissent seems to fear that the Court is returning to the days of *Lochner v. State of New York,* 198 U.S. 45, because it is imposing its own judgment on that of the legislature.

QUICKNOTES
CONNECTICUT BIRTH CONTROL LAW - Prohibits the use of any drug for the purpose of preventing conception.

PENUMBRA - A doctrine whereby authority of the federal government is implied pursuant to the Necessary and Proper Clause; one implied power may be inferred from the conferring of another implied power.

NOTES:

ROE v. WADE
Abortion ban challenger (P) v. State attorney general (D)
410 U.S. 113 (1973).

NATURE OF CASE: Review of challenge to state abortion law.

FACT SUMMARY: A state law absolutely prohibiting elective abortions was challenged as unconstitutional.

CONCISE RULE OF LAW: A state may not, consistent with the Constitution, absolutely prohibit elective abortions.

FACTS: Roe (P) was threatened with prosecution under a Texas law which prohibited all abortions other than those necessary to save a mother's life. Roe (P) later challenged the law as unconstitutional. The district and appellate courts held the law constitutional, and the Supreme Court granted review.

ISSUE: May a state constitutionally prohibit all elective abortions?

HOLDING AND DECISION: (Blackmun, J.) No. A state may not, consistent with the Constitution, absolutely prohibit elective abortions. State abortion laws do not enjoy the historical pedigree some believe. For the most part, they were passed in the second half of the nineteenth century, as a response to the high mortality rate of abortions in those days, a concern that is no longer relevant today. The Constitution gives no express right of privacy, but that right has been recognized since perhaps 1891. This right exists as a corollary to provisions of the First, Ninth, and Fourteenth Amendments. This Court believes that this right encompasses that of a woman to elect to terminate a pregnancy. Until such time as a fetus is viable, the state has no interest in the potential life the woman is carrying and cannot prohibit elective abortions. After viability, a state may take steps to protect the fetus, up to an including proscriptions of abortions. Reversed.

DISSENT: (Rehnquist, J.) The majority's decision to break pregnancy into three distinct terms and to outline the permissible restrictions the state may impose in each one partakes more of judicial legislation than it does of a determination of the intent of the draftors of the Fourteenth Amendment.

EDITOR'S ANALYSIS: The instant case represents probably the most controversial Supreme Court decision since the Dred Scott decision of the 1850s. It was hailed as a landmark for women's rights by some. It has been attacked from some quarters both for its result and for its reasoning, which pushed the edge of judicial activism. Despite the furor, the opinion has survived numerous legislative and political attacks.

NOTES:

PLANNED PARENTHOOD OF
SOUTHEASTERN PENNSYLVANIA v. CASEY
Abortion providers (P) v. State (D)
505 U.S. 833 (1992).

NATURE OF CASE: Appeal from the judgment upholding a state law regulating abortion in an action challenging the constitutionality of the law.

FACT SUMMARY: Responding to Pennsylvania's (D) enactment of its Abortion Control Act, Planned Parenthood (P), among others, challenged the constitutionality of five provisions of the Act.

CONCISE RULE OF LAW: A state may regulate abortion only where such regulation does not place an undue burden on a woman's ability to make a decision to terminate her pregnancy before viability.

FACTS: A number of cases challenging the constitutionality of five provisions of the Pennsylvania Abortion Control Act of 1982 were consolidated on appeal. The Act required that a woman seeking an abortion give an informed consent to the procedure and specified that she be provided with certain information at least 24 hours before the procedure was performed. A minor had to have the informed consent of one of her parents, although a judicial bypass option was provided. A married woman seeking an abortion had to notify her husband of the intended abortion. Compliance with the three previous requirements would be exempted in the event of a medical emergency as defined by the statute. Finally, the Act imposed certain reporting requirements on facilities that provided abortion services.

ISSUE: May a state regulate abortion only where such regulation does not place an undue burden on a woman's ability to make a decision to terminate her pregnancy before viability?

HOLDING AND DECISION: (O'Connor, J.) Yes. A state may regulate abortion only where such regulation does not place an undue burden on a woman's ability to make a decision to terminate her pregnancy before viability. An undue burden exists if a statute's purpose or effect is to place a substantial obstacle in the path of a woman seeking an abortion. If the information required to be made available to the woman is truthful and not misleading, it is not a substantial obstacle to obtaining an abortion, even where it expresses the state's preference for childbirth. Further, requiring a doctor to provide the information is not an undue burden. While the 24-hour waiting period is troubling in some respects, it has not been demonstrated that the waiting period constitutes an undue burden. Nor does the statute's definition of a medical emergency impose an undue burden on a woman's right to an abortion. However, because the spousal notification requirement is likely to prevent a significant number of women who are victims of regular physical and psychological

abuse at the hands of their husbands from obtaining an abortion, it is an undue burden and therefore invalid. A state may require a minor seeking an abortion to obtain the consent of a parent or guardian so long as there is an adequate judicial bypass procedure. Finally, the statute's record-keeping and reporting requirements are valid except for the provision requiring the reporting of a married woman's failure to give her husband notice.

CONCURRENCE AND DISSENT: (Blackmun, J.) The Constitution and decisions of this Court require that a state's abortion restrictions be subjected to the strictest of judicial scrutiny. Under this standard, the provisions requiring consent-based counseling, a 24-hour delay, informed parental consent, and reporting of abortion-related information must be invalidated.

CONCURRENCE AND DISSENT: (Rehnquist, C. J.) Because Roe v. Wade was wrongly decided, it can and should be overruled, consistent with this Court's traditional approach to stare decisis in constitutional cases. The challenged provisions of the statute should be upheld in their entirety.

EDITOR'S ANALYSIS: This opinion represents an unusual approach by the Court, in that the majority opinion was authored by three of the Justices, O'Connor, Kennedy, and Souter, with the other Justices joining in or dissenting from various parts of the opinion. The Court announced it was retaining the essential holding of *Roe v. Wade*. However, the opinion rejected *Roe's* trimester framework in favor of the "undue burden" standard. While it is the constitutional right of a woman to choose to terminate her pregnancy, the line is drawn at viability, the time at which there is a realistic possibility of maintaining and nourishing life outside the womb.

NOTES:

STENBERG v. CARHART
State official (D) v. Physician (P)
530 U.S. 914 (2000).

NATURE OF CASE: Appeal from a decision finding a partial-birth abortion statute unconstitutional.

FACT SUMMARY: The Court of Appeals found that a Nebraska statute criminalizing what it terms a partial birth abortion violates the Constitution as interpreted by the Supreme Court.

CONCISE RULE OF LAW: A statute criminalizing partial birth abortions violates the Constitution where it places a substantial obstacle in the path of a woman seeking an abortion of a nonviable fetus.

FACTS: This case concerns a Nebraska statute which imposes criminal penalties for what it terms "partial-birth abortions." The law defines such abortions as "deliberately and intentionally delivering into the vagina a living unborn child, or a substantial portion thereof, for the purpose of performing a procedure that the person performing the procedure knows will kill the unborn child and does kill the unborn child." The felony carries a prison term of up to 20 years, a fine of up to $25,000, and the automatic revocation of a doctor's license to practice medicine in Nebraska. Dr. Leroy Carhart (P), a Nebraska physician who performs abortions in a clinical setting, brought this lawsuit in federal district court seeking a declaration that the Nebraska statute violates the U.S. Constitution, and asking for an injunction forbidding its enforcement. The court of appeals found that the Nebraska statute does violate the Constitution.

ISSUE: Does a statute criminalizing partial birth abortions violate the Constitution where it places a substantial obstacle in the path of a woman seeking an abortion of a nonviable fetus?

HOLDING AND DECISION: (Breyer, J.) Yes. A statute criminalizing partial birth abortions violates the Constitution where it places a substantial obstacle in the path of a woman seeking an abortion of a nonviable fetus. The Nebraska statute in question lacks any exception for the preservation of the mother's health and imposes an undue burden on a woman's ability to choose this method of abortion of a nonviable fetus. This court's precedents in both *Casey* and *Roe* stand for the proposition that subsequent to viability, the State may regulate or even proscribe abortion except where necessary for the preservation of life or health of the mother. The Nebraska statute applies both pre- and postviability. Previability, the state's interest in preserving life is weaker than post-viability and the state's interest in this case is made ever weaker by the fact that the statute merely regulates a method of performing abortions and not abortions altogether. The court of appeals is affirmed.

CONCURRENCE: (Stevens, J.) Neither form of abortion described by the court is less gruesome, and thus it is irrational for the state of Nebraska to ban one and allow the other.

CONCURRENCE: (O'Connor, J.) Nebraska's statute is unconstitutional because it places an undue burden on a woman seeking to abort a nonviable fetus.

DISSENT: (Rehnquist, C.J.) *Planned Parenthood of Southeastern Pa. v. Casey,* 505 U.S. 833 (1992) was wrongly decided. Thus, the majority opinion in this case is also in error.

DISSENT: (Scalia, J.) The abortion issue is one of the most contentious issues in American society today. It is inappropriate for this court to act as an umpire in this debate, as there exists no constitutional text nor accepted tradition to root our position. This issue should be returned to the people and *Casey* should be overruled.

DISSENT: (Kennedy, J.) A central premise of *Roe v. Wade* was that the States retain a critical role in legislating on the issue of abortion. Today's decision ignores this premise by invalidating a state statute rooted in important state interests.

DISSENT: (Thomas, J.) *Casey's* undue burden analysis does not merit adherance. The majority erroneously abandons this court's precedence on statutory interpretation generally, and displaces the measured judgment of the people of Nebraska and 29 other states.

EDITOR'S ANALYSIS: The central argument between the majority and the dissent in *Stenberg* stems from the tension between the undue burden standard in *Planned Parenthood of Southeastern Pa. v. Casey* and its stated deference to the states' legitimate interest in promoting the life of the unborn child.

NOTES:

IN RE A.C.

Hospital (P) v. Unconscious patient (D)

D.C. Ct. App., 573 A.2d 1235 (1990).

NATURE OF CASE: Appeal of order mandating Caesarian section upon a terminally ill pregnant woman.

FACT SUMMARY: A court ordered that A.C., pregnant and dying, undergo a Caesarian section to save the baby.

CONCISE RULE OF LAW: A court may not order an individual to undergo a Caesarian section to save the baby's life.

FACTS: A.C., a chronic cancer patient, became pregnant. When she was twenty-five-weeks pregnant, she entered a hospital, complaining of pain. Tests revealed an inoperable tumor, and she was diagnosed as terminal. Based on conversations with doctors, she agreed to undergo a Caesarian section at twenty-eight weeks. However, her condition rapidly worsened, and by twenty-six weeks she had begun lapsing into and out of consciousness. Medical personnel believed that the only way to save the baby was an immediate C-section. However, they were not able to obtain A.C.'s consent, as she was mostly unconscious and not lucid when she was conscious. A court hearing was rapidly convened to determine what next to do. The court engaged in a balancing test between the state's interest in the fetus, the fetus' interests, and A.C.'s interests. The court ordered the C-section; unfortunately, the baby died, as did A.C. two days later. The district court of appeals reviewed the case.

ISSUE: May a court order an individual to undergo a Caesarian section to save the baby's life?

HOLDING AND DECISION: (Terry, J.) No. A court may not order an individual to undergo a Caesarian section to save the baby's life. It is a well-grounded common law rule that an individual is under no duty to take steps to save another's life. For instance, a person cannot be compelled to donate blood or an organ to save another's life. This rule applies with equal force in the context of a dying woman and her fetus: the woman cannot be compelled to undergo a procedure to save the fetus' life. Consent is required. If the woman is no longer competent, a court may hold an inquiry as to whether her consent would have been given were she competent. However, the scope of inquiry can only go so far as consent; the fetus' interests are not to be considered, nor those of the state, except perhaps in extraordinary circumstances. As the court considered those interests, it erred. Reversed.

CONCURRENCE AND DISSENT: (Belson, J.) The interests of the state and fetus are entitled to more weight than the court here gives them. In some cases, they may outweigh those of the mother.

EDITOR'S ANALYSIS: When a person is not capable of giving consent, it may be that the person had appointed a representative while they were still competent. If not, a court must try to divine what that person would have wanted. This requires an examination of all relevant circumstances, such as statements that the person might have made, as well as her value system. This inquiry is called "substituted judgment."

NOTES:

WHITNER v. SOUTH CAROLINA
Cocaine user (P) v. State (D)
S.C. Sup. Ct., 492 S.E.2d 777 (1997), cert. denied, 523 U.S. 1145 (1998).

NATURE OF CASE: Petition for post conviction relief following sentencing for child endangerment.

FACT SUMMARY: After pleading guilty to child endangerment because she had ingested cocaine during the third trimester of her pregnancy, Whitner (P) argued that the statute did not apply to fetuses.

CONCISE RULE OF LAW: The word "child" as used in South Carolina's child abuse and endangerment statute includes viable fetuses.

FACTS: Whitner (P) pled guilty to criminal child neglect for causing her baby to be born with cocaine in its system and she was sentenced to eight years in prison by the circuit court judge. Whitner (P) did not appeal her conviction, but later filed a petition for post conviction relief, pleading the circuit court's lack of subject matter jurisdiction to accept her guilty plea. Under South Carolina law, a circuit court lacked subject matter jurisdiction to accept a guilty plea to a nonexistent offense. For the sentencing court to have jurisdiction, criminal child neglect would have to include an expectant mother's use of crack cocaine after the fetus is viable. The State (D) contended that the statute encompassed maternal acts endangering a viable fetus. Whitner (P) argued that under the Children's Code, "child" meant a person under the age of eighteen.

ISSUE: Does the word "child" as used in the child abuse and endangerment statute include viable fetuses?

HOLDING AND DECISION: (Toal, J.) Yes. The word "child" as used in the child abuse and endangerment statute includes viable fetuses. There is no rational basis for finding a viable fetus is not a "person" in the present context. It would be absurd to recognize the viable fetus as a person for purposes of homicide laws and wrongful death statutes but not for purposes of statutes proscribing child abuse. Our holding that a viable fetus is a person rests primarily on the plain meaning of the word person in the light of existing medical knowledge. We do not believe the statute to be ambiguous and, therefore, the rule of lenity does not apply. Reversed.

DISSENT: (Finney, J.) It is apparent from a reading of the entire statute that the word "child" means a child in being and not a fetus. A plain reading of the entire child neglect statute reveals an intent to criminalize only acts directed at children, and not those which may harm fetuses.

DISSENT: (Moore, J.) The repeated failure of the legislature to pass proposed bills addressing the problem of drug use during pregnancy is evidence that the child abuse statute is not intended to apply in this instance. This court should not invade what is clearly the province of the legislative branch.

EDITOR'S ANALYSIS: This case differs from the majority of cases in other states. The legislature's intent usually is interpreted to preclude inclusion of fetuses in child endangerment statutes. All states also have child abuse reporting statutes requiring child protection authorities to be informed when abuse is witnessed.

NOTES:

FERGUSON v. CITY OF CHARLESTON
Obstetrical patients (P) v. City (D)
532 U.S. 67 (2001).

NATURE OF CASE: Appeal from complaint alleging that hospital policy concerning pregnant patients and drug abuse amounted to an unconstitutional search.

FACT SUMMARY: Obstetrical patients (P) who received care at the Medical University of South Carolina (MUSC) (D) were arrested after testing positive for cocaine. The patients filed suit against the City of Charleston (D), law enforcement officials (D) and MUSC representatives (D), alleging that the MUSC's (D) policy amounted to warrantless and non-consensual criminal searches. In the district court, the jury found for the defendants and petitioners appealed. The Fourth Circuit Court of Appeals affirmed and petitioners appeal.

CONCISE RULE OF LAW: A state hospital's performance of a diagnostic test to obtain evidence of a patient's criminal conduct for law enforcement purposes is an unreasonable search if the patient has not consented to the procedure.

FACTS: MUSC (D) is a state hospital. In the fall of 1988, MUSC (D) staff members became concerned about an apparent increase in the use of cocaine by patients who were receiving prenatal treatment. In response, as of April 1989, MUSC (D) began to order drug screens to be performed on urine samples from maternity patients (P) who were suspected of using cocaine. If a patient (P) tested positive, she was referred by MUSC (D) staff to the county substance abuse commission for counseling and treatment. Despite the referrals, the incidence of cocaine use did not change. After learning about the prosecution of pregnant users of cocaine in Greenville, South Carolina, MUSC (D) developed Policy M-7. Policy M-7 called for the testing of patients who met one or more of nine criteria for drug use. The policy also stated that a chain of custody should be followed when obtaining and testing urine samples to ensure that the results could be used in subsequent criminal proceedings. For patients who tested positive for drug use, the policy provided for education and referral to a substance abuse clinic under the threat of law enforcement intervention. If a patient was identified as a drug user after labor, the police were to be notified immediately, and the patient promptly arrested. The policy also set out procedures for the police to follow when a patient was arrested, and the precise offenses with which a woman could be charged. The policy did not, however, make any mention of any change in the prenatal care of such patients, nor did it prescribe any special treatment for newborns. The patients (P) were arrested after testing positive for cocaine at MUSC (D). The patients (P) filed suit against the City of Charleston (D), law enforcement officials (D) and MUSC representatives (D), alleging that the MUSC's (D) policy amounted to warrantless and nonconsensual criminal searches.

In the district court, the jury found for the defendants and petitioners appealed. The Fourth Circuit Court of Appeals affirmed and petitioners appeal.

ISSUE: Is a state hospital's performance of a diagnostic test to obtain evidence of a patient's criminal conduct for law enforcement purposes an unreasonable search if the patient has not consented to the procedure?

HOLDING AND DECISION: (Stevens, J.) Yes. A state hospital's performance of a diagnostic test to obtain evidence of a patient's criminal conduct for law enforcement purposes is an unreasonable search if the patient has not consented to the procedure. The reasonable expectation of privacy enjoyed by the typical patient undergoing diagnostic tests in a hospital is that the results of those tests will not be shared with nonmedical personnel without the patient's consent. The Fourth Amendment is applicable to MUSC (D) staff members' actions under Policy M-7. Because MUSC (D) is a state hospital, its staff members are state actors within the strictures of the Fourth Amendment. The urine tests performed by MUSC (D) staff members were searches within the meaning of the Fourth Amendment. Neither the district court nor the court of appeals concluded that any of the nine criteria used to identify the women to be searched provided either probable cause or reasonable suspicion of such use. The central and indispensable feature of Policy M-7 from its inception was the use of law enforcement to coerce the patients into substance abuse treatment. The policy devotes its attention to the chain of custody, the range of possible criminal charges, and the logistics of police notification and arrests. Further, through the development and application of Policy M-7, Charleston (D) prosecutors and police were extensively involved in its day-to-day administration. The immediate objective of Policy M-7 thus was to generate evidence for law enforcement purposes. The judgment of the court of appeals is reversed, and the case is remanded for further proceedings consistent with this opinion.

CONCURRENCE: (Kennedy, J.) The majority's decision should not operate to invalidate legitimate law enforcement procedures aimed at discovering information relating to drug abuse among expectant mothers. The medical profession can adopt acceptable criteria for testing expectant mothers for drug use in order to provide prompt and effective counseling.

Continued on next page.

DISSENT: (Scalia, J.) The police conduct involved in this case plainly does not violate the Fourth Amendment's prohibition of unreasonable searches and seizures. There exists no patient-physician privilege in South Carolina, and the patients (P) at issue in this case did not have a reasonable expectation that the urine samples they provided to their physicians would not be turned over to the authorities.

EDITOR'S ANALYSIS: The *Ferguson* case deals with the issue of maternal substance abuse. Thousands of children are born each year to women who have used tobacco, alcohol, or illegal drugs during pregnancy. There is some debate over whether the criminal prosecution for maternal substance abuse is the answer to this crisis.

NOTES:

J.B. v. M.B. & C.C.
Wife (P) v. Husband (D)
N.J. Ct. App., 783 A.2d 707 (2001).

NATURE OF CASE: Appeal from a summary judgment order on the issue of a divorced couples preembryos.

FACT SUMMARY: J.B. (P) filed for divorce and sought an order with regard to cryopreserved preembryos created during her marriage to M.B. (D). M.B. (D) counterclaimed, alleging that the couple agreed to donate the remaining preembryos to infertile couples. The district court granted J.B. (P) summary judgment on the preembryo issue and M.B. (D) appealed. The appellate division affirmed.

CONCISE RULE OF LAW: A court must only enforce agreements entered into at the time in vitro fertilization is begun, subject to the right of either party to change his or her mind about disposition up to the point of use or destruction of any preembryos.

FACTS: J.B. (P) and M.B. (D) were married in February of 1992. After J.B. (P) suffered a miscarriage early in the marriage, the couple encountered difficulty conceiving a child and sought medical advice. J.B. (P) learned that she had a condition which prevented her from becoming pregnant. Following this diagnosis, the couple decided to undergo an in vitro fertilization at the Cooper Center. The Cooper Center's consent form described the procedure and discussed the control and disposition of the preembryos. However, the consent form did not manifest a clear intent by J.B. (P) and M.B. (D) regarding disposition of the preembryos in the event of a dissolution of their marriage, just that the preembryos be relinquished to the Cooper Center, unless a court directs otherwise. The procedure was carried out in May 1995 and resulted in eleven preembryos. Four were transferred to J.B. (P) and seven were cryopreserved. J.B. (P) became pregnant and gave birth to the couple's daughter on March 19, 1996. In September of 1996, the couple separated and J.B. (P) informed M.B. (D) that she wished to have the remaining embryos discarded. M.B. (D) disagreed. J.B. (P) filed for divorce on November 25, 1996, seeking an order from the court regarding the preembryos. M.B. (D) counterclaimed, demanding that the remaining embryos be implanted or donated to other infertile couples. J.B. (P) filed a motion for summary judgment on the issue of the preembryos, which was granted. The appellate division affirmed. M.B. (D) appeals, contending that the judgment of the court below violated his constitutional rights to procreation and the care and companionship of his children.

ISSUE: Must a court enforce agreements entered into at the time in vitro fertilization is begun, subject to the right of either party to change his or her mind about disposition up to the point of use or destruction of any preembryos?

HOLDING AND DECISION: (Poritz, J.) Yes. A court must enforce agreements entered into at the time in vitro fertilization is begun, subject to the right of either party to change his or her mind about disposition up to the point of use or destruction of any preembryos. Ordinarily, the party choosing not to become a biological parent will prevail. In this case, M.B. (D) is a father and is capable of fathering additional children. Thus, M.B.'s (D) right to procreate is not lost if he is denied an opportunity to use or donate the preembryos. On the other hand, J.B.'s (P) right not to procreate may be lost through attempted use or donation of the prembryos. Implantation, if successful, would result in the birth of J.B.'s (P) biological child and could have life-long emotional and psychological repercussions. J.B. (P) does not object to continued storage of the preembryos if M.B. (D) wishes to pay any fees. If not, the preembryos are to be destroyed. The judgment of the appellate division is affirmed as modified.

CONCURRENCE: (Verniero, J.) The majority correctly disposed of this case in regards to all but one issue. The majority erroneously suggests in dicta that the right to procreate may depend on adoption as a consideration.

EDITOR'S ANALYSIS: There remains a question as to whether preembryos should be viewed as property or children in divorce proceedings, or whether they should occupy a wholly distinct category.

NOTES:

R.R. v. M.H.
Father (P) v. Surrogate mother (D)
Mass. Ct. App., 689 N.E.2d 790 (1998).

NATURE OF CASE: Action concerning the enforceability of a surrogacy agreement.

FACT SUMMARY: After signing a surrogacy agreement with R.R. (P), M.H.(D) changed her mind and decided to keep the child she was carrying. R.R. (P) commenced this action, seeking to enforce the surrogacy agreement.

CONCISE RULE OF LAW: Where compensation beyond pregnancy-related expenses is paid to a surrogate mother and the mother consents to the father's custody of the child before a suitable period has passed following the child's birth, a surrogacy agreement may not be upheld.

FACTS: R.R.'s (P) wife is infertile. Thus R.R. (P) and his wife sought to conceive through a surrogate mother. They entered into a contract with the New England Surrogate Parenting Advisors (NESPA), a for-profit corporation that helps match infertile couples with women willing to act as surrogates. They were matched with M.H. (D), a married woman with two children. M.H. (D) underwent psychological testing and was deemed solid, thoughtful, and well grounded and would have no problem giving her child up to R.R. (P) and his wife. Both parties signed a surrogacy agreement whereby, R.R. (P) would contribute the sperm to be inseminated into M.H. (D). The agreement acknowledged that M.H.'s (D) parental rights would not terminate if she permitted R.R. (P) to take the child home to live with him and his wife, and provided for compensation to the mother (D) in the amount of $10,000 for services rendered in carrying, caring and giving birth. There was no evidence of undue influence, and M.H. (D) made the decision of her own volition. M.H. (D) had herself inseminated on November 30 and December 1, 1996. The attempt at conception was successful and the lawyer for the father sent a check to M.H. (D) in December. In May, after receiving another payment from the father, M.H. (D) decided to keep the child, and returned the payment. She made no attempt to return any earlier payments. The father (P) then commenced this action seeking to establish his paternity, alleging breach of contract, and requesting a declaration of his rights under the surrogacy agreement.

ISSUE: Where compensation beyond pregnancy-related expenses is paid to a surrogate mother and the mother consents to the father's custody of the child before a suitable period has passed following the child's birth, may a surrogacy agreement be upheld?

DECISION AND HOLDING: (Wilkins, J.) No. Where compensation beyond pregnancy-related expenses is paid to a surrogate

mother and the mother consents to the father's custody of the child before a suitable period has passed following the child's birth, a surrogacy agreement may not be upheld. Under Massachusetts law, surrogate fatherhood is a recognized and accepted procedure. No statute decrees the consequences of the artificial insemination of a surrogate with the sperm of a fertile husband. Adoption legislation provides some guidance in this case. Although a consent to surrender custody is different from a consent to adoption, the legislative judgment that mother should have time to reflect on her wishes concerning the child weighs heavily in our consideration whether to give effect to a prenatal custody agreement. In this case, R.R. (P) paid compensation to M.H. (D) and had her sign onto the custody of the child prior to conception or delivery of the child. The surrogacy agreement may not be upheld.

EDITOR'S ANALYSIS: A significant minority of States have legislation addressing surrogacy agreements.

NOTES:

CULLITON v. BETH ISRAEL DEACONESS MEDICAL CENTER

Infertile couple (P) v. Medical center (D)
Mass. Ct. App., 756 N.E.2d 1133 (2001).

NATURE OF CASE: Appeal from dismissal of complaint seeking declaratory and injunctive relief.

FACT SUMMARY: The biological parents (P) and the gestational carrier (P) of twins sought an order from the district court to issue a prebirth order of parentage. The district court dismissed the declaratory and injunctive complaint, concluding that it could not order a prebirth order of parentage.

CONCISE RULE OF LAW: A district court has authority to issue a prebirth order of parentage where the plaintiffs are the sole genetic sources of the child in question, the gestational carrier agrees to the order sought, the proposed order is uncontested, and where the plaintiffs have waived any contradictory provisions in the contract.

FACTS: Marla and Steve Culliton (P) are married. Marla (P) is capable of conceiving a child, but cannot carry it to terms without placing herself in grave physical danger. As a result, Marla and Steve Culliton (P) entered into an agreement with Melissa Carroll (P) to have Carroll (P) act as a gestational carrier for them. Under the agreement, embryos created from the union of Steve Cullton's sperm and Marla Culliton's (P) ova would be implanted in Carroll's (P) uterus. Carroll (P) would carry the embryo to term and upon its birth, would permit the Cullitons (P) to have sole legal and physical custody of the child or children. Carroll (P) underwent the embryo implantation and became pregnant with twins. Months later, the Cullitons (P), with Carroll (P), filed a complaint in probate and family court, seeking an order of paternity and maternity, as well as a prebirth order directing the hospital (D) at which the gestational carrier was expected to deliver to designate the plaintiffs as the father and mother of the children on their birth certificates. Together with the complaint, the plaintiffs filed a stipulation for the entry of judgment in the plaintiffs' favor. The judge at the probate and family court ordered the entry of a judgment of dismissal, concluding that he did not have authority to issue a prebirth order of parentage. The plaintiffs appealed, and the appeals court entered a preliminary injunction enjoining the hospital (D) from issuing birth certificates until resolution of the appeal.

ISSUE: Does a district court have authority to issue a prebirth order of parentage where the plaintiffs are the sole genetic sources of the child in question, the gestational carrier agrees to the order sought, the proposed order is uncontested, and where the plaintiffs have waived any contradictory provisions in the contract?

HOLDING AND DECISION: (Greaney, J.) Yes. A district court has authority to issue a prebirth order of parentage where the plaintiffs are the sole genetic sources of the child in question, the gestational carrier agrees to the order sought, the proposed order is uncontested, and where the plaintiffs have waived any contradictory provisions in the contract. A protocol must be developed to deal with issues of parentage as infertile couples increasingly turn to emerging reproductive technologies. This is the province of the Legislature: to create a comprehensive set of laws that deal with the medical, legal, and ethical aspects of these practices. The judgment of dismissal is vacated and the preliminary injunction enjoining the hospital (D) from complying with its statutory obligations for the children is dissolved. A judgment is to enter declaring plaintiffs as the legal parents of the children and ordering the hospital (D), through its reporters, to place the plaintiffs' names on its records of birth, listing Marla (P) and Steve (P) as mother and father, respectively.

EDITOR'S ANALYSIS: According to *Culliton,* a gestational surrogate may enter into a binding agreement to forgo whatever parental rights she might have before the birth of the child.

NOTES:

8

CHAPTER 8
PUBLIC HEALTH LAW

QUICK REFERENCE RULES OF LAW

1. **Risk Assessment and Regulatory Competence.** Rulemaking requires a determination as to whether the restrictions imposed would materially reduce a significant workplace risk of human health without threatening massive dislocation to the health care industry. (American Dental Association v. Martin)

2. **The Source and Limit of Authority to Protect Public Health: Constitutional Principles.** The scope of the state's police power includes the authority to enact reasonable regulations to protect public health and safety. (Jacobson v. Commonwealth of Massachusetts)

3. **The Source and Limit of Authority to Protect Public Health: Disability Discrimination.** It is not sufficient to discriminate based on the fact that the person's physical impairment is contagious. (School Board of Nassau County v. Arline)

4. **Professional Licensure.** The words "prescribe and furnish medicine" include administering any substance or remedy in the treatment of an ailment or disease. (State v. Miller)

5. **Professional Licensure.** Findings of fact made by an administrative agency will not be disturbed on appeal unless such findings are contrary to the evidence or based on a mistake of law. (Modi v. West Virginia Board of Medicine)

6. **Regulating Access to Drugs.** In the treatment of any illness, terminal or otherwise, a drug is effective if it fulfills, by objective indices, its sponsor's claims of prolonged life, improved physical condition, or reduced pain. (United States v. Rutherford)

7. **Testing, Reporting, and Contact Tracing.** A warrantless search may be justified if the state's interest to be achieved outweighs the nature and scope of the intrusion on individuals' Fourth Amendment interests. (People v. Adams)

8. **Testing, Reporting, and Contact Tracing.** A patient-identification statute is a reasonable exercise of New York's broad police powers. (Whalen v. Roe)

9. **Testing, Reporting, and Contract Tracing.** Out-of-state AIDS testing labs are not similarly situated to physicians and dentists treating patients with AIDS or HIV for the purposes of the Equal Protection Clause. (Middlebrooks v. State Board of Health)

10. **Quarantine, Civil Commitment, and Mandatory Treatment.** Restrictions discriminating against a class of persons without justification are unconstitutional. (Wong Wai v. Williamson)

11. **Quarantine, Civil Commitment, and Mandatory Treatment.** A clear and convincing standard of proof is required by the Fourteenth Amendment to the Constitution in a civil proceeding brought under state law to commit an individual involuntarily for an indefinite period to a state mental hospital. (Addington v. Texas)

12. **Quarantine, Civil Commitment, and Mandatory Treatment.** Before a court can issue an order for an involuntary treatment, the petitioner must prove by clear and convincing evidence that the respondent is a person requiring treatment. (In the Interest of J.A.D.)

AMERICAN DENTAL ASSOCIATION v. MARTIN
Health care employer groups (P) v. Administrative agency (D)
984 F.2d 823 (7th Cir. 1993).

NATURE OF CASE: Challenge of the Occupational Safety and Health Administration's (OSHA) rule designed to protect health care workers from viruses.

FACT SUMMARY: When OSHA (D) promulgated a rule on occupational exposure to blood borne pathogens, some employers (P) challenged the rule.

CONCISE RULE OF LAW: Rulemaking requires a determination as to whether the restrictions imposed would materially reduce a significant workplace risk of human health without threatening massive dislocation to the health care industry.

FACTS: OSHA (D) adopted a rule imposing an extensive array of restrictions on the practice of medicine, nursing, and dentistry in order to protect health care workers against contracting AIDS and Hepatitis B. Three health care employer groups (P) challenged the rule on occupational exposure to blood borne pathogens promulgated by OSHA (D). The American Dental Association (P) alleged that OSHA (D) did not consider the reduction in medical care that might result from the rule's effect in making the practice of medicine more costly, and sought judicial review.

ISSUE: Does rulemaking require a determination as to whether rulemaking requires a determination as to whether the restrictions imposed would materially reduce a significant workplace risk of human health without threatening massive dislocation to the health care industry?

HOLDING AND DECISION: (Posner, J.) Yes. Rulemaking requires a determination as to whether the restrictions imposed would materially reduce a significant workplace risk of human health without threatening massive dislocation to the health care industry. The standard of review is reasonableness. We cannot say that the rule, viewed as a whole, flunks the test of material reduction of a significant risk to workplace health. Although OSHA (D) did not compare the benefits with the costs, its evaluation of the effects of the rule, relying as it did on the undoubted expertise of the Centers for Disease Control, cannot seriously be faulted, at least by judges. Affirmed.

CONCURRENCE AND DISSENT: (Coffey, J.) The rule can best be classified as an attempt to try to kill a fly with a sledgehammer. The rule was drafted partially in response to the public hysteria surrounding AIDS. The U.S. Congress must address the issue of whether there is a need to duplicate the efforts of the Centers for Disease Control and state health agencies, thus increasing health care costs.

EDITOR'S ANALYSIS: The judge in this case suggested in dictum that the whole concept of an occupational health and safety statute was unnecessary. The blood borne pathogen standard adopted was partially in reaction to the AIDS hysteria. Contagious diseases are at the core of public health regulation.

QUICKNOTES

29 C.F.R. § 910.1030 - Rule designed to protect health care workers from viruses causing Hepatitis B and AIDS.

NOTES:

JACOBSON v. COMMONWEALTH OF MASSACHUSETTS
Noncompliant citizen (D) v. State (P)
197 U.S. 11 (1905).

NATURE OF CASE: Review of conviction for refusal to be vaccinated.

FACT SUMMARY: A state statute requiring vaccination was alleged to be unconstitutional.

CONCISE RULE OF LAW: The scope of the state's police power includes the authority to enact reasonable regulations to protect public health and safety.

FACTS: A Massachusetts statute authorized cities to require that all city residents be vaccinated. The city of Cambridge adopted such a regulation. When Jacobson (D) refused to be vaccinated for smallpox, he was found guilty of noncompliance with the statute and jailed. Jacobson (P) appealed, alleging that his liberty was invaded, that a compulsory vaccination law was unreasonable, arbitrary and oppressive, and that the execution of such a law against a person who objected to vaccination was an assault against his person.

ISSUE: Does the scope of the state's police power include the authority to enact reasonable regulations to protect public health and safety?

HOLDING AND DECISION: (Harlan, J.) Yes. The scope of the state's police power includes the authority to enact reasonable regulations to protect public health and safety. The liberty secured by the Constitution to every person within its jurisdiction does not import an absolute right in each person to be, at all times and in all circumstances, wholly free from restraint. There are manifold restraints to which every person is necessarily subject for the common good. The means employed by Cambridge to stamp out smallpox have a real and substantial relation to the protection of the public health and the public safety. Nothing clearly appears that would justify this court in holding the statute to be unconstitutional and inoperative to Jacobson (D). Affirmed.

EDITOR'S ANALYSIS: This case has never been repudiated. The Court suggested that at times there simply is no liberty interest in conduct that may put others at risk. In the early part of the twentieth century, courts were extremely deferential to a state's power to protect the public health.

SCHOOL BOARD OF NASSAU COUNTY v. ARLINE
School officials (D) v. Discharged teacher (P)
480 U.S. 273 (1987).

NATURE OF CASE: Review of judgment for plaintiff in action filed pursuant to § 504 of the Rehabilitation Act of 1973 had been violated.

FACT SUMMARY: When Arline (P) was dismissed from her teaching position because of tuberculosis, she alleged that § 504 of the Rehabilitation Act of 1973 had been violated.

CONCISE RULE OF LAW: It is not sufficient to discriminate based on the fact that the person's physical impairment is contagious.

FACTS: The School Board of Nassau County, Florida (D) discharged Arline (P) from her teaching position after she suffered a third relapse of tuberculosis. Arline (P) successfully brought suit in federal court, alleging that the School Board (D) had violated § 504 of the Rehabilitation Act prohibiting discrimination on the basis of physical impairment. The School Board (D) appealed, alleging that Arline (P) had been dismissed because of the threat that her relapses of tuberculosis posed to the health of others and that her impairment was irrelevant.

ISSUE: Is it sufficient to discriminate based on the fact that the person's physical impairment is contagious?

HOLDING AND DECISION: (Brennan, J.) No. It is not sufficient to discriminate based on the fact that the person's physical impairment is contagious. Allowing discrimination based on the contagious effects of a physical impairment would be inconsistent with the basic purpose of § 504, which is to ensure that handicapped individuals are not denied jobs or other benefits because of the prejudiced attitudes or the ignorance of others. Whether Arline (P) is otherwise qualified for the job of elementary schoolteacher is for the district court to determine on remand. The judgment of the court of appeals is affirmed.

EDITOR'S ANALYSIS: The Rehabilitation Act of 1973 applies only to federal government employees, and those who contract with or are funded by the federal government. Congress later enacted the Americans with Disabilities Act to expand protection against discrimination by private employers. Employers are allowed to discriminate against a disabled person only if he poses a "direct threat" to the health or safety of others.

QUICKNOTES
REHABILITATION ACT OF 1973 - Statute prohibiting a federally funded state program from discriminating against a handicapped individual solely by reason of his or her handicapped.

STATE v. MILLER
State (P) v. Alternative medicine practitioner (D)
Iowa Sup. Ct., 542 N.W.2d 241 (1995).

NATURE OF CASE: Appeal from convictions for practicing medicine without a license.

FACT SUMMARY: When a jury found Miller (D) guilty of seven counts of practicing medicine without a license, he contended that the natural vitamins he had recommended to clients were not medicines, but food.

CONCISE RULE OF LAW: The words "prescribe and furnish medicine" include administering any substance or remedy in the treatment of an ailment or disease.

FACTS: Miller (D) treated people in his home by evaluating their ailments and then selling or recommending natural vitamins or nutrients. Miller (D) was charged and found guilty of practicing medicine without a license. He appealed, alleging that there was insufficient evidence to prove him guilty beyond a reasonable doubt. Miller (D) asserted that he had not violated the Iowa unlicensed statute prohibiting the practice of medicine because he never publicly professed to be a physician and never advertised. Moreover, he claimed that he did not fit the jury instruction definition of a person engaged in the practice of medicine because he did not "prescribe and furnish medicine," he only furnished food.

ISSUE: Do the words "prescribe and furnish medicine" include administering any substance or remedy in the treatment of an ailment or disease?

HOLDING AND DECISION: (Andreasen, J.) Yes. The words "prescribe and furnish medicine" include administering any substance or remedy in the treatment of an ailment or disease. The jury's verdict must be upheld unless the record lacks substantial evidence to support the charges. Substantial evidence is evidence that would convince a rational jury that the defendant is guilty of the crimes charged beyond a reasonable doubt. Miller's (D) actions of selling or recommending natural vitamins to his customers constituted furnishing a substance or remedy for treating their ailments. Therefore there is sufficient evidence to convince a rational jury beyond a reasonable doubt that Miller (D) was guilty of practicing medicine without a license. Affirmed.

EDITOR'S ANALYSIS: The practice of medicine without a license is a criminal offense. The practice of medicine is usually defined very broadly in the statutes. However, these statutes have been challenged on grounds of vagueness.

MODI v. WEST VIRGINIA BOARD OF MEDICINE

Psychiatrist (P) v. Disciplinary board (D)

W. Va. Sup. Ct., 465 S.E.2d 230 (1995).

NATURE OF CASE: Appeal from circuit court order vacating fine and public reprimand in a professional disciplinary action.

FACT SUMMARY: The west Virginia Board of Medicine (D) disciplined Dr. Modi (P), a psychiatrist, for practicing so-called depossession treatment on a patient.

CONCISE RULE OF LAW: Findings of fact made by an administrative agency will not be disturbed on appeal unless such findings are contrary to the evidence or based on a mistake of law.

FACTS: Modi (P) was a psychiatrist licensed in West Virginia. The West Virginia Board of Medicine (D) initiated an administrative proceeding against her because of her alleged care and treatment of a patient by the use of a technique known as depossession therapy. Depossession therapy involved the use of hypnosis to "exorcize" patients who believed they were possessed. Modi (P) filed an answer admitting the use of depossession therapy but denying any conduct justifying disciplinary action. The hearing examiner's report found that Modi (P) had used an experimental therapy without first obtaining a full, informed, and written consent from the patient and recommended sanctions. The Board then found that Modi (P) was unqualified to practice medicine without certain limitations and adopted the hearing examiner's recommendations for sanctions. Modi (P) appealed. The circuit court of Ohio reversed and vacated the Board's (D) order upon a finding that it was arbitrary and an abuse of discretion. The Board of Medicine (D) appealed.

ISSUE: Must a disciplinary board address the findings of fact and conclusions of law proposed by the parties and make a reasoned, articulate decision?

HOLDING AND DECISION: (Albright, J.) Yes. Findings of fact made by an administrative agency will not be disturbed on appeal unless such findings are contrary to the evidence or based on a mistake of law. In this case, the Board (D) utterly failed to rule on the proposed findings and conclusions of law and its order is barely intelligible. The circuit court was correct in finding that the Board (D) made inadequate findings of fact and incorrect conclusions of law. Also, the court properly concluded that the sanctions were arbitrary and capricious. However, the court below should have remanded to the Board (D) for reconsideration of the issue of the use of an experimental therapy without written consent. Affirmed in part, reversed in part, and remanded.

EDITOR'S ANALYSIS: This case involved three charges made against Dr. Modi (P). First, she was charged with failing to follow accepted medical practice. Second, she was charged with the ethical violation of providing experimental treatment without informed consent. Third, she was charged with filing a false report for insurance reimbursement when she described her use of depossession therapy as psychotherapy.

NOTES:

UNITED STATES v. RUTHERFORD

Administrative agency (D) v. Cancer patients (P)
442 U.S. 544 (1979).

NATURE OF CASE: Review of court order permitting use of a drug not approved by the Food and Drug Administration (FDA).

FACT SUMMARY: When terminally ill cancer patients (P) were granted limited permission to use Laetrile, a non-approved drug, the FDA (D) appealed.

CONCISE RULE OF LAW: In the treatment of any illness, terminal or otherwise, a drug is effective if it fulfills, by objective indices, its sponsor's claims of prolonged life, improved physical condition, or reduced pain.

FACTS: Rutherford (P) and other terminally ill patients (P) and their spouses (P) brought an action to enjoin the government (D) from interfering with the interstate shipment and sale of Laetrile, a drug not approved for distribution under the Federal Food, Drug, and Cosmetic Act. Finding that Laetrile was nontoxic and effective, the district court ordered the government (D) to permit limited purchases of the drug by a plaintiff. The court of appeals instructed the district court to remand the case to the Food and Drug Administration (D) for determination whether Laetrile was a "new" drug under the Act. The Commissioner (D) found that Laetrile in its various forms constituted a new drug and the district court sustained his determination but held that, by denying cancer patients the right to use a nontoxic substance in connection with their personal health, the Commissioner (D) had infringed constitutionally protected privacy interests. The court of appeals approved the district court's injunction permitting use of Laetrile by cancer patients certified as terminally ill because there were no realistic standards to measure the safety and effectiveness of a drug upon that class of individuals. The government (D) appealed.

ISSUE: In the treatment of any illness, terminal or otherwise, is a drug effective if it fulfills, by objective indices, its sponsor's claims of prolonged life, improved physical condition, or reduced pain?

HOLDING AND DECISION: (Marshall, J.) Yes. In the treatment of any illness, terminal or otherwise, a drug is effective if it fulfills, by objective indices, its sponsor's claims of prolonged life, improved physical condition, or reduced pain. No implicit exemption for drugs used by the terminally ill is necessary to attain Congressional objectives. Nothing in the history of the 1938 Food, Drug, and Cosmetic Act or of the 1962 Amendments suggests that Congress intended protection only for persons suffering from curable diseases. To accept the proposition that the safety and efficacy standards of the Act have no relevance for terminal patients is to deny the Commissioner's (D) authority over all drugs, however toxic or ineffectual, for such individuals. Reversed.

EDITOR'S ANALYSIS: The power to regulate public health is derived from the federal government's power to regulate interstate commerce. States have criminalized the sale of nonapproved drugs and discipline health care professionals. The FDA often delays approval of new drugs and Congress has enacted legislation to speed up the development of new drugs by pharmaceutical companies.

QUICKNOTES

1938 FOOD, DRUG, AND COSMETIC ACT - Federal statute prohibiting interstate distribution of any "new drug" unless approved by the Secretary of Health, Education and Welfare.

NOTES:

PEOPLE v. ADAMS

State (P) v. Convicted prostitute (D)

III. Sup. Ct., 597 N.E.2d 574 (1992).

NATURE OF CASE: Appeal from circuit court judgment that a state statute was unconstitutional.

FACT SUMMARY: When Adams (D) was convicted of prostitution and ordered to undergo medical testing for HIV under the Unified Code of Corrections, she challenged the statute as unconstitutional.

CONCISE RULE OF LAW: A warrantless search may be justified if the state's interest to be achieved outweighs the nature and scope of the intrusion on individuals' Fourth Amendment interests.

FACTS: Adams (D) was convicted of prostitution and had to undergo medical testing to determine whether she carried the HIV virus. The trial court found that the testing procedure represented an illegal search and seizure and denied Adams (D) equal protection. The State (P) appealed.

ISSUE: May a warrantless search be justified if the state's interest to be achieved outweighs the nature and scope of the intrusion on individuals' Fourth Amendment interests?

HOLDING AND DECISION: (Miller, J.) Yes. A warrantless search may be justified if the state's interest to be achieved outweighs the nature and scope of the intrusion on individuals' Fourth Amendment interests. Traditionally the states have been allowed broad discretion in the formulation of measures designed to protect and promote public health. Like other measures intended to enhance public health and community well-being, governmental action designed to control the spread of disease falls within the scope of the state's police power. The Fourth Amendment only proscribes those searches and seizures that are unreasonable. Special government needs may need to be balanced against the nature and scope of the intrusion. The actual physical intrusion required by the HIV testing is relatively slight and poses no threat to health or safety. The challenged statute is not an unreasonable search and seizure under the U.S. and state Constitutions. Reversed and remanded.

EDITOR'S ANALYSIS: The court went on to find that there was no violation of the Equal Protection Clause either. Since no suspect class or fundamental right was involved, the rational basis test was applied. The testing requirement was found to bear a rational relationship to the state interest in combating the spread of AIDS.

QUICKNOTES

UNIFIED CODE OF CORRECTIONS - Requires convicts to undergo testing to determine whether they are carriers of the human immunodeficiency virus (HIV).

NOTES:

WHALEN v. ROE

Patients (P) v. State health commissioner (D)
429 U.S. 589 (1977).

NATURE OF CASE: Appeal from order enjoining enforcement of portions of the New York State Controlled Substances Act of 1972.

FACT SUMMARY: Patients (P) contended that a statutorily mandated computer file of all persons who obtained prescriptions of certain drugs infringed their constitutionally protected rights of privacy.

CONCISE RULE OF LAW: A patient-identification statute is a reasonable exercise of New York's broad police powers.

FACTS: The New York State Controlled Substances Act required the recording, in a centralized computer file, of the name and addresses of all persons who had obtained certain prescription drugs for which there was both a lawful and an unlawful market. A group of patients (P) regularly receiving prescription for Schedule II drugs, i.e., opium and opium derivatives, commenced this litigation. After a trial, the district court found that the State (D) had been unable to demonstrate the necessity for the patient-identification requirement. The New York Health Commissioner (D) appealed.

ISSUE: Is a patient-identification statute a reasonable exercise of New York's broad police powers?

HOLDING AND DECISION: (Stevens, J.) Yes. A patient-identification statute is a reasonable exercise of New York's broad police powers. The New York program does not, on its face, pose a sufficiently grievous threat to any interest to establish a constitutional violation. Neither the immediate nor the threatened impact of the patient-identification requirements in the Act on either the reputation or independence of patients for whom Schedule II drugs are medically indicated is sufficient to constitute an invasion of any right or liberty protected by the Fourteenth Amendment. Reversed.

EDITOR'S ANALYSIS: The plaintiffs in this case had alleged that they feared being stigmatized as "drug addicts." They also alleged a violation of their zone of privacy. Privacy usually involves two interests: the individual interest in avoiding disclosure of personal matters, and the interest in independence in making certain kinds of important decisions.

QUICKNOTES

CONTROLLED SUBSTANCES ACT - New York law requiring the state to record the names and addresses of all persons who obtain a prescription for certain opium and opium derivatives, cocaine, methadone, amphetamines, or methaqualone.

NOTES:

MIDDLEBROOKS v. STATE BOARD OF HEALTH

Physician (D) v. State agency (P)
Ala. Ct. App., 710 So.2d 891 (1998).

NATURE OF CASE: Appeal from an order compelling disclosure under a state statute.

FACT SUMMARY: The State Board of Health (P) filed an action against Dr. Middlebrooks (D) for violating a state statute requiring disclosure of cases or suspected cases of AIDS and HIV, including disclosure of the names and addresses of those infected. The trial court compelled disclosure and Dr. Middlebrooks appealed.

CONCISE RULE OF LAW: Out-of-state AIDS testing labs are not similarly situated to physicians and dentists treating patients with AIDS or HIV for the purposes of the Equal Protection Clause.

FACTS: An Alabama state statute requires physicians, dentists, and certain other persons to report cases or suspected cases of diseases such as HIV and AIDS to the Alabama State Board of Health. Dr. Mark Middlebrooks, a physician practicing in Jefferson County, must report under this statute. In July 1993, Dr. Middlebrooks (D) was contacted by officials of the Jefferson County Health Department, who requested that he comply with the reporting mandate of the statute and with the rules of the State Board of Health. Dr. Middlebrooks provided certain statistical data, as the statute and regulatory rules required, but he refused to provide the names and addresses of his patients. In September of 1994, the State Board of Health (P) filed this action against Dr. Middlebrooks (D), seeking to compel him to disclose the names and addresses of his HIV and AIDS patients. The trial court entered an order compelling disclosure and Dr. Middlebrooks (D) appealed.

ISSUE: Does a state statute requiring physicians, dentists, and certain other persons, not including out-of state AIDS testing labs, to report cases or suspected cases of diseases and conditions such as HIV and AIDS violate the Equal Protection Clause?

HOLDING AND DECISION: (Maddox, J.) No. A state statute requiring physicians, dentists, and certain other persons, not including out-of-state AIDS testing labs, to report cases or suspected cases of diseases and conditions such as HIV and AIDS does not violate the Equal Protection Clause. The prevention of the spread of HIV and AIDS is a legitimate government interest. Thus, the state may require disclosure to representatives of the state having responsibility for the health of the community. The disclosure in this case does not amount to an impermissible invasion of privacy. Dr. Middlebrooks' (D) Equal Protection Clause argument must also fail. The purpose of the Equal Protection Clause is to prevent states from enacting legislation that treats persons "similarly situated" differently. The out-of-state labs who confidentially sell and analyze the results of AIDS and HIV tests distributed in the state of Alabama are not similarly situated to physicians treating persons with AIDS or HIV in the state.

EDITOR'S ANALYSIS: Most states now require physicians and others to report the names of persons testing positive for HIV.

NOTES:

WONG WAI v. WILLIAMSON
Asian resident (P) v. City officials (D)
103 F. 1 (C.C.N.D. Cal. 1900).

NATURE OF CASE: Motion for an injunction restraining health officials.

FACT SUMMARY: When Asian resident Wai (P) was singled out for vaccination and quarantine, he sued San Francisco government officials (D).

CONCISE RULE OF LAW: Restrictions discriminating against a class of persons without justification are unconstitutional.

FACTS: The Board of Health in San Francisco (D) placed restrictions on Asian residents' travel because they were allegedly considered to be more vulnerable to the plague than other residents. They were also required to be inoculated. Wong Wai (P) alleged that the rules discriminated unreasonably against him and other Chinese residents and he sought to enjoin the application of the rules.

ISSUE: Are restrictions discriminating against a class of persons without justification unconstitutional?

HOLDING AND DECISION: (Morrow, J.) Yes. Restrictions discriminating against a class of persons without justification are unconstitutional. The Board (D) has not established any fact from which an inference might be drawn that any particular class of persons were liable to develop, or in danger of developing, the plague. It has failed to provide suitable rules and regulations on emergencies affecting the public health. The rules adopted appear to be without legislative authority, but assuming they had the sanction of a general order, they still could not be sustained. They were not based upon any established distinction in the conditions that are supposed to attend the plague, or the persons exposed to its contagion, but they were boldly directed against the Asiatic or Mongolian race as a class, without regard to the previous condition, habits, exposure to disease or residence of the individual. No evidence has been presented that this particular race is more liable to the plague than others and it is not known to be a fact. This explanation must therefore be dismissed as unsatisfactory. Motion for injunction is granted.

EDITOR'S ANALYSIS: This case involved several public health measures. Persons of Chinese ancestry were required to undergo inoculation against the bubonic plague. Uninoculated Chinese were prohibited from traveling outside the city.

ADDINGTON v. TEXAS
Civilly committed person (D) v. State (P)
441 U.S. 418 (1979).

NATURE OF CASE: Review of standard of proof used by trial court for involuntary commitment.

FACT SUMMARY: When Addington (D) was found to be mentally ill, he challenged the standard of proof used at the trial.

CONCISE RULE OF LAW: A clear and convincing standard of proof is required by the Fourteenth Amendment to the Constitution in a civil proceeding brought under state law to commit an individual involuntarily for an indefinite period to a state mental hospital.

FACTS: Addington (D) had a long history of temporary commitments as mentally ill and was arrested on charges of assault and threats against his mother. His mother filed a petition for indefinite commitment. At trial, he was found mentally ill and subject to commitment under the law based upon "clear, unequivocal and convincing evidence." The Texas Supreme Court upheld the commitment and the applicable standard of proof. Addington (D) appealed, alleging that due process required use of the criminal law's standard of proof—beyond a reasonable doubt.

ISSUE: Is a clear and convincing standard of proof required by the Fourteenth Amendment to the Constitution in a civil proceeding brought under state law to commit an individual involuntarily for an indefinite period to a state mental hospital?

HOLDING AND DECISION: (Burger, C.J.) Yes. A clear and convincing standard of proof is required by the Fourteenth Amendment to the Constitution in a civil proceeding brought under state law to commit an individual involuntarily for an indefinite period to a state mental hospital. However, determination of the precise burden equal to or greater than the "clear and convincing" standard which this Court holds is required to meet due process guarantees is a matter of state law. Remanded to the Texas supreme court for further proceedings. Vacated and remanded.

EDITOR'S ANALYSIS: The Court also discussed the reasonable-doubt standard used in criminal cases. Psychiatric diagnosis is not based on specific, knowable facts as criminal law is, and therefore the beyond-a-reasonable-doubt standard would not be appropriate. Within the medical discipline, the traditional standard for "factfinding" is a "reasonable medical certainty."

IN THE INTEREST OF J.A.D.
State (P) v. Mentally ill individual (D)
N.D. Sup. Ct., 492 N.W.2d 82 (1992).

NATURE OF CASE: Appeal from order requiring hospitalization and treatment.

FACT SUMMARY: When J.A.D. was ordered to be involuntarily hospitalized, he appealed, alleging that there was no clear and convincing evidence to support the findings of the trial court.

CONCISE RULE OF LAW: Before a court can issue an order for an involuntary treatment, the petitioner must prove by clear and convincing evidence that the respondent is a person requiring treatment.

FACTS: J.A.D. was mentally ill and the trial court issued an order requiring him to be hospitalized after hearing testimony that he was homeless and would not be able to find adequate shelter during the winter. J.A.D. appealed, alleging that the evidence presented at trial did not reach the clear and convincing level required by the statutes.

ISSUE: Before a court can issue an order for an involuntary treatment, must the petitioner prove by clear and convincing evidence that the respondent is a person requiring treatment?

HOLDING AND DECISION: (Vande Walle, J.) Yes. Before a court can issue an order for an involuntary treatment, the petitioner must prove by clear and convincing evidence that the respondent is a person requiring treatment. The court must first find that the individual is mentally ill and then the court must find that there is a reasonable expectation that if the person is not hospitalized there exists serious risk of harm to himself, others, or property. The record is tenuous as to whether J.A.D. poses a danger to himself because of his homelessness. His physician's testimony that J.A.D. was in need of treatment as defined by the statutes was not clear and convincing evidence. There is no presumption that J.A.D., as a homeless person, will neither be able to fend for himself during the winter nor be able to take care of his needs. Reversed.

CONCURRENCE: (Erickstad, J.) Through our very careful review of the facts and our analysis of the possible consequences of the facts, this court may have deprived J.A.D. of treatment crucial to his future welfare, without providing him with a safety net of any kind, at a time, considering the season of the year, when survival as a homeless person in North Dakota could be hazardous, to say the very least.

EDITOR'S ANALYSIS: This case demonstrates that a higher burden of proof is required for civil commitments. This standard in most states is applied to both aspects of the state's case. The diagnosis of mental illness and the requirement of dangerousness are often intertwined.

NOTES:

9

CHAPTER 9
HEALTH CARE FINANCING AND REFORM

QUICK REFERENCE RULES OF LAW

1. **Sources of Health Insurance: The Right to Health Care.** The defense of necessity is not applicable when one has a choice of several courses of action. (United States v. Milligan)

2. **Insurance and HMO Regulation.** A company that does not bear the risk of loss by its members, but merely agrees to make "best efforts" to minimize such losses, is not an insurer. (Jordan v. Group Health Ass'n)

3. **Insurance and HMO Regulation.** A state HMO Act is a law directed toward the insurance industry and as such is saved from ERISA preemption. (Rush Prudential HMO v. Moran)

4. **ERISA Preemption.** ERISA preempts state law and assures that federal regulation will be exclusive. (American Medical Security, Inc. v. Bartlett)

5. **ERISA Preemption.** Congress did not intend that ERISA circumscribe employers' control over the content of benefits plans they offered to their employees. (McGann v. H & H Music Co.)

6. **Health Insurance Coverage: Rationing and Discrimination.** An otherwise qualified handicapped individual must be provided with meaningful access to the benefit that the grantee of federal funding offers. (Alexander v. Choate)

7. **Health Insurance Coverage: Determining What Is Medically Appropriate.** Only the treating physician can determine what the appropriate treatment should be for any given condition. (Mount Sinai Hospital v. Zorek)

8. **Health Insurance Coverage: Determining What Is Medically Appropriate.** Congress never intended ERISA to dictate the content of welfare benefit plans; the discretion to make decisions concerning the content of the Plan rest with the Plan administrator. (Bechtold v. Physicians Health Plan of Northern Indiana)

9. **Cost-Based Reimbursement.** The amount paid to any provider of Medicare services shall be the reasonable cost of such services, and when costs for services are compared, they must comprise the same basic elements. (Memorial Hospital/Adair County Health Center v. Bowen)

10. **Capitation Payment.** Treatment decisions made by a health maintenance organization, acting through its physicians, are not fiduciary acts within the meaning of the Employee Retirement Income Security Act of 1974 (ERISA). (Pegram v. Herdrich)

11. **Economic and Regulatory Theory.** Advertising restrictions arguably protecting patients from misleading or irrelevant advertising regarding professional services where significant challenges exist to informed decisionmaking by customers require more than a cursory review under antitrust law. (California Dental Ass'n v. Federal Trade Commission)

UNITED STATES v. MILLIGAN
Federal government (P) v. Insured (D)
17 F.3d 177 (6th Cir. 1994).

NATURE OF CASE: Appeal from convictions for criminal fraud.

FACT SUMMARY: When a friend who had no health insurance was injured, Milligan (D) took him to a hospital and identified the victim as himself in order to receive his health insurance benefits.

CONCISE RULE OF LAW: The defense of necessity is not applicable when one has a choice of several courses of action.

FACTS: The victim of an accident was taken to a hospital by Milligan (D), who had health insurance provided by his employer. Since the accident victim did not have health insurance, Milligan (D) identified the victim as himself so medical assistance would be provided to him. At trial, Milligan (D) raised necessity as a defense, but the jury convicted him of fraud. Milligan (D) appealed.

ISSUE: Is the defense of necessity applicable when one has a choice of several courses of action?

HOLDING AND DECISION: (Keith, J.) No. The defense of necessity is not applicable when one has a choice of several courses of action. Here Milligan (D) had the choice to reveal the victim's uninsured status and request treatment, and failed to pursue this alternative. The choice was not foreclosed because each of the treatment facilities had policies requiring treatment of uninsured patients. Nor did Milligan (D) cease the criminal offense as soon as a safe opportunity arose. Affirmed.

EDITOR'S ANALYSIS: The court asserted that health institutions should not be punished by allowing persons who consciously defraud health care providers to receive more lenient sentencing. By choosing to deny the fraud, an unplanned reaction to a desperate situation was converted into a fraudulent scheme and conspiracy to avoid payment of medical bills. Milligan (D) alleged that the health care system reserves the best medical services for the insured and relegates uninsured patients to marginal care.

JORDAN v. GROUP HEALTH ASS'N
*Insurance superintendent (P) v.
Health maintenance organization (D)*
107 F.2d 239 (D.C. Cir. 1939).

NATURE OF CASE: Appeal from determination that defendant health organization was not subject to laws regulating insurance industry.

FACT SUMMARY: Jordan (P), the Superintendent of Insurance for the District of Columbia, brought suit against Group Health (D), a non-profit corporation that arranged for health care services for its members, alleging noncompliance with insurance regulations.

CONCISE RULE OF LAW: A company that does not bear the risk of loss by its members, but merely agrees to make "best efforts" to minimize such losses, is not an insurer.

FACTS: Group Health (D), in return for monthly dues payments by its members, contracted with independent medical practitioners and hospitals for the provision of medical services to members and their dependents. Group Health (D) did not regulate or control the physicians, nor did it determine what services would be made available to members in each case. Jordan (P) brought suit, alleging that Group Health (D) was an insurance company within the meaning of the D.C. Code, and had failed to comply with the requirements of the Code. The district court found in favor of Group Health (D), and Jordan (P) appealed.

ISSUE: Is a company that does not bear the risk of loss by its members properly characterized as an insurance company?

HOLDING AND DECISION: (Rutledge, J.) No. A company that does not bear the risk of loss by its members, but merely agrees to make "best efforts" to minimize such losses, is not an insurer. Group Health (D) assumed no liability if unable to provide services when called upon do so. Its only obligation, if a contracting physician failed to perform services or to perform them properly, was to use "best efforts to procure the needed services from another source." The primary purpose of Group Health (D) was to reduce the cost of medical services to its members by purchasing them in quantity, not to assume the risk of loss in exchange for payment. It lacked a critical attribute of insurers, and was therefore not subject to the insurance statutes. Affirmed.

EDITOR'S ANALYSIS: *Jordan,* an early case involving the legal rights and obligations of HMOs, no longer states the law. Modern HMO enabling statutes impose modified insurance regulations on HMOs, recognizing them as serving the combined functions of insurer and service provider, and imposing lower capital reserve requirements upon such organizations.

RUSH PRUDENTIAL HMO v. MORAN
HMO (D) v. HMO Beneficiary (P)
122 S. Ct. 2151 (2002).

NATURE OF CASE: Appeal from the reversal of a state court judgment enforcing an HMO Act.

FACT SUMMARY: On remand from federal court, a state court ordered Rush Prudential (D) to comply with a state statute providing a right to independent medical review for its beneficiary, Moran (P). Rush (D) continued to deny Moran's (P) claim and the court of appeals reversed.

CONCISE RULE OF LAW: A state HMO Act is a law directed toward the insurance industry and as such is saved from ERISA preemption.

FACTS: Debra Moran (P) is a beneficiary of an employee welfare benefit plan provided by Rush Prudential HMO (Rush) (D) and sponsored by her husband's employer. In 1996, Moran (P) began to have pain and numbness in her right shoulder. Moran's (P) primary care physician, Dr. LaMarre, unsuccessfully administered conservative treatments. In October 1997, Dr. LaMarre recommended that Rush (D) approve surgery by an unaffiliated specialist, Dr. Terzis, who had developed an unconventional treatment for Moran's (P) condition. Rush (D) denied the request, despite Dr. LaMarre's assurances that Moran (P) would be best served by this treatment. Rush (D) proposed that Moran (P) undergo standard surgery by a Rush-affiliated physician. In January 1998, Moran (P) made a written demand for an independent medical review of her claim. Rush (D) failed to provide an independent review, and Moran (P) filed a state court action demanding compliance with a state HMO Act providing a right to independent medical review of certain denials of benefits. Rush (D) removed the claim to federal court, arguing that a cause of action was completely preempted under the Employment Retirement Income Security Act (ERISA). While her suit was pending, Moran (P) had the surgery by Dr. Terzis at her own expense and submitted a $94,841.27 reimbursement claim to Rush (D). Rush (D) commenced a new inquiry to determine coverage. The federal court remanded the case to a state court, which enforced the state statute. The doctor selected for the independent review found the treatment to be medically necessary, but Rush (D) continued to deny Moran's (P) claim for coverage. The Seventh Circuit Court of Appeals reversed.

ISSUE: Is a state HMO statute providing a right to independent medical review of certain denials of benefits preempted by the Employment Retirement Income Security Act?

HOLDING AND DECISION: (Souter, J.) No. A state HMO statute providing a right to independent medical review of certain denials of benefits is not preempted by the Employment Retirement Income Security Act. The ERISA Statute preempts state laws that relate to employee benefit plans. Moran (P) is a beneficiary of an employee benefit plan. However, the ERISA statute has a savings clause stating that it is not meant to relieve any person from any law of any state which regulates insurance, banking, or securities. Rush's (D) argument that HMOs are not insurers falls short. HMOs have taken over much of the business formerly performed by traditional indemnity insurers, and they are almost universally regulated as insurers under state law. The HMO Act in question here is directed toward the insurance industry and thus is saved from ERISA preemption.

EDITOR'S ANALYSIS: The ERISA statute, as drafted, leaves much doubt as to its interpretation and a myriad issues for the courts to determine.

NOTES:

AMERICAN MEDICAL SECURITY, INC. v. BARTLETT
Insurance companies (P) v. Insurance regulator (D)
111 F.3d 358 (4th Cir. 1997).

NATURE OF CASE: Appeal in declaratory judgment action to invalidate health insurance regulation.

FACT SUMMARY: The Maryland Insurance Commissioner (D) sought to regulate the business of insurance and the insurance companies (P) sought to take advantage of the Employee Retirement Income Security Act's of 1974 (ERISA) preemption and deemer clauses to remove self-funded plans from the reach of state insurance regulation.

CONCISE RULE OF LAW: ERISA preempts state law and assures that federal regulation will be exclusive.

FACTS: Three Maryland employers (P) sponsoring self-funded employee health insurance plans subject to ERISA with stop-loss insurance and whose employee benefits plans contained less than the twenty-eight health benefits required by ERISA sought to bypass state mandates and sought a declaration that some regulations were invalid.

ISSUE: Does ERISA preempt state law and assure that federal regulation will be exclusive?

HOLDING AND DECISION: (Niemeyer, J.) Yes. ERISA preempts state law and assures that federal regulation will be exclusive. A preempted law is saved from preemption if it regulates insurance, but state insurance regulation may not directly or indirectly regulate self-funded ERISA plans. A regulation relates to an employee benefit plan when it has a "connection with or reference to such a plan." The state regulations at issue here therefore do "relate" to ERISA plans. Although the regulations are carefully drafted to focus directly on insurance companies issuing stop-loss insurance, Maryland is violating the ERISA provision that no ERISA plan "shall be deemed to be an insurance company for purposes of any law of any state purporting to regulate insurance companies or insurance contracts." These efforts impermissibly intrude on the relationship between an ERISA plan and its participants and beneficiaries. Maryland is without authority to fill any regulatory gaps left by ERISA.

EDITOR'S ANALYSIS: This case demonstrates that only Congress can address the problem of employers attempting to circumvent state regulation. The states are powerless to do so. Maryland cannot be concern itself with the benefits that ERISA plans choose to provide to their participants and beneficiaries.

QUICKNOTES

ERISA - Comprehensive federal statute regulating private pension plans and also covering other employee fringe benefit plans, including plans providing medical or other health benefits.

PREEMPTION - Doctrine stating that certain matters are of a national character so that federal laws preempt or take precedence over state or local laws.

STOP-LOSS INSURANCE - Provides coverage to self-funded plans above a certain level of risk absorbed by the plan.

NOTES:

MCGANN v. H & H MUSIC CO.

Employee (P) v. Employer (D)

946 F.2d 401 (5th Cir. 1991).

NATURE OF CASE: Appeal from summary judgment for defendant in action alleging retaliation in violation of ERISA.

FACT SUMMARY: McGann (P), an AIDS victim, alleged that his employer (D) was retaliating against him by lowering maximum health benefits in the company health plan.

CONCISE RULE OF LAW: Congress did not intend that ERISA circumscribe employers' control over the content of benefits plans they offered to their employees.

FACTS: McGann (P) discovered that he had AIDS and submitted claims for reimbursement under his employer's, H & H Music Company (D), group medical plan. A short time later benefits payable for AIDS-related claims were limited to a lifetime maximum of $5,000. McGann (P) sued H & H Music (D) under ERISA provisions prohibiting discharge or discrimination against a plan participant for exercising any rights to which he was entitled under a benefit plan. McGann (P) failed to make a showing sufficient to establish that a genuine issue existed as to H & H Music's (D) specific intent to retaliate against McGann (P) for filing AIDS-related claims or to interfere with any right to which he may have become entitled. H & H Music's (D) motion for summary judgment was granted by the district court and McGann (P) appealed.

ISSUE: Did Congress intend that ERISA circumscribe employers' control over the content of benefits plans they offered to their employees?

HOLDING AND DECISION: (Garwood, J.) No. Congress did not intend that ERISA circumscribe employers' control over the content of benefits plans they offered to their employees. ERISA does not broadly prevent an employer from discriminating in the creation, alteration, or termination of employee benefits plans. McGann's (P) allegations showed no promised benefit because the H & H Music Company's (D) Plan expressly provided that it "may terminate or amend the Plan at any time or terminate any benefit under the Plan at any time." Affirmed.

EDITOR'S ANALYSIS: McGann (P) could not show that he had become entitled to any benefits since the Plan never promised that any benefit would be "permanent." An employer can reserve the right to amend a medical plan. To succeed with his claim, McGann (P) had to show both that the employer was retaliating and that his benefits had "vested."

ALEXANDER v. CHOATE
Medicaid program directors (D) v. Medicaid recipients (P)
469 U.S. 287 (1985).

NATURE OF CASE: Review of alleged violation of federal anti-discrimination statute.

FACT SUMMARY: When cost-cutting measures threatened handicapped patients' medical services in Tennessee, a class action was filed under the Rehabilitation Act of 1973, a federal statute.

CONCISE RULE OF LAW: An otherwise qualified handicapped individual must be provided with meaningful access to the benefit that the grantee of federal funding offers.

FACTS: The directors of the Tennessee Medicaid program decided to institute cost-cutting measures. One measure was the reduction from twenty to fourteen in the number of inpatient hospital days per fiscal year that Tennessee Medicaid would pay hospitals on behalf of a Medicaid recipient. Before the new measures took effect, a class action was brought by Choate (P), on behalf of Tennessee Medicaid recipients, requesting declaratory and injunctive relief. Choate (P) alleged that the proposed limitation on inpatient coverage would have a discriminatory effect on the handicapped and would violate § 504 of the Rehabilitation Act of 1973.

ISSUE: Must an otherwise qualified handicapped individual be provided with meaningful access to the benefit that the grantee of federal funding offers?

HOLDING AND DECISION: (Marshall, J.) Yes. An otherwise qualified handicapped individual must be provided with meaningful access to the benefit that the grantee of federal funding offers. Proof of discriminatory animus is not required to establish a violation of § 504. Discrimination against the handicapped was perceived by Congress to be most often the product, not of invidious animus, but rather of thoughtlessness and indifference—of benign neglect. To determine which disparate impacts § 504 make actionable, a balance must be struck between the statutory rights of the handicapped to be integrated into society and the legitimate interests of federal grantees in preserving the integrity of their programs. While a grantee need not be required to make "fundamental" or "substantial" modifications to accommodate the handicapped, it may be required to make "reasonable" ones. The benefit itself cannot be defined in a way that effectively denies otherwise qualified handicapped individuals the meaningful access to which they are entitled. To assure meaningful access, reasonable accommodations in the grantee's program or benefit may have to be made. In this case, the 14-day limitation will not deny Choate (P) meaningful access to Tennessee Medicaid services or exclude him from those services.

EDITOR'S ANALYSIS: This case balanced the state's right to limit expenses against the rights of the handicapped. Tennessee was not required to redefine its Medicaid program. Federal law prohibits discrimination against the handicapped which comes about by effect, rather than by design.

QUICKNOTES

REHABILITATION ACT OF 1073 - Federal statute providing that no otherwise qualified handicapped individual shall, by reason of his handicap, be excluded from any federally funded program.

NOTES:

MOUNT SINAI HOSPITAL v. ZOREK
Hospital (P) v. Patient (D) and insurer (D)
N.Y. Civ. Ct., 271 N.Y.S.2d 1012 (1966).

NATURE OF CASE: Complaint seeking payment from a third-party defendant insurance company.

FACT SUMMARY: When Zorek's (D) hospital bill for obesity treatments was not paid by Blue Cross, Mount Sinai Hospital (P) sued her insurer, Associated Hospital Service (D).

CONCISE RULE OF LAW: Only the treating physician can determine what the appropriate treatment should be for any given condition.

FACTS: Zorek (D) was hospitalized at Mount Sinai Hospital (P) under her physician's orders for treatment of obesity. The third-party defendant, Associated Hospital Service of New York (AHS) (D), with whom Zorek (D) had a family Blue Cross contract, refused payment. AHS (D) claimed that obesity was not within the coverage of the contract and that Zorek's (D) hospital confinement was not necessary for the treatment of her condition.

ISSUE: Can only the treating physician determine what the appropriate treatment should be for any given condition?

HOLDING AND DECISION: (Greenfield, J.) Yes. Only the treating physician can determine what the appropriate treatment should be for any given condition. Although AHS (D) argued that obesity is neither a disease nor an injury, it is clear that Blue Cross coverage is not limited only to those calamities. The diagnosis and treatment of a patient are matters peculiarly within the competence of the treating physician. Once the treating physician has decided on the treatment, a court may review his judgment as to whether hospitalization was necessary. In this case, evidence was presented that the Duncan regime prescribed for Zorek (D) was a dangerous course of treatment. Not only was hospitalization necessary once the Duncan regime was decided upon, it would have been medically irresponsible to have had anything less. Mount Sinai Hospital (P) is entitled to a judgment in the amount of the Zorek's (D) hospital bill.

EDITOR'S ANALYSIS: The court construed the Blue Cross contract. When multiple courses of treatment are available, whether for the obese, the alcoholic, or the addicted, if the physician chooses that treatment for which hospitalization is required, there is full coverage for the hospital stay. It was medical necessity and not cosmetic vanity that dictated the hospital stay.

BECHTOLD v. PHYSICIANS HEALTH PLAN OF NORTHERN INDIANA
Patient (P) v. Insurance company (D)
19 F.3d 322 (7th Cir. 1994).

NATURE OF CASE: Appeal from judgment for defendant denying a claim for the payment of medical expenses by an insurance company.

FACT SUMMARY: When cancer treatment was not covered under a medical insurance plan, Bechtold (P), the patient, sued the insurance company, Physicians Health Plan of Northern Indiana (D).

CONCISE RULE OF LAW: Congress never intended ERISA to dictate the content of welfare benefit plans; the discretion to make decisions concerning the content of the Plan rests with the Plan administrator.

FACTS: Bechtold (P) was diagnosed with breast cancer and underwent surgery which was covered by her employer's health plan administered by Physicians Health Plan of Northern Indiana (PHP) (D). Her oncologist later recommended chemotherapy and an autologous bone marrow transplant (HDC/ABMT). Before proceeding with the treatment, PHP (D) informed Bechtold (P) that the HDC/ABMT treatment was not a covered service under the plan. Bechtold (P) appealed the denial of benefits and received a hearing before a committee who recommended that the PHP (D) change its policy and authorize payment for the procedure. PHP (D) did not agree with the committee's recommendation and refused to pay, stating that it had lived up to its obligations under the clear and unambiguous language of the contract. Bechtold (P) appealed, alleging a violation of ERISA because the PHP (D) plan was operating under a conflict of interest.

ISSUE: Did Congress intend ERISA to dictate the content of welfare benefit plans?

HOLDING AND DECISION: (Coffey, J.) No. Congress never intended ERISA to dictate the content of welfare benefit plans; the discretion to make decisions concerning the content of the Plan rests with the Plan administrator. A claim for benefits under an ERISA-governed plan is a matter of contract interpretation. Even under a less deferential de novo review, the clear and unambiguous language of the policy dictated that Physicians Health Plan of Northern Indiana (D) properly denied coverage for the HDC/ABMT treatment. Affirmed.

EDITOR'S ANALYSIS: This case demonstrates that a higher standard of review applies for ERISA-governed plans when there is a conflict of interest. Bechtold (P) alleged that the higher cost of the experimental treatment was a factor in PHP's (D) decision not to cover it. Insufficient data existed, however, to establish the efficacy of the ABMT procedure.

MEMORIAL HOSPITAL/ADAIR COUNTY HEALTH CENTER v. BOWEN

Hospital (P) v. Administrative agency (D)
829 F.2d 111 (D.C. Cir., 1987).

NATURE OF CASE: Appeal from summary judgment in favor of defendant in action challenging refusal to reimburse.

FACT SUMMARY: When Memorial Hospital's (P) pharmacy expenses were not reimbursed, Memorial (P), a Medicare provider hospital (P), sued the Secretary for Health and Human Services, Bowen (D).

CONCISE RULE OF LAW: The amount paid to any provider of Medicare services shall be the reasonable cost of such services, and when costs for services are compared, they must comprise the same basic elements.

FACTS: The Secretary of Health and Human Services, Bowen (D), denied full payment for pharmacy services rendered to Medicare patients by a rural Oklahoma hospital (P). The hospital, Memorial Hospital/Adair County Health Center (P), filed complaints challenging the decisions. Blue Cross had audited the reimbursement claim by comparing the costs of each hospital with other institutions in the same area which were similar in size, scope of services and other factors. In this case, Memorial's (P) pharmacy provided state-of-the-art services whose cost was out of line with the peer group's costs. On cross motions for summary judgment, the district court concluded that the Secretary's (D) decisions were not irrational. Memorial (P) appealed.

ISSUE: Must the amount paid to any provider of Medicare services be the reasonable cost of such services and, when costs for services are compared, must they comprise the same basic elements?

HOLDING AND DECISION: (Buckley, J.) Yes. The amount paid to any provider of Medicare services shall be the reasonable cost of such services and, when costs for services are compared, they must comprise the same basic elements. Here, the Secretary (D) denied Memorial (P) reimbursement of actual per diem pharmacy costs that were in excess of the highest per diem pharmacy costs in the peer hospital groups, even though none of the comparison hospitals used a pharmacist-supervised intravenous admixture program that accounted for most of Memorial's (P) purportedly excessive costs. On remand, Memorial's (P) pharmacy costs must be compared with those incurred by peer groups offering comparable IV and other pharmacy services. Reversed and remanded.

EDITOR'S ANALYSIS: The reasonable cost of services varies by geographic area. Peer groups are created to compare costs within one geographic area. Following the inception of Medicare, the net income of hospitals increased.

NOTES:

PEGRAM v. HERDRICH

Physician (D) v. Patient (P)

530 U.S. 211 (2000).

NATURE OF CASE: Review of medical malpractice action.

FACT SUMMARY: The appellate court found that HMOs were acting as fiduciaries when their physicians made medical decisions and could be held liable for breach of fiduciary duties.

CONCISE RULE OF LAW: Treatment decisions made by a health maintenance organization, acting through its physicians, are not fiduciary acts within the meaning of the Employee Retirement Income Security Act of 1974 (ERISA).

FACTS: Pegram (D), the HMO treating plan physician, examined Herdrich (P) but failed to immediately order an ultrasound. When Pegram (D) ultimately ordered the ultrasound, Herdrich (P) had to go to a distant facility owned by the HMO. Because of the delay, Herdrich's (P) appendix ruptured, causing peritonitis. Herdrich (P) sued Pegram (D) and the HMO (D) in state court for medical malpractice and later added two counts charging state-law fraud. The HMO (D) and Pegram (D) asserted that ERISA preempted the new counts and removed the case to federal court where they then sought summary judgment on the state law fraud counts. The court dismissed one count, but allowed Herdrich (P) to amend the one remaining. Herdrich (P) then alleged that provision of medical services under the terms of the HMO, rewarding physicians for limiting medical care, entailed an inherent or anticipatory breach of an ERISA fiduciary duty. The district court granted the HMO's (D) motion to dismiss the ERISA count for failure to state a claim upon which relief may be granted. The Court of Appeals of the Seventh Circuit reversed. The U.S. Supreme Court granted certiorari.

ISSUE: Are treatment decisions made by a health maintenance organization, acting through its physicians, fiduciary acts within the meaning of ERISA?

HOLDING AND DECISION: (Souter, J.) No. Treatment decisions made by a health maintenance organization, acting through its physicians, are not fiduciary acts within the meaning of ERISA. Since courts are not in a position to differentiate among the various types of HMOs and their organizational structures, all decisions by HMOs acting through their owner or employee physicians are to be judged by the same standards and subject to the same claims. Congress did not intend any HMO to be treated as a fiduciary to the extent that it makes mixed eligibility decisions acting through its physicians. The congressional policy of allowing HMO organizations would be threatened by ERISA fiduciary claims portending wholesale attacks on existing HMOs solely because of their structure, untethered to claims of concrete harm. For all practical purposes, every such claim of fiduciary breach by an HMO physician would boil down to a malpractice claim. Reversed.

EDITOR'S ANALYSIS: The court here found that in most cases, the eligibility decision and the treatment decision were inextricably mixed. Such mixed decisions include physicians' recommendations of tests, decisions about referrals and consultations with other physicians or facilities, proper standards of care, etc. Decisions involving medical judgment were found not to be related to ERISA.

QUICKNOTES

ERISA - 29 U.S.C. § 1001 - enacted in 1974, a comprehensive statute designed to benefit the interests of employees and their beneficiaries in employee benefit plans.

MEDICAL MALPRACTICE - Conduct on the part of a doctor falling below that demonstrated by other doctors of ordinary skill and competency under the circumstances, resulting in damages to patients.

NEGLIGENCE - Conduct falling below the standard of care that a reasonable person would demonstrate under similar conditions.

NOTES:

CALIFORNIA DENTAL ASS'N v. FEDERAL TRADE COMMISSION

Nonprofit association of dentists (D) v. Federal agency (P)

526 U.S. 756 (1999).

NATURE OF CASE: Appeal from an administrative law judge's finding of an FTC violation.

FACT SUMMARY: The Federal Trade Commission (FTC) (P) brought an FTC action against the California Dental Ass'n (D) based upon a Code of Ethics provision. An administrative law judge found a violation of the FTC Act.

CONCISE RULE OF LAW: Advertising restrictions arguably protecting patients from misleading or irrelevant advertising regarding professional services where significant challenges exist to informed decisionmaking by customers require more than a cursory review under antitrust law.

FACTS: The California Dental Association (CDA) (D) is a voluntary nonprofit association of local dental societies, to which three quarters of the dentists practicing in California belong. The members of the CDA (D) abide by a Code of Ethics which includes several advertising restrictions. The CDA (D) advised its members on how to comply with these restrictions and advised them on the disclosures they must make when engaging in discount advertising. The FTC (P) brought a complaint against the CDA (D), alleging that it had unreasonably restricted two types of advertising: price advertising, particularly discounted fees, and advertising relating to the quality of dental services. An administrative law judge found a violation of the FTC Act.

ISSUE: Do advertising restrictions arguably protecting patients from misleading or irrelevant advertising regarding professional services where significant challenges exist to informed decisionmaking by customers require more than a cursory review under antitrust law?

HOLDING AND DECISION: (Souter, J.) Yes. Advertising restrictions arguably protecting patients from misleading or irrelevant advertising regarding professional services where significant challenges exist to informed decisionmaking by customers require more than a cursory review under antitrust law. The CDA (D) restrictions are aimed at combatting false advertising in a market characterized by striking disparities between the information available to the professional and the patient. The quality of professional services tends to resist monitoring by individual patients or clients. The cursory review of these restrictions did not examine these unique features of professional services. Reversed and remanded.

EDITOR'S ANALYSIS: *California Dental Ass'n* raises questions about the role of the market in the delivery of healthcare.

NOTES:

CHAPTER 10
REGULATION OF HEALTH CARE FACILITIES AND TRANSACTIONS

QUICK REFERENCE RULES OF LAW

1. **Licensure and Accreditation.** The Department of Health and Human Services must enforce compliance with the Medicaid Act by focusing on patient care. (Estate of Smith v. Heckler)

2. **Licensure and Accreditation.** Where decisions of a private accrediting body are subject to full review by a public official, there is no improper delegation of authority. (Cospito v. Heckler)

3. **Certificate of Need Regulation.** State officials may not disregard at will a federally mandated State Health Plan for the distribution of hospitals. (Statewide Health Coordinating Council v. General Hospitals of Humana, Inc.)

4. **Nonprofit and Public Entities.** An organization incorporated for charitable purposes is impressed with a trust by virtue of the express declaration of the corporation's purposes. (Queen of Angels Hospital v. Younger)

5. **Charitable Tax Exemption.** The term "charitable" is not limited to those organizations that provide relief to the poor. (Eastern Kentucky Welfare Rights Organization v. Simon)

6. **Charitable Tax Exemption.** A hospital may be considered nonprofit and still not be entitled to a tax exemption. (Utah County v. Intermountain Health Care, Inc.)

7. **Charitable Tax Exemption.** A hospital operated almost exclusively for the benefit of a limited group of associated physicians is not operated exclusively for charitable purposes. (Harding Hospital, Inc. v. United States)

8. **The Corporate Practice of Medicine.** The practice of medicine by a profit corporation debases the profession and is unlawful as against public policy. (Bartron v. Codington County)

9. **The Corporate Practice of Medicine.** A hospital is authorized to practice medicine through its physicians and is excepted from the corporate practice of medicine doctrine. (Berlin v. Sarah Bush Lincoln Health Center)

10. **Medical Staff Bylaws.** The medical staff bylaws of a medical center constitute a binding contract. (St. John's Hospital Medical Staff v. St. John Regional Medical Center)

11. **Medical Staff Bylaws.** The medical staff bylaws of a hospital do not trump the Board of Directors' ability to make administrative decisions. (Mahan v. Avera St. Lukes)

12. **Medical Staff Disputes.** A hospital regulation automatically excluding osteopaths fully licensed by the state to practice medicine and otherwise qualified is void as against public policy. (Greisman v. Newcomb Hospital)

13. **Medical Staff Disputes.** Although a hospital need not wait for a disruptive doctor to harm a patient before terminating his or her privileges, more is required than general complaints of a physician's inability to cooperate with others. (Nanavati v. Burdette Tomlin Memorial Hospital)

14. **Membership in Managed Care Networks.** When an insurer who possesses power so substantial that removal from its preferred provider list significantly impairs the ability of an ordinary, competent physician to practice medicine or a medical specialty in a particular geographic area, thereby affecting an important, substantial economic interest, decides to remove a doctor from its preferred provider list, the insurer must comply with the common law right to fair procedure. (Potvin v. Metropolitan Life Ins. Co.)

15. **Medical Staff Boycotts.** The exclusion of osteopaths from a hospital medical staff based on the use of unequal and unreasonable procedures constitutes an illegal group boycott. (Weiss v. York Hospital)

16. **Medical Staff Boycotts.** A boycott that negatively impacts individuals does not violate the antitrust laws unless it harms competition in the overall market. (Hassan v. Independent Practice Associates)

17. **Medical Staff Boycotts.** Advertising restrictions arguably protecting patients from misleading or irrelevant advertising regarding professional services where significant challenges exist to informed decisionmaking by customers require more than a cursory review under antitrust law. (California Dental Ass'n v. Federal Trade Commission)

18. **Price-Fixing Law.** An agreement on maximum fees for specific medical services constitutes a per se antitrust violation. (Arizona v. Maricopa County Medical Society)

19. **Price-Fixing Law.** The practices of an insurance provider that involve contracts with subscribers are exempt from scrutiny under the antitrust laws. (Ocean State Physicians Health Plan, Inc. v. Blue Cross & Blue Shield of Rhode Island)

20. **Antitrust Merger Law.** Courts should refrain from intervening in a competitive situation which may upset the balance of the market in cases where there exists no evidence of barriers constraining normal operation of the market. (Federal Trade Commission v. Tenet Health Care Corp.)

21. **Referral Fee Laws.** A payment to a referring physician, if done to induce future referrals, is illegal even if the payment is compensatory. (United States v. Greber)

22. **Referral Fee Laws.** Where physicians receive limited partnership profit shares under a scheme to knowingly induce referrals to consortium labs, the profit-sharing plan violates § 1128(b)(2) of the Social Security Act. (The Hanlester Network v. Shalala)

ESTATE OF SMITH v. HECKLER

Nursing home patients (P) v. Administrative agency (D)

747 F.2d 583 (10th Cir. 1984).

NATURE OF CASE: Appeal from denial of injunction to compel compliance with federal statute.

FACT SUMMARY: A class of nursing-home patients challenged the Department of Health and Human Services' (D) practice of enforcing compliance with the Medicaid Act by focusing on homes' facilities rather than patient care.

CONCISE RULE OF LAW: The Department of Health and Human Services must enforce compliance with the Medicaid Act by focusing on patient care.

FACTS: A class-action suit was filed on behalf of nursing-home patients residing in Colorado against Heckler (D), the Secretary of Health and Human Services (HHS). In essence, the suit alleged that Heckler (D) was under a duty to enforce compliance with the federal Medicaid Act by considering the quality of care actually provided to patients, rather than by looking only to the facilities offered by such homes. The district court concluded that Heckler (D) was acting consistently with the statute in effecting a "facility-oriented" compliance review and dismissed. An appeal was taken.

ISSUE: Must the Department of Health and Human Services enforce compliance with the Medicaid Act by focusing on patient care?

HOLDING AND DECISION: (McKay, J.) Yes. The Department of Health and Human Services must enforce compliance with the Medicaid Act by focusing on patient care. Nothing in the Medicaid Act indicates that Congress intended the physical facilities to be the end product of the Act. Rather, the Act repeatedly focuses on the care to be provided. For example, the Act provides that health standards are to be developed and maintained and also provides that states must inform the secretary of what methods they use to ensure quality care. In light of this, the Secretary (D) must look to patient care actually rendered. The current review system, as implemented by Heckler (D), which looks to facilities only and, therefore, only the potential of care, is insufficient. Reversed.

EDITOR'S ANALYSIS: The Medicaid Act is found at 42 U.S.C. § 1396. The purpose of the Act is to assist states in providing quality care to the disabled. To receive funding, a state must submit a plan to HHS which meets the Act's requirements. These requirements were at issue here.

COSPITO v. HECKLER

Patients (P) v. Administrative agency (D)

742 F.2d 72 (3d Cir. 1984).

NATURE OF CASE: Appeal from summary judgment that plaintiffs had suffered no unconstitutional loss of federal benefits.

FACT SUMMARY: Cospino (P) and other plaintiffs lost the federally funded benefits they had been receiving as patients of a qualified psychiatric hospital when the hospital lost its certification.

CONCISE RULE OF LAW: Where decisions of a private accrediting body are subject to full review by a public official, there is no improper delegation of authority.

FACTS: Trenton Psychiatric Hospital lost its accreditation from the Joint Commission on Accreditation of Hospitals (JCAH) (D), a corporation formed for the purpose of creating and maintaining standards for hospitals. As a result, Heckler (D), the Secretary of the Department of Health, Education and Welfare, terminated various federally funded benefits contingent on the patients (P) receiving treatment at a qualified psychiatric hospital. The patients (P) argued that the Medicare, Medicaid and Supplemental Social Security Income programs improperly delegated authority to JCAH (D) in derogation of Congress' ultimate responsibility to establish federal policy.

ISSUE: May Congress delegate authority to a private entity to prescribe standards for accreditation if the private organization's decisions are subject to full review by a public official?

HOLDING AND DECISION: (Garth, J.) Yes. Where decisions of a private accrediting body are subject to full review by a public official, there is no improper delegation of authority. The Secretary (D) was empowered to decertify the hospital despite a JCAH (D) decision to grant the hospital accreditation. On the other hand, he could establish lower standards than JCAH (D), certifying the hospital for federal benefits even if it did not meet the JCAH (D) requirements. Congress has provided a "distinct part" survey as a mechanism for allowing the Secretary (D) to independently determine whether a hospital is qualified. There has thus been no real delegation of authority to JCAH (D), and the summary judgment in its favor is affirmed.

EDITOR'S ANALYSIS: The district court granted summary judgment on a different issue, that of procedural due process. Finding that patients had no settled interest in receiving benefits at any particular facility, the court determined that the patients had not been deprived of any protectable property interest.

STATEWIDE HEALTH COORDINATING COUNCIL v. GENERAL HOSPITALS OF HUMANA, INC.

State officials (P) v. Hospital owner (D)

Ark. Sup. Ct., 660 S.W.2d 906 (1983).

NATURE OF CASE: Appeal from circuit court's upholding of state agency's decision to authorize defendant to construct and operate a hospital.

FACT SUMMARY: Humana (D) sought and received a certificate of need from the Arkansas Health Planning and Development Agency to build a 150-bed community hospital.

CONCISE RULE OF LAW: State officials may not disregard at will a federally mandated State Health Plan for the distribution of hospitals.

FACTS: The federal government, in an effort to control rising hospital patient costs, and finding that competition among hospitals actually increased hospital charges, required each state to pass a State Health Plan dividing the state into health service areas and limiting the distribution of hospitals. Desiring to build a new hospital in Arkansas, Humana (D) applied for a certificate of need, the procedure by which the state health agency was empowered to make exceptions to the State Health Plan's limits on the maximum number of hospital beds allocated to an area. The certificate was granted; the Arkansas Social Services Agency independently reviewed and upheld the certificate, and the circuit court affirmed that decision.

ISSUE: May state officials disregard at will a federally mandated State Health Plan for the distribution of hospitals?

HOLDING AND DECISION: (Smith, J.) No. State officials may not disregard at will a federally mandated State Health Plan for the distribution of hospitals. The State Health Plan is not inflexible, and permits the maximum bed limits in an area to be exceeded to meet exceptional conditions. However, no such conditions were found here. Instead, Humana (D) argued that the federal and state efforts to control hospital proliferation were mere guidelines. They are not, and therefore the judgment of the circuit court is reversed.

DISSENT: (Purtle, J.) This is a case of overregulation. Competition will drive the cost of hospitalization down, not up. Furthermore, human lives may be at stake; acutely ill persons in north Pulaski County may not survive the trip to other area hospitals.

EDITOR'S ANALYSIS: Certificate-of-need laws have apparently had little impact on hospital patient costs. One problem is that they control entry to the market, but not pricing. Savings from the regulations limiting the number of beds in an area are simply moved to operating expenses, such as the purchase of new services and equipment. The costs are then passed to the consumer as always.

NOTES:

QUEEN OF ANGELS HOSPITAL v. YOUNGER

Hospital (P) v. State attorney general (D)
Cal. Sup. Ct., 136 Cal. Rptr. 36 (1977).

NATURE OF CASE: Appeal from declaratory relief action against attorney general to determine validity of lease agreement.

FACT SUMMARY: Queen of Angels Hospital (P) leased its hospital, excepting an outpatient clinic and convent house, with the intention of establishing additional outpatient clinics.

CONCISE RULE OF LAW: An organization incorporated for charitable purposes is impressed with a trust by virtue of the express declaration of the corporation's purposes.

FACTS: Queen (P), a hospital founded in connection with the Catholic Church, operated an outpatient clinic within the hospital. It subsequently leased the hospital to another service provider, except for the outpatient clinic and a convent house. Queen (P) intended to use the lease proceeds to establish and operate additional outpatient clinics to dispense free medical care, and aid and advice to the needy. It filed a declaratory relief action against Younger (D), the state attorney general, to declare the lease valid, which the lower court did.

ISSUE: May a corporation incorporated as a charitable organization for tax purposes cease to perform the charitable purpose for which it was created?

HOLDING AND DECISION: (Kaus, J.) No. An organization incorporated for charitable purposes is impressed with a trust by virtue of the express declaration of the corporation's purposes. Queen (P), in its articles of incorporation and in a statement to the Franchise Tax Board, has stated that it is in the business of running a hospital. It is not disputed that an outpatient clinic is not functionally equivalent to a hospital. Nor is it disputed that an outpatient clinic to serve the poor serves a worthy purpose. The question is not whether Queen (P) can divert some of its assets to purposes other than the operation of a hospital, but whether it can abandon the hospital business altogether, thereby ceasing to perform the charitable function for which it was expressly created. It may not do so and retain control over its assets. Reversed.

EDITOR'S ANALYSIS: The doctrine of ultra vires was held to bind Queen (P) to the charitable purpose for which it was created. However, it was not required to do so if running a hospital would result in its financial ruin. The rule of cy pres—as near as possible—would permit Queen (P) to pursue charitable purposes of the same general type when the original purpose was impossible or highly impractical.

NOTES:

EASTERN KENTUCKY WELFARE RIGHTS ORGANIZATION v. SIMON

Health and welfare organization v. Tax commissioner (D)
506 F.2d 1278 (D.C. Cir. 1974).

NATURE OF CASE: Appeal from determination that regulation broadening definition of charitable organizations was valid.

FACT SUMMARY: Eastern Kentucky Welfare Rights Organization (P) challenged an IRS (D) ruling that made it easier for nonprofit hospitals to qualify as charitable organizations for tax purposes.

CONCISE RULE OF LAW: The term "charitable" is not limited to those organizations that provide relief to the poor.

FACTS: The IRS (D) had long held that hospitals could only qualify as tax-exempt charitable organizations under IRS Code § 501(c)(3) if they provided services to those unable to pay to the extent of the hospital's financial ability. In 1969, the IRS (D) issued Revenue Ruling 69-545, defining charitable in terms of "community benefit" and stating that the provision of health care benefited the entire community, even if those unable to pay for hospital services received no direct benefit. Under the new definition, a nonprofit hospital could qualify as charitable by keeping its emergency room open to all, regardless of ability to pay, and by admitting any person able to pay, either directly or through third party reimbursement. Eastern Kentucky Welfare Rights Organization (P) sued to declare Ruling 69-545 invalid and to enjoin its implementation. The district court refused to invalidate the Ruling, and the Organization (P) appealed.

ISSUE: Is the term "charitable," for tax purposes, properly limited to those organizations that provide no-cost or low-cost services to the poor?

HOLDING AND DECISION: (Jameson, J.) No. The term "charitable" is not limited to those organizations that provide relief to the poor. Such a definition fails to recognize the changing economic, social, and technological precepts and values of contemporary society. Hospitals no longer, as once they did, serve almost exclusively the sick poor. The introduction of Medicare and Medicaid has greatly reduced the number of people requiring free or below-cost services. Thus the rationale on which the definition of "charitable organizations" was originally predicated has largely disappeared. Furthermore, the new regulation requires that hospitals wishing to qualify as charitable must provide emergency room services to all, regardless of ability to pay. This is a service of great importance to the indigent. Affirmed.

EDITOR'S ANALYSIS: The charitable tax exemption is of great importance to hospitals. They generally own considerable real estate subject to property tax and often generate millions of dollars in revenues that would otherwise be subject to state and federal corporate income tax. Furthermore, tax-exempt hospitals can take advantage of tax-exempt bond financing and are eligible to receive tax-deductible gifts. The value of hospital tax exemptions has been estimated to be as much as $8 billion.

QUICKNOTES

IRS CODE § 501 - Exempts from federal income tax corporations operated exclusively for charitable purposes.

NOTES:

UTAH COUNTY v. INTERMOUNTAIN HEALTH CARE, INC.

County (P) v. Hospital operator (D)

Utah Sup. Ct., 709 P.2d 265 (1985).

NATURE OF CASE: Appeal of granting of tax exemption.

FACT SUMMARY: Utah County (P) contended that Intermountain Health Care (D), operating two nonprofit hospitals, was not entitled to tax-exempt status.

CONCISE RULE OF LAW: A hospital may be considered nonprofit and still not be entitled to a tax exemption.

FACTS: Intermountain Health Care (D) operated two hospitals, which were classified as nonprofit. The hospitals were funded almost exclusively through insurance, government assistance, and fees; very little income came from gifts. Income exceeded expenses, and free services amounted to less than 1% of revenues. Employees of the hospitals worked on a voluntary basis, but the hospitals used the services of numerous paid contractors. The Utah County (P) Board of Equalization denied IHC (D) tax-exempt status. The State Tax Commission reversed, and Utah County (P) appealed.

ISSUE: May a hospital be considered nonprofit and still not be entitled to a tax exemption?

HOLDING AND DECISION: (Durham, J.) Yes. A hospital may be considered nonprofit and still not be entitled to a tax exemption. Under the Utah constitution, an entity is entitled to a property tax exemption only if it is a charitable institution. Whether an institution is charitable does not depend on a nonprofit nomenclature. Rather, the workings of the institution must be analyzed against the standard of what constitutes a charitable institution. Factors include (1) whether the entity provides services without expectation of material reward, (2) the extent to which it is supported by donations, (3) the extent to which recipients are expected to pay for services, (4) whether income exceeds expenses, (5) restrictions upon beneficiaries, and (6) whether financial benefits are available to those involved. Here, free services accounted for less than 1% of the hospitals' revenues, only a small amount of revenue came from donations, patients were charged, income exceeded expenses, indigents were discouraged from seeking treatment, and although employees were unpaid, contractors (who often were also employees) were often utilized. In light of these considerations, charitable status appeared inappropriate. Reversed.

DISSENT: (Stewart, J.) The legal concept of charity does not require that an institution incur a deficit. As the evidence shows that not one cent of revenues went toward paying employees, officers, or directors, the hospitals should be entitled to tax-exempt status.

EDITOR'S ANALYSIS: In years past, most hospitals were charitable in that they were affiliated with a church or philanthropic organization and were money-losers. In the twentieth century, for-profit hospitals became the norm. While still having indicia of charitable institutions, they are run like businesses. Where charity ends and business begins is not always clear.

NOTES:

HARDING HOSPITAL, INC. v. UNITED STATES
Hospital (P) v. Federal government (D)
505 F.2d 1068 (6th Cir. 1974).

NATURE OF CASE: Appeal from district court determination that plaintiff did not qualify as charitable organization for tax purposes.

FACT SUMMARY: Harding Hospital (P), a psychiatric institution, sought tax-exempt status under I.R.S. Code § 501(c)(3) as a charitable organization.

CONCISE RULE OF LAW: A hospital operated almost exclusively for the benefit of a limited group of associated physicians is not operated exclusively for charitable purposes.

FACTS: The Harding Hospital (P), an Ohio corporation originally incorporated as a for-profit corporation, then as a non-profit organization, entered into contracts with the Harding-Evans Medical Associates. The Associates, a partnership of seven doctors, treated 90 to 95% of the Hospital's (P) patients, in return for an annual payment. The Associates paid the Hospital (P) rent for office space, equipment and office services. In 1968, the rent was reduced to a point well below the appraised value of the office space alone. It argued, unsuccessfully, that it should be entitled to tax exemptions under § 501(c)(3) of the Code, which exempts charitable organizations.

ISSUE: May a hospital operated almost exclusively for the financial benefit of a limited group of physicians qualify as a charitable organization for tax purposes?

HOLDING AND DECISION: (Phillips, J.) No. A hospital operated almost exclusively for the benefit of a limited group of associated physicians is not operated exclusively for charitable purposes, and therefore does not meet the requirements of I.R.S. Code § 501(c)(3). Harding Hospital (P) treated almost exclusively paying patients. The Associates enjoyed a virtual monopoly on the treatment of patients at the Hospital (P). The Associates also benefited from the payment of the Hospital (P) for their services, and from the reduced rate charged by the Hospital (P) for office space and services. I.R.S. Code § 501(a) requires that a corporation may only qualify as charitable for tax purposes if no part of its net earnings benefits a private individual. Such is not the case here. Affirmed.

EDITOR'S ANALYSIS: The court stated that several factors, none of which was crucial to its holding, when taken together indicated that Harding's (P) relationship with the Associates had seriously compromised its status as a charitable organization. Rather than laying down a general rule to be followed in such cases, the court leaned in the direction of a case-by-case, fact-driven approach to determining when a hospital was operated primarily for the private benefit of its physicians rather than for charitable purposes.

NOTES:

BARTRON v. CODINGTON COUNTY
Clinic (P) v. County (D)
S.D. Sup. Ct., 2 N.W.2d 337 (1942).

NOTES:

NATURE OF CASE: Appeal from determination that it is unlawful for a corporation to practice medicine.

FACT SUMMARY: The Bartron Clinic (P), a corporation formed for profit, operated a hospital and clinic, and employed doctors, nurses, and other duly licensed persons.

CONCISE RULE OF LAW: The practice of medicine by a profit corporation debases the profession and is unlawful as against public policy.

FACTS: The Bartron Clinic (P), a for-profit corporation, contracted with Codington County (D) to provide medical and surgical services as well as medicines to indigent residents of the county. The County (D) refused to pay a bill for medicines provided by Bartron (P) to the county indigent. All services, except for a small item provided by an intern, were provided by licensed physicians; and all medicines were prescribed by doctors, pursuant to the directions and orders of the county commissioners. Bartron (P) brought suit, but the court refused to enforce the contracts. Barton (P) appealed.

ISSUE: May a profit corporation engage in the practice of medicine?

HOLDING AND DECISION: (Smith, J.) No. The practice of medicine by a profit corporation debases the profession and is unlawful as against public policy. Although the trial court found the Bartron Clinic (P) innocent of any unethical intention or practice, we are concerned with the tendency of the challenged practice. That tendency, it seems, is toward an undue emphasis on making money, and commercial exploitation of professional services. Insofar as the contracts between Bartron (P) and the County (D) dealt with professional services, they were illegal and unenforceable. Affirmed.

EDITOR'S ANALYSIS: A basis for the corporate practice of medicine doctrine, which forbids corporations to have any connection with medical activities, has been found in the Medical Practice Act and in public policy. The two bases are rarely distinguished; however, the *Bartron* court drew the distinction, finding the literal terms of the Act insufficient for a corporate practice challenge. Instead, the court relied heavily on the common law public policy argument.

BERLIN v. SARAH BUSH LINCOLN HEALTH CENTER

Physician (P) v. Hospital (D)

Ill. Sup. Ct., 688 N.E.2d 106 (1997).

NATURE OF CASE: Appeal from summary judgment in favor of plaintiff in action to invalidate employment agreement.

FACT SUMMARY: Berlin (P) left the Sarah Bush Lincoln Health Center (D) to practice elsewhere, and alleged that his employment agreement with the Health Center (D), which contained a covenant not to compete nearby, was unenforceable.

CONCISE RULE OF LAW: A hospital is authorized to practice medicine through its physicians and is excepted from the corporate practice of medicine doctrine.

FACTS: Berlin (P) and the Health Center (D) entered into a written agreement for Berlin (P) to practice medicine for the hospital for five years. The agreement contained a restrictive covenant barring Berlin (P) from providing health services within fifty miles of the Health Center (D) for two years after the end of the agreement. Berlin (P) resigned less than two years after signing the agreement, and accepted employment immediately at a clinic located approximately one mile from the Health Center. The court determined that the Health Center (D), by hiring Berlin (P) to practice medicine, had violated the prohibition against corporations practicing medicine. Therefore it found the entire employment agreement unenforceable. The Health Center (D) appealed.

ISSUE: Is a hospital barred from practicing medicine because of its corporate status, rendering employment agreements with its staff physicians unenforceable?

HOLDING AND DECISION: (Nickles, J.) No. A hospital is authorized to practice medicine through its physicians and is excepted from the corporate practice of medicine doctrine. The rationale underlying the doctrine is that a corporation, unable to meet the educational and character screening requirements of the profession, cannot obtain a license to practice and therefore cannot practice medicine. However, numerous jurisdictions have found exceptions to the doctrine, allowing hospital corporations to employ physicians. The hospital licensing statutes clearly authorize, and at times require, licensed hospitals to provide medical services. Further, the Medical Practice Act, from which the corporate practice of medicine doctrine is inferred, contains no express prohibition on the corporate employment of physicians by hospitals. The employment agreement is therefore valid, and the judgment for Berlin (P) is reversed.

DISSENT: (Harrison, J.) The most that can be said of the hospital licensing statutes is that they authorize hospitals to operate facilities for the diagnosis and care of patients. They do not authorize hospitals to employ physicians directly; it is presumed that they will staff their facilities by granting staff privileges to licensed private physicians.

EDITOR'S ANALYSIS: Other rationales were mentioned in the Berlin decision as excepting hospitals from the corporate practice of medicine doctrine. One was the viewpoint that hospitals do not practice medicine, but merely make it available; another, that the public policy arguments supporting the doctrine ought not apply to nonprofit hospitals and health associations.

NOTES:

ST. JOHN'S HOSPITAL MEDICAL STAFF v. ST. JOHN REGIONAL MEDICAL CENTER

Hospital staff (P) v. Hospital (D)
S.D. Ct. App., 245 N.W.2d 472 (1976).

NATURE OF CASE: Appeal from dismissal of complaint seeking declaratory and injunctive relief.

FACT SUMMARY: St. John Regional Medical Center (D) unilaterally amended medical staff bylaws and attempted to bind the medical staff (P) to the new bylaws.

CONCISE RULE OF LAW: The medical staff bylaws of a medical center constitute a binding contract.

FACTS: St. John's Hospital Medical Staff (P) is an unincorporated association whose members hold medical staff privileges at the St. John Regional Medical Center (D) in South Dakota. In October 1947, the Sisters of the Franciscan Order proposed certain medical staff bylaws to regulate the affairs of the physicians using the hospital. According to the terms of these bylaws, they could be amended only if the amendment was agreed to by both medical staff (P) and the hospital (D). In 1972, the hospital (D) wished to amend the medical staff bylaws. The attempted changes were unacceptable to the medical staff (P), leading to an impasse in negotiations. Despite this breakdown, the board of directors of the hospital (D) moved ahead and unilaterally adopted the amended bylaws disapproved of by the medical staff (P). The hospital (D) then attempted to bind the medical staff (P). The medical staff (P) objected.

ISSUE: Do the medical staff bylaws of a medical center constitute a binding contract?

HOLDING AND DECISION: [Judge not stated in casebook excerpt.] Yes. The medical staff bylaws of a medical center constitute a binding contract. The bylaws of a corporation constitute a binding contract between the corporation and its shareholders. In this case, the 1947 medical staff bylaws of St. John (D) constitute a contract which is, by its express terms, subject to amendment when amendment is agreed to by both the medical staff (P) and the hospital (D). The medical center (D) thus is bound by the provisions in these bylaws. By amending the bylaws without medical staff (P) consent, the medical center (D) breached its contractual relationship with the staff (P).

EDITOR'S ANALYSIS: Many courts have agreed with the decision in *St. John's* that medical staff bylaws constitute a contract and cannot be amended or ignored unilaterally by the hospital board.

NOTES:

MAHAN v. AVERA ST. LUKES

Physician (P) v. Medical center (D)

S.D. Ct. App., 621 N.W.2d 150 (2001).

NATURE OF CASE: Appeal from finding of breach of contract.

FACT SUMMARY: The circuit court found that Avera St. Lukes (ASL) (D) did not have the right to initiate actions that affect the privileges of medical staff such as Dr. Mahan (P) where they had previously delegated this authority.

CONCISE RULE OF LAW: The medical staff bylaws of a hospital do not trump the Board of Directors' ability to make administrative decisions.

FACTS: Avera St. Luke's (ASL) (D) is part of a regional health care system sponsored by the Sisters of the Presentation of the Blessed Virgin Mary of Aberdeen, South Dakota. Since 1901, the Presentation Sisters have provided quality health services to the Aberdeen community. In mid-1996, ASL's (D) neurosurgeon left Aberdeen. During the process of recruiting his replacement, ASL (D) learned that most neurosurgeon applicants would not be interested in coming to Aberdeen if there was already an orthopedic surgeon practicing in the area. ASL (D) successfully recruited a neurosurgeon in December of 1996. Around this time, ASL (D) learned that OSS (P), a group of Aberdeen orthopedic surgeons, had decided to build a day surgery center that would directly compete with ASL (D). During the first seven months that OSS' (P) surgery center was open, ASL (D) suffered a 1000 hour loss of operating room usage. In response, ASL (D) closed ASL's (D) medical staff with respect to physicians requesting privileges for spine surgery, and closed its medical staff to applicants for orthopedic surgery privileges. In the summer of 1998, OSS (P) recruited Dr. Mahan (P), a spine-fellowship trained orthopedic surgeon engaged in the practice of orthopedic surgery. Mahan (P) applied for staff privileges at ASL (D) but was denied. Mahan (P) and OSS (P) commenced this action against ASL (D), challenging the Board's decision to close the staff. The circuit court determined that ASL (D) breached the Staff Bylaws which delegated power regarding medical staff issues by closing the staff without first consulting the staff. ASL (D) appealed.

ISSUE: Does a delegation of authority in medical staff bylaws concerning staff privileges trump a hospital Board's authority to make business decisions relating to staff privileges?

HOLDING AND DECISION: [Judge not stated in casebook excerpt.] No. The medical staff bylaws of a hospital do not trump the Board of Directors' ability to make administrative decisions. This is not a case concerning issues delegated to the expertise of medical staff concerning appointments and privileges. Rather, it was an adminisitrative decision by ASL's (D) Board to close ASL's (D) staff for certain procedures to ensure ASL's (D)

economic survival. Allowing the medical staff to pass upon valid business decisions by the Board as to any issue that incidentally affects the medical staff would render the Board ineffectual. Hospitals have a duty of responsibility with regards to hiring competent physicians. To impose this duty and leave hospital boards powerless to make any decisions regarding medical staff as the lower court suggests would lead to illogical results.

EDITOR'S ANALYSIS: Despite the arguments made in *Mahan* that hospital boards should not just act as a rubber stamp in approving physicians for staff privileges that are approved or recommended by staff, this is how most hospitals actually function.

NOTES:

GREISMAN v. NEWCOMB HOSPITAL
Osteopath (P) v. Hospital (D)
N.J. Sup. Ct., 192 A.2d 817 (1963).

NATURE OF CASE: Appeal from determination that plaintiff was entitled to consideration of his application for admission to defendant's courtesy staff.

FACT SUMMARY: Greisman (P), a doctor of osteopathic medicine, was rejected by Newcomb Hospital (D) because of a hospital bylaw requiring courtesy staff applicants to have graduated from an American Medical Association-approved medical school.

CONCISE RULE OF LAW: A hospital regulation automatically excluding osteopaths fully licensed by the state to practice medicine and otherwise qualified is void as against public policy.

FACTS: Greisman (P) possessed an unqualified license to practice medicine in New Jersey. He applied for application to Newcomb's (D) courtesy staff, but his application was rejected without consideration. The rejection was based on a hospital bylaw requiring applicants to have graduated form a medical school approved by the American Medical Association. On appeal, Newcomb (D) contended that as a private hospital, its staff admission policies were entirely discretionary.

ISSUE: May a hospital lawfully enforce a regulation excluding osteopaths otherwise fully qualified from admission to the medical staff?

HOLDING AND DECISION: (Jacobs, J.) No. A hospital regulation automatically excluding osteopaths fully licensed by the state to practice medicine and otherwise qualified is void as against public policy. The courts have long recognized the need for judicial regulation of private businesses and professions that serve the common good. Such approaches have been used in the case of railroads, insurance, the milk industry, and other businesses. Certainly the services provided by Newcomb (D) are no less dedicated to the public good. The public interest and issues of fairness require that Newcomb (D) consider Greisman's (P) application, to determine whether admitting him to the staff would best serve the needs of the hospital and the community.

EDITOR'S ANALYSIS: Note that *Greisman* was not decided on constitutional due process or equal protection grounds, but on a common law fairness theory, based on the quasi-public nature of private hospitals. Only public hospitals have been subject to regulation under the constitutional due process clause. It is unclear how far this common law doctrine extends; the courts have not yet addressed such issues as whether private hospitals owe duties of fairness to employed physicians or whether such duties extend to patients.

QUICKNOTES

OSTEOPATH - A physician who specializes in the practice of medicine emphasizing the interrelationship between the musculoskeletal system and the rest of the body.

NOTES:

NANAVATI v. BURDETTE TOMLIN MEMORIAL HOSPITAL
Dismissed cardiologist (P) v. Hospital (D)
N.J. Sup. Ct., 526 A.2d 697 (1987).

NATURE OF CASE: On petition for certification to determine whether actual interference with patient care is required to terminate a physician's staff privileges.

FACT SUMMARY: Dr. Nanavati (P), a cardiologist on the staff of Burdette Tomlin Memorial Hospital (D), became embroiled in a dispute with the chief cardiologist at Burdette (D), leading to his dismissal.

CONCISE RULE OF LAW: Although a hospital need not wait for a disruptive doctor to harm a patient before terminating his or her privileges, more is required than general complaints of a physician's inability to cooperate with others.

FACTS: Dr. Sorensen, the chief cardiologist at Burdette (D), enjoyed a virtual monopoly on the lucrative practice of reading electrocardiograms (EKGs) at Burdette (D). Dr. Nanavati (P) was allowed to read EKGs one day a week, but when he requested an additional day, Dr. Sorensen refused his request. A feud between the doctors began and escalated. After Nanavati (P) allegedly violated a Hospital (D) bylaw requiring a staff doctor to "be of a temperament and disposition that will enable him to work in harmony with his colleagues on the Medical Staff," the hospital executive committee voted to revoke his staff privileges.

ISSUE: May a hospital terminate a staff doctor solely on the basis of the doctor's disruption of the harmonious work relationship with other hospital staff?

HOLDING AND DECISION: (Pollock, J.) Yes. A hospital may terminate a doctor for disrupting the harmonious work relationship with other staff. Although a hospital need not wait for a disruptive doctor to harm a patient before terminating his or her privileges, more is required than general complaints of a physician's inability to cooperate with others. If a hospital is to care for its patients, the staff must work together. A bylaw providing that the inability of a doctor to work with other doctors or nurses is grounds for terminating staff privileges is therefore lawful. Such termination should take place only upon the presentation of concrete evidence of specific instances of misbehavior likely to adversely affect health care delivery. The judgment is affirmed as modified and the cause is remanded to the Hospital (D).

EDITOR'S ANALYSIS: The courts have frequently stated that the selection and retention of doctors should be a matter left to hospital boards, subject to minimal judicial review. The rationale is that human lives are at stake, and that the professional skill of doctors is better evaluated by their peers. By requiring that the Burdette Hospital (D) present concrete evidence of specific instances of disruptive behavior, is the court appears to be involved on a substantive level, rather than merely requiring procedural fairness.

NOTES:

POTVIN v. METROPOLITAN LIFE INS. CO.
Physician (P) v. Managed care organization (D)
Cal. Sup. Ct., 997 P.2d 1153 (2000).

NATURE OF CASE: Appeal from summary judgment for defendant.

FACT SUMMARY: Potvin (P) sued MetLife (D) when his name was removed from the list of preferred provider physicians.

CONCISE RULE OF LAW: When an insurer who possesses power so substantial that removal from its preferred provider list significantly impairs the ability of an ordinary, competent physician to practice medicine or a medical specialty in a particular geographic area, thereby affecting an important, substantial economic interest, decides to remove a doctor from its preferred provider list, the insurer must comply with the common law right to fair procedure.

FACTS: Potvin (P), an obstetrician and gynecologist, had practiced medicine for over 35 years when he contracted with MetLife (D) to be placed on its list of preferred providers. MetLife (D) later terminated Potvin's (P) preferred provider status without cause. When Potvin (P) insisted on an explanation, he was told that he did not meet their standard for malpractice history because he had been sued four times for malpractice. After MetLife (D) refused to respond to Potvin's (P) request for a hearing, Potvin (P) filed a complaint alleging violation of the common law right to fair procedure. The district court granted MetLife's (D) motion for summary judgment, but the appellate court reversed. MetLife (D) appealed to the state Supreme Court for review.

ISSUE: When an insurer who possesses power so substantial that removal from its preferred provider list significantly impairs the ability of an ordinary, competent physician to practice medicine or a medical specialty in a particular geographic area, thereby affecting an important, substantial economic interest, decides to remove a doctor from its preferred provider list, must the insurer comply with the common law right to fair procedure?

HOLDING AND DECISION: (Kennard, J.) Yes. When an insurer who possesses power so substantial that removal from its preferred provider list significantly impairs the ability of an ordinary, competent physician to practice medicine or a medical specialty in a particular geographic area, thereby affecting an important, substantial economic interest, decides to remove a doctor from its preferred provider list, the insurer must comply with the common law right to fair procedure. Potvin (P) alleged that the adverse effects of removal from MetLife's (D) preferred provider lists included rejection by physician groups and devastation of his practice. The "without cause" termination clause in the contract was unenforceable to the extent it purported to limit an otherwise existing right to fair procedure under the common law. Affirmed.

DISSENT: (Brown, J.) The standard announced today is unworkable because it will be unpredictable. The standard purports to draw distinctions based on an insurer's share of the market in a particular geographic area which would lead to uncertain results. The "without cause" termination provision should be enforced because there was no showing of bad faith.

EDITOR'S ANALYSIS: The dissent argued that the court was concerned with maintaining the physician's guaranteed minimum income. MetLife (D) would not include physicians who had more than two malpractice lawsuits on its preferred provider lists. The American Medical Association and the California Medical Association were amici curiae for Potvin (P) in this matter.

QUICKNOTES

AMICUS CURIAE - A third party, not implicated in the suit, which seeks to file a brief containing information for the court's consideration in conformity with its position.

COMMON LAW - A body of law developed through the judicial decisions of the courts as opposed to the legislative process.

FIDUCIARY - Person holding a legal obligation to act for the benefit of another.

FUNDAMENTAL RIGHT - A liberty that is either expressly or impliedly provided for in the United States Constitution, the deprivation or burdening of which is subject to a heightened standard of review.

NOTES:

WEISS v. YORK HOSPITAL
Osteopath (P) v. Hospital (D)
745 F.2d 786 (3d Cir. 1984).

NATURE OF CASE: Antitrust lawsuit claiming exclusion from defendant's medical staff violated the Sherman Act.

FACT SUMMARY: Weiss (P), an osteopath, applied for staff privileges at York Hospital (D), which had formerly admitted only allopaths (M.D.s); his application was considered and denied.

CONCISE RULE OF LAW: The exclusion of osteopaths from a hospital medical staff based on the use of unequal and unreasonable procedures constitutes an illegal group boycott.

FACTS: Weiss (P) and another osteopath applied for staff privileges at York (D). Weiss (P) informed York (D) staff representatives that if York (D) excluded him because of is osteopathic status, he would institute legal action. York (D) considered the applications of the two osteopaths, but did not initially approve either one. Instead, it took the step, never before taken by York (D), of making extensive inquiries regarding the professional competence and moral character of the applicants. The investigation turned up some evidence, apparently hearsay, about Weiss's (P) competence. On that basis, his application was denied; the application of the other osteopath was approved. He then brought a class action suit against York (D). The district court found that the medical staff violated Sherman Act § 1. An appeal followed.

ISSUE: May a hospital exclude osteopaths from its medical staff by applying unequal procedures in considering the applications of osteopaths for staff privileges?

HOLDING AND DECISION: (Becker, J.) No. The exclusion of osteopaths from a hospital medical staff based on the use of unequal and unreasonable procedures constitutes an illegal group boycott. The actions of the doctors on the committee that rejected Dr. Weiss's (P) application may be analogized to the classic "concerted refusal to deal." In the traditional retail context, a retailer may use the threat, implicit or explicit, of not dealing with a supplier or customer unless the supplier or customer does not deal with the retailer's competitors. Because York (D) admitted other osteopaths, the analogy is not perfect. However, the second-class treatment given osteopaths applying for staff privileges would seem to adversely impact or discourage such applicants, and thereby constitute a per se antitrust violation, the conspiracy requirement having also been met. The judgment of the district court for Weiss (P) is affirmed.

EDITOR'S ANALYSIS: The Supreme Court has adopted an exception to application of the per se rule of illegal boycotts where the case involves a "learned profession," such as medicine, and the boycott is justified on the grounds of public service or ethical norms. However, York (D) did not raise any defenses based on public service or ethics, so the exception did not apply.

QUICKNOTES

SHERMAN ACT - Prohibits a contract, combination, or conspiracy in restraint of trade and having an dffect on interstate commerce.

NOTES:

HASSAN v. INDEPENDENT PRACTICE ASSOCIATES

Allergists (P) v. Physicians group (D)
698 F. Supp. 679 (E.D. Mich. 1988).

NATURE OF CASE: Motion for summary judgment by HMO-affiliated physicians group accused of illegally boycotting plaintiffs.

FACT SUMMARY: Doctors Shawky Hassan (P) and Fikria Hassan (P), allergists, were associated with Independent Practice Associates (D) until their membership in the group was terminated.

CONCISE RULE OF LAW: A boycott that negatively impacts individuals does not violate the antitrust laws unless it harms competition in the overall market.

FACTS: The Hassans (P) were member doctors of IPA (D), an organization whose sole purpose was to provide care to customers of Health Plus, a health maintenance organization. Billing records revealed a high incidence of lab tests by the Hassans (P). A review of patient charts failed to satisfy the IPA (D) that the level of testing was justified. Health Plus sent out a notice that subscribers could no longer see the Hassans (P), and IPA (D) subsequently denied the Hassans' (P) request to provide emergency care to IPA (D) members in their new clinic. The Hassans (P) sued, charging that IPA (D) had engaged in an illegal group boycott. IPA (D) moved for summary judgment.

ISSUE: Does a boycott that negatively impacts individuals violate the antitrust laws if it does not affect competition in the overall market?

HOLDING AND DECISION: (Newblatt, J.) No. A boycott that negatively impacts individuals does not violate the antitrust laws unless it harms competition in the overall market. The antitrust laws were not intended to protect individual competitors. There is no evidence to show that IPA (D) had significant market power, nor that the Hassans' (P) exclusion from IPA (D) had an impact on market competition. IPA's (D) motion for summary judgment is granted.

EDITOR'S ANALYSIS: Although the Hassans (P) lost, the court acknowledged that the rule of reason, long used to determine whether hospital exclusion of staff physicians constituted an illegal boycott, applied equally to similar actions by insurers and managed care organizations.

CALIFORNIA DENTAL ASS'N v. FEDERAL TRADE COMMISSION

Nonprofit association of dentists (D) v. Federal agency (P)
526 U.S. 756 (1999).

NATURE OF CASE: Appeal from an ALJ finding of an FTC violation.

FACT SUMMARY: The Federal Trade Commission (P) brought an FTC action against the California Dental Ass'n (D) based upon a Code of Ethics provision. An administrative law judge found a violation of the FTC Act.

CONCISE RULE OF LAW: Advertising restrictions arguably protecting patients from misleading or irrelevant advertising regarding professional services where significant challenges exist to informed decisionmaking by customers require more than a cursory review under antitrust law.

FACTS: The California Dental Association (CDA) (D) is a voluntary nonprofit association of local dental societies, to which three quarters of the dentists practicing in California belong. The members of the CDA (D) abide by a Code of Ethics which includes several advertising restrictions. The CDA (D) advised its members on how to comply with these restrictions and advised them on the disclosures they must make when engaging in discount advertising. The FTC (P) brought a complaint against the CDA (D), alleging that it had unreasonably restricted two types of advertising: price advertising, particularly discounted fees, and advertising relating to the quality of dental services. An administrative law judge found a violation of the FTC Act.

ISSUE: Do advertising restrictions arguably protecting patients from misleading or irrelevant advertising regarding professional services where significant challenges exist to informed decisionmaking by customers require more than a cursory review under antitrust law?

HOLDING AND DECISION: (Souter, J.) Yes. Advertising restrictions arguably protecting patients from misleading or irrelevant advertising regarding professional services where significant challenges exist to informed decisionmaking by customers require more than a cursory review under antitrust law. The CDA (D) restrictions are aimed at combating false advertising in a market characterized by striking disparities between the information available to the professional and the patient. The quality of professional services tends to resist monitoring by individual patients or clients. The cursory review of these restrictions did not examine these unique features of professional services. Reversed and remanded.

EDITOR'S ANALYSIS: *California Dental Ass'n* raises questions about the role of the market in the delivery of healthcare.

ARIZONA v. MARICOPA COUNTY MEDICAL SOCIETY

State (P) v. Medical societies (D) and foundations (D)
457 U.S. 332 (1982).

NATURE OF CASE: Appeal from denial of summary judgment in action challenging a medical fee schedule.

FACT SUMMARY: An agreement on maximum fees for specific medical services was challenged as a per se antitrust violation.

CONCISE RULE OF LAW: An agreement on maximum fees for specific medical services constitutes a per se antitrust violation.

FACTS: The Maricopa Foundation for Medical Care (D) was an Arizona corporation composed of doctors engaging in private practice. About 70% of Maricopa County's doctors were members. The Pima Foundation (D) was a similar corporation consisting of 400 doctors. Each organization had adopted a schedule of fees imposing a maximum amount that member doctors could charge. This practice was challenged by the State of Arizona (P) as price-fixing in violation of the Sherman Act. This district court, declining to apply a per se rule of illegality , denied Arizona's (P) motion for summary adjudication. The Ninth Circuit affirmed, and the Supreme Court granted review.

ISSUE: Does an agreement on maximum fees for specific medical services constitute a per se antitrust violation?

HOLDING AND DECISION: (Stevens, J.) Yes. An agreement on maximum fees for specific services constitutes a per se antitrust violation. Most actions in restraint of trade are subject to a "rule of reason" requiring extensive inquiry into their purposes and effects. However, some categories of restraint have been deemed so inherently anticompetitive that a per se rule of illegality applies. Horizontal price-fixing is one such category. Here, horizontal price-fixing is what is being effected, so the per se rule would at first glance appear applicable. However, Maricopa (D) and Pima (D) argued that an agreement to fix maximum rather than minimum prices is not anticompetitive. This is not true. Price ceilings and price floors may have different economic consequences, but price ceilings still have anticompetitive effects, as they may severely intrude upon the ability of competitors to survive in the market. Maricopa (D) and Pima (D) also argued that the health care field should not be included in the per se rule. This Court is unconvinced. The economic analysis for the medical profession is essentially the same as for business in general. For these reasons, the courts below were incorrect in failing to apply the per se rule. Reversed.

DISSENT: (Powell, J.) The term "price-fixing" is not to be applied in a talismanic fashion to every agreement restricting prices. The system here appears to benefit consumers and should be analyzed under the rule of reason.

EDITOR'S ANALYSIS: At first glance, price ceilings do not have the sinister, conspiratorial air that price floors do. However, price ceilings can have anticompetitive effects which in the long run will harm consumers. Generally speaking, restrictions on price lead to decreases in supply, which in turn lead to shortages, which certainly don't help the public.

QUICKNOTES

PER SE ANTITRUST VIOLATION - Business transactions that in themselves constitute restraints on trade, obviating the need to demonstrate an injury to competition in making out an antitrust case.

NOTES:

OCEAN STATE PHYSICIANS HEALTH PLAN, INC. v. BLUE CROSS & BLUE SHIELD OF RHODE ISLAND

Health maintenance organization (P) v. Insurer (D)
883 F.2d 1101 (1st Cir.1989).

NATURE OF CASE: Appeal from judgment n.o.v. that was exempt from antitrust laws.

FACT SUMMARY: Ocean State (P) alleged that Blue Cross (D) violated the Sherman Act by programs and policies designed to create a monopoly.

CONCISE RULE OF LAW: The practices of an insurance provider that involve contracts with subscribers are exempt from scrutiny under the antitrust laws.

FACTS: Blue Cross (D) has long been the largest health insurer in Rhode Island. Ocean State (P), an HMO, captured many of Blue Cross's (D) subscribers by providing more coverage and lower premiums. Blue Cross (D) responded by launching its own HMO, HealthMate, offering benefits and prices similar to Ocean State (P). It then instituted a policy by which rates were lowest for employers that offered only Blue Cross (D), and highest for employers that offered a competing HMO such as Ocean State (P), but declined to offer HealthMate. Ocean State (P) sued under the Sherman Act, and the jury ruled in its favor. The judge granted Blue Cross' (D) motion for judgment n.o.v., and Ocean State (P) appealed.

ISSUE: Are the practices of an insurance provider that involve contracts with subscribers subject to scrutiny under the antitrust laws?

HOLDING AND DECISION: (Campbell, J.) No. The practices of an insurance provider that involve contracts with subscribers are exempt from scrutiny under the antitrust laws. Both HealthMate and the pricing policy are exempt under the test applied by the Supreme Court; they involve the spreading of risk; the relationships between insurer and insured; and are limited to entities within the insurance industry. This must be distinguished from contracts between an insurer and its health care providers, which are contracts for goods and services and not intrinsic to the "business of insurance." Affirmed.

EDITOR'S ANALYSIS: Testimony was offered to the effect that Blue Cross's (D) president "had expressed—in none-too-polite terms—a desire to emasculate Ocean State." On the basis of this and other evidence, the court said, a jury could have concluded that Blue Cross (D) wanted to put Ocean State (P) out of business. However, the desire to crush a competitor, unaccompanied by unlawful conduct, was held insufficient to constitute a violation of the antitrust laws.

QUICKNOTES

JUDGMENT N.O.V. - A judgment entered by the trial judge reversing a jury verdict if the jury's determination has no basis in law or fact.

NOTES:

FEDERAL TRADE COMMISSION v. TENET HEALTH CARE CORP.

Federal agency (P) v. Health care corporation (D)
186 F.3d 1045 (8th Cir. 1999).

NATURE OF CASE: Appeal from an order enjoining the merger of two hospitals.

FACT SUMMARY: The district court found a substantial likelihood that the merger of of a Tenet hospital (D) with another hospital would substantially lessen competition between acute care hospitals in Poplar Bluff, Missouri.

CONCISE RULE OF LAW: Courts should refrain from intervening in a competitive situation which may upset the balance of the market in cases where there exists no evidence of barriers constraining normal operation of the market.

FACTS: Lucy Lee Hospital and Doctors' Regional Medical Center are the only two hospitals in Poplar Bluff, aside from a Veteran's Hospital. Tenet Healthcare Corporation (Tenet) (D) owns Lucy Lee Hospital, a general acute care hospital that provides primary and secondary care services in Poplar Bluff. Lucy Lee has 201 licensed beds and operates ten outpatient clinics in the surrounding counties. Doctors' Regional Medical Center in Poplar Bluff is also a general acute care hospital providing primary and secondary services. Doctors' Regional has 230 beds and also operates several rural health clinics in the area. Tenet (D) entered into an agreement to purchase Doctors' Regional for over forty million dollars, to operate it as a long-term care facility and to consolidate inpatient services at Lucy Lee. Pursuant to the Hart-Scott-Rodino Act, the hospitals filed a premerger certification with the Federal Trade Commission (FTC) (P). Shortly thereafter, the FTC (P) filed a complaint alleging that the hospitals' merger would lessen competition for primary and secondary inpatient hospitalization services in the area.

ISSUE: Should courts refrain from intervening in a competitive situation which may upset the balance of the market in cases where there exists no evidence of barriers constraining normal operation of the market?

DECISION AND HOLDING: (Beam, J.) Yes. Courts should refrain from intervening in a competitive situation which may upset the balance of the market in cases where there exists no evidence of barriers constraining normal operation of the market. A relevant market, consisting of a product market and a geographic market, must be defined before a court finds an antitrust violation. The FTC (P) in this case proposes a relevant geographic market that matches its service area. A service area and a merging firm's geographic market are not necessarily the same, however. Because the FTC (P) failed to demonstrate a well-defined relevant market, it failed to show that the merged

entity would possess market power. Patients may use hospitals outside the service area that may be closer to such residents or provide higher quality services in the patients' minds. Also, the potential efficiencies gained by the merger in this case should have been examined by the lower court to determine if this might have enhanced competition in the greater Southeast Missouri area. Reversed.

EDITOR'S ANALYSIS: The FTC has played a major role in subjecting the healthcare industry to antitrust scrutiny.

NOTES:

UNITED STATES v. GREBER

Federal government (P) v. Osteopathic physician (D)

760 F.2d 68 (3rd Cir. 1985).

NATURE OF CASE: Appeal of conviction for Medicare and mail fraud.

FACT SUMMARY: Greber (D), a specialist, compensated referring physicians in an amount in excess of the work performed by such physicians, with the intent to induce future referrals.

CONCISE RULE OF LAW: A payment to a referring physician, if done to induce future referrals, is illegal even if the payment is compensatory.

FACTS: Greber (D) was an osteopathic physician who was board certified in cardiology. He organized a company, Cardio-Med, Inc., to provide diagnostic services. Cardio-Med billed Medicare for some such services. The Government (P) eventually charged Greber (D) with Medicare fraud in violation of 42 U.S.C. § 1395nn(b)(2)(B), as well as mail fraud. The charges stemmed from Cardio-Med's practice of paying referring physicians kickbacks from Medicare funds for the purpose of obtaining future referrals. Greber (D) contended that the payments were for work performed by the physicians and that future referrals was only one purpose of the payments. Greber (D) was convicted, and he appealed.

ISSUE: Is a payment to a referring physician done to induce future referrals illegal even if the payment is compensatory?

HOLDING AND DECISION: (Weis, J.) Yes. A payment to a referring physician done to induce future referrals is illegal even if the payment is compensatory. Section 1395nn(b)(2) provides that anyone who knowingly and willfully offers any remuneration to induce the recipient thereof to arrange for such service shall be guilty of felony. This section clearly provides that, when Medicare is involved, no payment of any kind, either gratuitous or compensatory in nature, can be used with the intent of securing a referral. Such referral need not be the sole reason for the payment; for a violation, it need be only a factor in the payment. Here, that is how the jury was charged, so no error occurred. Affirmed.

EDITOR'S ANALYSIS: Earlier versions of § 1395nn(b)(2) only prohibited "kickbacks." The term "kickback" is somewhat imprecise; some courts construed it to refer only to gratuitous payments. In 1982, the word "renumeration" was added, with the intent to cover compensatory payments made to secure referrals.

NOTES:

THE HANLESTER NETWORK v. SHALALA

General partnership (P) v. Administrative agency (D)

51 F.3d 1390 (9th Cir. 1995).

NATURE OF CASE: Review of summary judgment upholding exclusion from Medicare and Medicaid participation.

FACT SUMMARY: The Hanlester Network (P), which held interests in several medical labs, sold limited partnership interests in labs to physicians, having the indirect effect of compensating partner-physicians for referrals.

CONCISE RULE OF LAW: Where physicians receive limited partnership profit shares under a scheme to knowingly induce referrals to consortium labs, the profit-sharing plan violates § 1128B(b)(2) of the Social Security Act.

FACTS: The Hanlester Network (P), a California general partnership, was formed in 1987. Hanlester (P) had an ownership interest in several medical labs. Hanlester (P) began selling limited partnership shares in joint venture labs to physicians. Payments to physician-partners was on the basis of shares held, not the number of referrals of lab services to joint venture labs. An agent of Hanlester (P) told prospective limited partners that the number of shares they could purchase would be contingent on the volume of business they referred to the labs. In 1989, Hanlester (P) was notified by the Inspector General of the Department of Health and Human Services that it had violated § 1128B(b)(2) of the Social Security Act by paying remuneration to induce referrals to labs. Hanlester (P) was notified that it would be excluded from the Medicare and state health care programs. An administrative law judge found that Hanlester (P) violated § 1128B(b)(2), but declined to impose permissive exclusions from Medicare or Medicaid based on the violations. An appellate panel ruled that more violations had occurred and ordered the imposition of permissive exclusions on remand. Hanlester (P) appealed to district court. The district court granted Secretary Shalala's (D) motion for summary judgment. Hanlester (P) appealed.

ISSUE: Does payment to physicians of limited partnership profit shares constitute a violation of § 1128B(b)(2) of the Social Security Act by improperly offering or paying remuneration to induce referrals to the labs?

HOLDING AND DECISION: (Tanner, J.) Yes. Where physicians receive limited partnership profit shares under a scheme to knowingly induce referrals to consortium labs, the profit-sharing plan violates § 1128B(b)(2) of the Social Security Act. To have violated § 1128B(b)(2), remuneration must have been knowingly and willfully paid or offered to induce proscribed referrals of program-related business. In this case, the partnership intended to allow physicians to profit indirectly from referrals when they could not do so directly. The arrangement was not a per se violation of the law. However, there is ample evidence that Hanlester (P) intended to encourage limited partners to refer business to joint venture labs. But a high rate of return for high volume referrals is not enough to show a violation of § 1128B(b)(2). The statements to potential investors were clearly intended to induce referrals to joint venture labs. Partnership shares were to be sold based upon the volume of referrals to the labs. These statements clearly connected partnership payments with referral volume. Hanlester (P) is liable for the statements made by its agents on the theory of respondeat superior. There is no evidence, however, that the conduct of Hanlester (P) and its labs harmed Medicare or Medicaid programs. Since the liability is strictly vicarious, emanating from their agent, the untrustworthiness of the joint venture ended when the agent left. Exclusion from the health care programs is unnecessary to meet the remedial purposes of the Social Security Act. The district court summary judgment is reversed, and the ALJ's original ruling is reinstated.

EDITOR'S ANALYSIS: The ruling in this case has become irrelevant, for the most part. Legislation has since made it improper for a physician, or a family member of the physician, to have an ownership or investment interest in an entity to which he refers business, and at the same time to receive Medicare or Medicaid payments for such services. However, the holding still covers other business arrangements not specifically covered by the Stark Amendment legislation.

QUICKNOTES

SOCIAL SECURITY ACT - Prohibits solicitation or receipt of remuneration in return for the referral of program-related business.

RESPONDEAT SUPERIOR - Rule that the principal is responsible for tortious acts committed by its agents in the scope of their agency or authority.

NOTES:

GLOSSARY
COMMON LATIN WORDS AND PHRASES ENCOUNTERED IN THE LAW

A FORTIORI: Because one fact exists or has been proven, therefore a second fact that is related to the first fact must also exist.

A PRIORI: From the cause to the effect. A term of logic used to denote that when one generally accepted truth is shown to be a cause, another particular effect must necessarily follow.

AB INITIO: From the beginning; a condition which has existed throughout, as in a marriage which was void ab initio.

ACTUS REUS: The wrongful act; in criminal law, such action sufficient to trigger criminal liability.

AD VALOREM: According to value; an ad valorem tax is imposed upon an item located within the taxing jurisdiction calculated by the value of such item.

AMICUS CURIAE: Friend of the court. Its most common usage takes the form of an amicus curiae brief, filed by a person who is not a party to an action but is nonetheless allowed to offer an argument supporting his legal interests.

ARGUENDO: In arguing. A statement, possibly hypothetical, made for the purpose of argument, is one made arguendo.

BILL QUIA TIMET: A bill to quiet title (establish ownership) to real property.

BONA FIDE: True, honest, or genuine. May refer to a person's legal position based on good faith or lacking notice of fraud (such as a bona fide purchaser for value) or to the authenticity of a particular document (such as a bona fide last will and testament).

CAUSA MORTIS: With approaching death in mind. A gift causa mortis is a gift given by a party who feels certain that death is imminent.

CAVEAT EMPTOR: Let the buyer beware. This maxim is reflected in the rule of law that a buyer purchases at his own risk because it is his responsibility to examine, judge, test, and otherwise inspect what he is buying.

CERTIORARI: A writ of review. Petitions for review of a case by the United States Supreme Court are most often done by means of a writ of certiorari.

CONTRA: On the other hand. Opposite. Contrary to.

CORAM NOBIS: Before us; writs of error directed to the court that originally rendered the judgment.

CORAM VOBIS: Before you; writs of error directed by an appellate court to a lower court to correct a factual error.

CORPUS DELICTI: The body of the crime; the requisite elements of a crime amounting to objective proof that a crime has been committed.

CUM TESTAMENTO ANNEXO, ADMINISTRATOR (ADMINISTRATOR C.T.A.): With will annexed; an administrator c.t.a. settles an estate pursuant to a will in which he is not appointed.

DE BONIS NON, ADMINISTRATOR (ADMINISTRATOR D.B.N.): Of goods not administered; an administrator d.b.n. settles a partially settled estate.

DE FACTO: In fact; in reality; actually. Existing in fact but not officially approved or engendered.

DE JURE: By right; lawful. Describes a condition that is legitimate "as a matter of law," in contrast to the term "de facto," which connotes something existing in fact but not legally sanctioned or authorized. For example, de facto segregation refers to segregation brought about by housing patterns, etc., whereas de jure segregation refers to segregation created by law.

DE MINIMUS: Of minimal importance; insignificant; a trifle; not worth bothering about.

DE NOVO: Anew; a second time; afresh. A trial de novo is a new trial held at the appellate level as if the case originated there and the trial at a lower level had not taken place.

DICTA: Generally used as an abbreviated form of obiter dicta, a term describing those portions of a judicial opinion incidental or not necessary to resolution of the specific question before the court. Such nonessential statements and remarks are not considered to be binding precedent.

DUCES TECUM: Refers to a particular type of writ or subpoena requesting a party or organization to produce certain documents in their possession.

EN BANC: Full bench. Where a court sits with all justices present rather than the usual quorum.

EX PARTE: For one side or one party only. An ex parte proceeding is one undertaken for the benefit of only one party, without notice to, or an appearance by, an adverse party.

EX POST FACTO: After the fact. An ex post facto law is a law that retroactively changes the consequences of a prior act.

EX REL.: Abbreviated form of the term ex relatione, meaning, upon relation or information. When the state brings an action in which it has no interest against an individual at the instigation of one who has a private interest in the matter.

FORUM NON CONVENIENS: Inconvenient forum. Although a court may have jurisdiction over the case, the action should be tried in a more conveniently located court, one to which parties and witnesses may more easily travel, for example.

GUARDIAN AD LITEM: A guardian of an infant as to litigation, appointed to represent the infant and pursue his/her rights.

HABEAS CORPUS: You have the body. The modern writ of habeas corpus is a writ directing that a person (body) being detained (such as a prisoner) be brought before the court so that the legality of his detention can be judicially ascertained.

IN CAMERA: In private, in chambers. When a hearing is held before a judge in his chambers or when all spectators are excluded from the courtroom.

IN FORMA PAUPERIS: In the manner of a pauper. A party who proceeds in forma pauperis because of his poverty is one who is allowed to bring suit without liability for costs.

INFRA: Below, under. A word referring the reader to a later part of a book. (The opposite of supra.)

IN LOCO PARENTIS: In the place of a parent.

IN PARI DELICTO: Equally wrong; a court of equity will not grant requested relief to an applicant who is in pari delicto, or as much at fault in the transactions giving rise to the controversy as is the opponent of the applicant.

IN PARI MATERIA: On like subject matter or upon the same matter. Statutes relating to the same person or things are said to be in pari materia. It is a general rule of statutory construction that such statutes should be construed together, i.e., looked at as if they together constituted one law.

IN PERSONAM: Against the person. Jurisdiction over the person of an individual.

IN RE: In the matter of. Used to designate a proceeding involving an estate or other property.

IN REM: A term that signifies an action against the res, or thing. An action in rem is basically one that is taken directly against property, as distinguished from an action in personam, i.e., against the person.

INTER ALIA: Among other things. Used to show that the whole of a statement, pleading, list, statute, etc., has not been set forth in its entirety.

INTER PARTES: Between the parties. May refer to contracts, conveyances or other transactions having legal significance.

INTER VIVOS: Between the living. An inter vivos gift is a gift made by a living grantor, as distinguished from bequests contained in a will, which pass upon the death of the testator.

IPSO FACTO: By the mere fact itself.

JUS: Law or the entire body of law.

LEX LOCI: The law of the place; the notion that the rights of parties to a legal proceeding are governed by the law of the place where those rights arose.

MALUM IN SE: Evil or wrong in and of itself; inherently wrong. This term describes an act that is wrong by its very nature, as opposed to one which would not be wrong but for the fact that there is a specific legal prohibition against it (malum prohibitum).

MALUM PROHIBITUM: Wrong because prohibited, but not inherently evil. Used to describe something that is wrong because it is expressly forbidden by law but that is not in and of itself evil, e.g., speeding.

MANDAMUS: We command. A writ directing an official to take a certain action.

MENS REA: A guilty mind; a criminal intent. A term used to signify the mental state that accompanies a crime or other prohibited act. Some crimes require only a general mens rea (general intent to do the prohibited act), but others, like assault with intent to murder, require the existence of a specific mens rea.

MODUS OPERANDI: Method of operating; generally refers to the manner or style of a criminal in committing crimes, admissible in appropriate cases as evidence of the identity of a defendant.

NEXUS: A connection to.

NISI PRIUS: A court of first impression. A nisi prius court is one where issues of fact are tried before a judge or jury.

N.O.V. (NON OBSTANTE VEREDICTO): Notwithstanding the verdict. A judgment n.o.v. is a judgment given in favor of one party despite the fact that a verdict was returned in favor of the other party, the justification being that the verdict either had no reasonable support in fact or was contrary to law.

NUNC PRO TUNC: Now for then. This phrase refers to actions that may be taken and will then have full retroactive effect.

PENDENTE LITE: Pending the suit; pending litigation underway.

PER CAPITA: By head; beneficiaries of an estate, if they take in equal shares, take per capita.

PER CURIAM: By the court; signifies an opinion ostensibly written "by the whole court" and with no identified author.

PER SE: By itself, in itself; inherently.

PER STIRPES: By representation. Used primarily in the law of wills to describe the method of distribution where a person, generally because of death, is unable to take that which is left to him by the will of another, and therefore his heirs divide such property between them rather than take under the will individually.

PRIMA FACIE: On its face, at first sight. A prima facie case is one that is sufficient on its face, meaning that the evidence supporting it is adequate to establish the case until contradicted or overcome by other evidence.

PRO TANTO: For so much; as far as it goes. Often used in eminent domain cases when a property owner receives partial payment for his land without prejudice to his right to bring suit for the full amount he claims his land to be worth.

QUANTUM MERUIT: As much as he deserves. Refers to recovery based on the doctrine of unjust enrichment in those cases in which a party has rendered valuable services or furnished materials that were accepted and enjoyed by another under circumstances that would reasonably notify the recipient that the rendering party expected to be paid. In essence, the law implies a contract to pay the reasonable value of the services or materials furnished.

QUASI: Almost like; as if; nearly. This term is essentially used to signify that one subject or thing is almost analogous to another but that material differences between them do exist. For example, a quasi-criminal proceeding is one that is not strictly criminal but shares enough of the same characteristics to require some of the same safeguards (e.g., procedural due process must be followed in a parol hearing).

QUID PRO QUO: Something for something. In contract law, the consideration, something of value, passed between the parties to render the contract binding.

RES GESTAE: Things done; in evidence law, this principle justifies the admission of a statement that would otherwise be hearsay when it is made so closely to the event in question as to be said to be a part of it, or with such spontaneity as not to have the possibility of falsehood.

RES IPSA LOQUITUR: The thing speaks for itself. This doctrine gives rise to a rebuttable presumption of negligence when the instrumentality causing the injury was within the exclusive control of the defendant, and the injury was one that does not normally occur unless a person has been negligent.

RES JUDICATA: A matter adjudged. Doctrine which provides that once a court of competent jurisdiction has rendered a final judgment or decree on the merits, that judgment or decree is conclusive upon the parties to the case and prevents them from engaging in any other litigation on the points and issues determined therein.

RESPONDEAT SUPERIOR: Let the master reply. This doctrine holds the master liable for the wrongful acts of his servant (or the principal for his agent) in those cases in which the servant (or agent) was acting within the scope of his authority at the time of the injury.

STARE DECISIS: To stand by or adhere to that which has been decided. The common law doctrine of stare decisis attempts to give security and certainty to the law by following the policy that once a principle of law as applicable to a certain set of facts has been set forth in a decision, it forms a precedent which will subsequently be followed, even though a different decision might be made were it the first time the question had arisen. Of course, stare decisis is not an inviolable principle and is departed from in instances where there is good cause (e.g., considerations of public policy led the Supreme Court to disregard prior decisions sanctioning segregation).

SUPRA: Above. A word referring a reader to an earlier part of a book.

ULTRA VIRES: Beyond the power. This phrase is most commonly used to refer to actions taken by a corporation that are beyond the power or legal authority of the corporation.

ADDENDUM OF FRENCH DERIVATIVES

IN PAIS: Not pursuant to legal proceedings.

CHATTEL: Tangible personal property.

CY PRES: Doctrine permitting courts to apply trust funds to purposes not expressed in the trust but necessary to carry out the settlor's intent.

PER AUTRE VIE: For another's life; in property law, an estate may be granted that will terminate upon the death of someone other than the grantee.

PROFIT A PRENDRE: A license to remove minerals or other produce from land.

VOIR DIRE: Process of questioning jurors as to their predispositions about the case or parties to a proceeding in order to identify those jurors displaying bias or prejudice.

REV 1-95

CASENOTE LEGAL BRIEFS